JEPHTHAH'S CHILDREN

Gay parenting has been a huge and risky social experiment: only a generation later can the outcomes be fully visible. But now that time has passed and we need to listen to the voices of those who have grown up in families headed by same-sex parents. The voice of ex-gays has been all but silenced in the UK; we cannot allow the same to happen to the voices of those who have been launched into life by gay parenting. There is a powerful case here for a serious re-think.

Rev Dr John Nolland, Visiting Professor, University of Bristol

This is the book everyone would be reading if they wanted to have an honest and intelligent conversation about the sex and gender issues roiling society today. It opens our eyes like Judith Wallerstein's *The Unexpected Legacy of Divorce*...only 25 years ahead of schedule.

Helen M. Alvare, Professor of Law, Scalia Law School, George Mason University, Virginia

It's been a joy to watch Bobby Lopez, who loved his lesbian mother, grow from reluctant story teller to fierce teller of truth, growing deeper in knowledge and understanding of this complex issue with every stroke of his pen. Dr. Lopez has assembled a brilliant group of people ... each with their own story to tell. Unique and compelling ... there's nothing quite like *Jephthah's Children*.

Sandy Rios, Director of Governmental Affairs, American Family Association

This is a very disturbing book. Don't read it if you want to remain in your comfort zone and close your ears to the cries of the little ones in the affluent West suffering injustice. In our time God is calling prophets to unveil the truth about the sexual revolution and its effects, especially on children. Robert Lopez is such a prophet. Like the author of the story of Jephthah's daughter and other horrific narratives from the dark days of Israel's history, or like Jeremiah or Ezekiel, he provides narratives that are raw and unvarnished, revealing sometimes in just a few shocking lines the depths of human sin. Lust, pride, cruelty, manipulation and other examples of adult selfishness are relentlessly paraded. The reader is often left asking: "where is the happy ending? Where is the redemption?" Tragically, for many of those brought up in dysfunctional homes with lies, abuse and corruption of innocence, there is only silent torment. But Lopez and other narrators who have emerged from such situations, who have had the courage to speak out about them, show in their own life stories how even in the worst situations God is present with his judgment and his transforming grace. Many people, even in the church, still cling to the myth that Judaeo-Christian sexual ethics on which our civilization is based are somehow outmoded, prudish and oppressive. This book shows, in a series of snapshots and sharp comments, something of the destructive and toxic effects of widespread sexual immorality, and how we desperately need to re-lay the foundations by commending and modelling the biological family, for the sake of our future.

Rev Andrew Symes, Executive Secretary, Anglican Mainstream

JEPHTHAH'S CHILDREN

The Innocent Casualties of Same-Sex Parenting

Editors
Robert Oscar López
Brittany Klein

Wilberforce Publications
London

The first edition of this book entitled Jephthah's Daughters
was published in Los Angeles, USA in 2015 by
International Children's Rights Institute
9250 Reseda Blvd. #165
Northridge, CA 91324
whose permission is gratefully acknowledged

This edition published in Great Britain in 2016 by
Wilberforce Publications Limited
70 Wimpole Street, London W1G 8AX
Wilberforce Publications Limited is a wholly owned subsidiary of Christian Concern

ISBN 978-0-9575725-9-1

Printed in Great Britain by Imprint Digital, Exeter
and worldwide by CreateSpace

Contents

Note to readers: Throughout this text, the term "ligbitist" is sometimes used to describe the ideology espoused by people who use the term LGBT. The term ligbitist is used to distinguish LGBT advocacy from gay people themselves, and also to avoid the awkwardness of repeating the capitalised acronym too many times.

PREFACE

Robert Oscar Lopez

This book is an uncensored chronicle of everything that has gone wrong because of the movement to normalise same-sex parenting. Brittany Klein and I compiled the first edition of this book, *Jephthah's Daughters* (2015) with many other contributors. We have firsthand experience with the seeming "side issues" that became entangled in the war for marriage "equality". Those side issues ended up being more important than the legal status of same-sex relationships; hence, this book. We can help the general reader understand why something viewed by so many as beneficial was actually harmful to so many more. This book is not *just* our story; it is our story plus a whole lot of other people's stories, gathered into a broader picture of everything that backfired. It offers a few theories as to why multiple societies had such a lapse in judgment: Propaganda was powerful. Complex issues were prone to oversimplification. Sexuality was an easy proxy issue on which to project economic frustrations. There is no catch-all explanation.

Brittany Klein and I are less philosophers than narrators, less ethicists than chroniclers, less experts than storytellers. Our discipline is literature and our appetites lean toward the episodic and personal. There will be no shortage of statistics and citations in *Jephthah's Daughters*—brace yourself for hundreds upon hundreds of endnotes—but as literary critics we have a habit of not liking spoilers. We prefer to let you reach the ending with an air of suspense and a chance to be surprised. We are also partial to the role of editor and compiler, allowing a cacophony of other people's voices to be heard alongside ours.

Please do not view the life stories and reflections in this book as theological orthodoxy, and I hope you will forgive the sometimes colourful language. The authors have sought to be true to their heartfelt and painful personal experiences which illustrate deep truths about the nature of human life and the created order.

Brittany and I were both raised by lesbians; she grew up to become a radical feminist, and I grew up to be queer. She descended from Jews who survived ghastly persecution in Europe, while I descended from colonised subjects in the Philippines and from slaves in the Caribbean. Controversy was never a strictly intellectual matter for us; it was raw and visceral, for our families and for us.

There is only so much distance Brittany and I can assume from the question of same-sex marriage. When we talk about the marriage war, we are talking about people we love. We are talking also about ourselves. We inhabited the battlefields of the marriage war long before we became scholars. Having grown up in peculiar circumstances and having seen things around us that few people can relate to their own experience, we are distrustful of generalisations and all-encompassing categories. Consensus and common sense have never been safe zones for us, because we never seem to fit in with other people's paradigms.

There are many voices in this book besides ours. Still, it is inevitable that the structure and content of the book are colored by where we are coming from. As children we learned how to stay focused in jarring circumstances. Such is the methodology we have hoped to employ here. The book is a journey from vignette to vignette. None is fictional. Many vignettes challenge the postulations in other vignettes. All demonstrate the damages caused by the war for marriage "equality."

Whatever views are held about same-sex relationships, same-sex marriage, and in the UK civil partnership (which preceded it), have been, and are, a social disaster for the children affected. Same-sex marriage was premised on falsehoods. It was pushed on unwilling populations using nefarious tactics ranging from half-true propaganda to criminal intimidation and racketeering. It took protections away from the most vulnerable people in the world—particularly but not exclusively children—and empowered the most privileged people in the world (particularly but not exclusively wealthy white men).

It required changing laws, culture, and global relations in multiple bad directions. Sex and gender had to be uncoupled from one another, sometimes through dangerous surgery, sometimes through Orwellian language policing. Sexual choices and self-mastery had to be replaced by biological determinism and peer pressure. Free will itself was discredited in favour of being "born this way". Self-determination was mandated (for transsexuals) or forbidden (to ex-gays), depending on how one's urge to change oneself matched the identity politics of opinionated elites.

Ancient life cycles were overturned for fashionable social theories less than a decade old. Childhood had to be hyper-sexualised. Parenthood had to be totally de-sexualised and replaced with systems of buying and selling offspring. Science and academic research fell prey to groupthink, false assertions, and consensus by duress. Schools, courts, city halls, and popular culture faced catastrophic reprisal if they did not agree to promote the fallacies used to justify the same-sex marriage movement.

The discredited logic behind slavery, cultural genocide, and eugenics snuck back into the zeitgeist, under the noses of the progressive critics who usually felt most superior to the slavers, settlers, and Nazis who practiced those historic evils in earlier times. Resources for serious social-justice movements – such as women's rights, economic aid to the global poor, critical anti-racism, sexual assault intervention, and refugee assistance – shifted from urgent flashpoints toward hubs of wealthy professionals seeking fulfillment in their personal sex lives.

None of this is alarmism, paranoia, or even speculation. Our research has been careful and thorough. This book will show whom the same-sex marriage movement and same-sex parenting have harmed. In Section I, a range of essays will demonstrate how children's most fundamental birthright – the right to their mother and father, indeed their heritage – has been cast to the flames to make a small gay lobby happy, and few on the left or right seemed to notice or care. Section II will describe the toll taken on vulnerable parties in society, particularly women, because of the move toward "reconstructing families" according to emerging LGBT consumer tastes. Section III will examine more broadly the global effect of imposing same-sex marriage on multiple continents, a process that enhances unhealthy power dynamics among different races and classes, as well as between the United States and the rest of the world.

A society that compels people to think things that aren't true, say things they do not believe, and live in fear of retaliation, is one that will lose whatever war it thinks it is waging. Same-sex marriage did not have to be this way. As it was originally introduced to the American public, it was a question of honouring relationships between consenting adults.

11

"It doesn't hurt anyone", went the honest expression of the movement's early claims. But this core of honesty was adulterated by a series of rash decisions made by gay rights leaders. Suddenly same-sex parenting was thrown into the mix as a bait and switch.

With the sleight of hand that yoked marriage to parenting, a host of earnest questions became taboo. What about the children placed in gay homes who have biological parents somewhere outside the home? What about those excluded biological parents? What about the people whose children are taken away by the state? What about the cousins, grandparents, siblings, and neighbours who find eugenics unethical, and who want to be tied to their kin? What about people who cannot remain silent when they see children being trafficked, engineered, or forcibly removed from their origins? What about all of society, careering toward a future in which human beings will be designed in laboratories and children will be bought and sold?

Haste makes waste. The old saying turns out to be true, like so many clichés. We have learned, once again, the lesson that the Jewish warrior Jephthah learned, in the eleventh chapter of the Book of Judges.

The rash vow: Jephthah's lesson
As an ex-queer father, I cannot help but read the character Jephthah as sharing some characteristics with the queer. He appears in the Book of Judges as an intriguing figure, a bastard born of a whore. In the *New Oxford Annotated Bible,* "Gilead was the father of Jephthah", though Gilead is the name of an entire region. Some scholars have proposed that perhaps this reference implies that his mother was so promiscuous that literally all the men of the province had used her, making his paternity shameful as well as uncertain.[1]

Stigmatised and abused by his "brothers," Jephthah runs away to "the land of Tob" and gathers "worthless fellows" around himself. They go "raiding" together.[2] He lives the life of the outcast, the exile, the border-crosser. There is no mention in the text of Jephthah marrying or seducing a woman, but he ends up having one child somehow, a daughter.

Where did the girl come from? The mystery of his family is one of the intriguing holes in the Bible. My guess has always been that Jephthah adopted her, perhaps stealing her from a village he raided, or saving her on a foray that orphaned her. However it happens, he is a father without a wife when his half-brothers come to find him one day in Tob. The brothers come and beg Jephthah to return to his birth town and bear arms against the Ammonites, who are at war with Israel. Apparently he has a reputation for being a mighty fighter.[3]

Jephthah taunts his half-brothers, asking, "Did you not hate me and drive me out of my father's house?" His brothers seek to reconcile themselves with him, saying that if he comes back and fights against Ammon, they will make him the leader over all of Gilead. He has the chance to go from being the lowest reject of his native land to being its highest authority.[4]

Jephthah's decision to return to Israel and fight is not a wise one, for he ends up exposing himself to great harm for the honour and survival of a country that treated him with scorn. But we must consider what must have been going through his mind. He knows what it means to be unaccepted, denied one's rightful place in society. He is aware that he is worthy of far more than he was once given. Now is his chance to get everything that was denied him. He can prove himself. He gets to be somebody.

There is a powerful allegory for queerness here. Jephthah is dangerously vulnerable to overcompensation. There is a streak of vindictiveness in him, even as he tries to be enthusiastic. Having been an outsider, he savours the thrill of being at the forefront of legitimate society. He throws himself into soldiering with the zeal of the converted. God is with him. The text says:

> Then the Spirit of the LORD came upon Jephthah, and he passed through Gilead and Manasseh, and passed on to Mizpah of Gilead, and from Mizpah of Gilead he passed on to the Ammonites. And Jephthah made a vow to the LORD and said, 'If thou wilt give the Ammonites into my hand, then whoever comes forth from the doors of my house to meet me, when I return victorious from the Ammonites, shall be the LORD's, and I will offer him up for a burnt offering.' [5]

"With a very great slaughter," Jephthah gets what he wants and what Israel wants—he vanquishes the Ammonites and liberates his homeland.

He returns as a conquering hero. Who is the first one to rush out of the house to greet him?

> Behold, his daughter came out to meet him with timbrels and with dances; she was his only child; beside her he had neither son nor daughter. And when he saw her, he rent his clothes and said, 'Alas, my daughter! You have brought me very low, and you have become the cause of great trouble for me; for I have opened my mouth to the LORD, and I cannot take back my vow.'[6]

Of course his daughter was the first one to rush out of the house to greet him. She was happy to see him. She was proud that her dad was now a general rather than a rapscallion.

Jephthah is confronted with the consequences of the rash vow he made in order to go from the margins to the center of society. He realises that he can only gain a "seat at the table" by destroying an innocent human being whom he loves dearly.

No kindness would have been greater to her father, than refusing to be sacrificed. Yet Jephthah's aspirations seem to have infected his daughter; she has internalised his war and subordinated her selfhood to his obsessions.

> "Let this thing be done to me; let me alone two months, that I may go and wander on the mountains, and bewail my virginity, I and my companions...." She had never known a man.[7]

No doubt when Jephthah sends his daughter away to the mountains, he prays that she will not come back. A daughter who lives on as a disobedient runaway is better than a daughter who dies out of a sense of duty.

This narrative is one of the most fitting for the maze of difficult topics tied to same-sex marriage, because Judges 11 does not automatically flatter a Christian or anti-Christian attitude. It forces readers to dwell in complexity and even confusion, which is perhaps a good way to destabilise people from their routine assumptions. A religious press told Brittany and me that they liked the general idea for this book, but the choice of Jephthah's family as an opening allegory was unwise and theologically reckless. This tale is one of the hardest for Jews and Christians alike to interpret with confidence.

However, we decided to stick with Jephthah. What better way to open a book about a confusing and rash charge into same-sex parenting than Judges 11? The outcome of the story is unsatisfying, even for devoutly religious readers who strive to see the daughter's submission to her father's will as a saintly presaging of the New Testament. The story of Jephthah calls attention to the perversion of child sacrifice. While the Christ narrative relies upon the notion that God sacrificed his only son to save the world from sin, this class of child immolation is reserved for a deity. Christ *is* God. Christ's crucifixion is miles apart from what happened to Jephthah's daughter. For a mortal father to offer up his child's life so that *he* can be glorified, one would have to distort the logic of Christ until it is not recognisable anymore. The intended sacrifice of Isaac in Genesis is thwarted by God; Jephthah's rashness stands unique in the Bible as one of the grossest misjudgments by a parent. It is shocking that God never intervenes to stop the girl's burning, but these are, perhaps, mysteries for theologians.

For lay people, the lesson is clear regardless. Parenthood was designed to entail grown-ups sacrificing their own ambitions and desires for the sake of children. *Not the other way around.* War perverts everything, including the proper configuration of parent to child. Had she run away, as her father once did, to a fringe town to live among "worthless fellows", she would have given Jephthah the gift to make him happy. She would have had the chance to make love to a man, have children, carry on his line, and proceed as if he had not made his rash vow. For the best interests of everyone, she should have rebelled against her father to save him.

That is not how it works out. She returns from the mountains a virgin and her father must kill her as a burnt sacrifice, a holocaust. She never has children, so he has no descendants. The sacred order of society collapses in on itself. Some might argue that this is only fair to her, for she wanted the chance to contribute to Israel's victory the way a male heir would have, through physical danger. I do not see it that way. Everyone loses out because everyone is consumed with a distorted consciousness. Jephthah's failure to question himself and deal with his bitterness over past exile leads to his overly zealous spirit during war and his abuse of the one person who might have truly loved him. Shortly after this episode in the Bible, Jephthah orders the slaughter of men from another tribe of Israel with whom he has a dispute, identifying them by their inability to say the word "shibboleth". 42,000 fellow Israelites are killed. The darkness of his loss does not lift; he dies after ruling over Israel but six years.[8]

In the Book of Judges it says that there was a custom in Israel that for four days every year, all the daughters of Israel went away to lament the daughter of Jephthah. They did not want her to be forgotten. Perhaps they saw in her an allegory for being anyone's daughter, or anyone's child. Tragedy ensues when a parent's ambitions consume the whole family and when the child is so eager to please the parent that child sacrifice becomes thinkable and even doable.

We are all Jephthah's children now

The debate over same-sex marriage was not really a debate. It was a war. Its polemic rhythms paralleled blitzkrieg and social weapons of mass destruction. It was less violent than the battle Jephthah waged in Mizpah, but Mizpah was one small stretch of Israel. To satisfy the gay movement's desires, same-sex marriage had to be imposed on the entire world, a globe of seven billion people. The argument over its implementation remains visceral. The camps are tribal. Some of the tactics are as unscrupulous and vicious as one would expect were we exchanging gunfire.

Marriage means a great deal to the modern-day Jephthahs—those queers who were once relegated to live among worthless fellows in the land of Tob and now see a precious chance to gain respectability. To have been called a bastard and shunned, one develops a thick skin but a sensitive heart. Shown the chance to do away with the alienation and inferiority of the past, any marginalised community can be forgiven for going too far.

So in some ways I cannot blame queers for wanting same-sex marriage. There is not really much point in blaming anyone for the disastrous way the struggle over matrimony and family has played out. In reflecting upon Jephthah's story, I cast a blameful eye on Jephthah's daughter. She owed it to Jephthah, herself, and all of Israel, to say no. The brave act would have been, not running to the mountains, but rather staying in the public square and declaring herself, her body, her ethics, and her descendants off limits from a distorted and vindictive ideology.

All of us are in *her* position now, not Jephthah's. Albeit mostly by force of judicial fiat, the war has largely been fought and won for same-sex marriage and parenting. During the fog of war, the gay lobby demanded and was promised the right to have other people's children, as well as the assurance that anyone who criticised gay families would be punished. Those rash vows can only be kept by hurting people who will have to be sacrificed, not to a god but to men. Will we allow the gay lobby's obsession with marriage to seize our minds so much, that we will be okay with sacrificing ourselves to the gospel of "marriage equality"? If we go that far and offer ourselves up as sacrifices, we are not only sacrificing ourselves. We are sacrificing many others who stand to be hurt in the aftermath.

It is easy to be rash. It is difficult to be brave. It is shameful to be cowardly. We must choose—will we be like Jephthah's daughter, or will we do the right thing?

Notes
[1] *New Oxford Annotated Bible*, ed. Michael D. Coogan (Oxford: Oxford University Press, 2001). Judges 11-12, 373-5.
[2] Ibid.
[3] Ibid.
[4] Ibid.
[5] Ibid.
[6] Ibid.
[7] Ibid.
[8] Ibid.

SECTION ONE

CHILDREN

Introduction

Alana Newman

In 1976, African-American author Alex Haley published the best-selling book *Roots*—about his decade-long search to uncover his genealogy. Relying on stories from his relatives and a lot of genius detective work, Haley was able to trace his ancestry all the way back to Gambia, where his ancestor Kunta Kinte was kidnapped and trafficked into slavery.[1]

Roots was turned into a film that became the most-watched TV miniseries in American history.* Haley's work spurred a revolution in family reunions and stressed the importance of knowing whom and where you come from as a part of healthy human development.

Haley also transcribed the biography for Malcolm X—one of America's most celebrated civil rights figures. The "X" for his last name is a symbolic statement criticising the way in which slave traders removed people from their biological kin and cultural heritage.[2]

We have failed to learn the lessons of recent history. Today, we're destroying kinship bonds all over again through sperm and egg harvesting.

For any child who grows up without a biological parent in the home—whatever the reason—there remains a longing. *Why aren't they here for me?*

---

* There remains some controversy about the authenticity of some of Mr. Haley's claims. See: Molly Driscall, "5 Famous Plagiarism and Fraud Accusations in the Book World", *Christian Science Monitor*, Books (December 8, 2011) www.csmonitor.com (Accessed February 4, 2015)

The answer to that question matters a great deal. More and more, the answer we offspring are getting is: *Because your parents were not willing to love each other*.

I'm uncomfortable addressing gay parenting. I do so because, like Professor Lopez, I know where this enterprise leads and feel a responsibility to put on the brakes. The way the term "gay" perniciously augments the word "parenting" is especially harmful in public discussions regarding family forms because those three tiny letters connote cosmically different associations.

When some say, "I support gay parenting" what they likely mean is:

I believe in a person's right to reproduce. I believe LGBT people can fulfil parental responsibilities and chores as effectively as heterosexual people. The kinds of families that gay people desire to form are morally indistinguishable between the kinds of families mainstream heterosexuals are forming. I believe gratifying sex is an important part of human flourishing.

When a gay marriage/gay parenting supporter comes across a person who does not share their conclusions, it often comes across as unfathomable—they might believe *only* hatred can be responsible for any opposition. But to millions of people around the globe "gay parenting" conflicts with deeply held values such as:

Mothers are irreplaceable and essential for a child's total ability to thrive. Fathers are irreplaceable and essential for a child's total ability to thrive. Genealogical bewilderment and identity loss is a human tragedy that should be avoided. Pregnancy and procreation are sacred and therefore should never be commercialised.

There is another word, often augmented by the term "gay". It is Pride. There is a lot to be said about pride. It is sometimes defined this way:

Pride: a feeling or deep pleasure or satisfaction derived from one's own achievements, the achievements of those with whom one is closely associated, or from qualities or possessions that are widely admired.

Sounds like a good thing, does it not? But then there are also these definitions:

Pride: the absence of humility as darkness is the absence of light and a vacuum is the absence of atmosphere; a particular kind of insanity caused by a lack of humility. A desire to take the place of God. If there is contention, there is pride behind it. It is difficult to hurt the feelings of a humble person but easy to hurt the feelings of the proud.

A large book could be written describing the many consequences of gamete donation and surrogacy, to the offspring, to the parents, to society. The sexual orientation of the custodial parents is not the underlying problem. This has been described as a fight about the "gay" in gay parenting. It's not primarily about that. This is also not a fight about third-party reproduction—the use of sperm and egg donors. Nor is it about adoption. Eventually there will be a technology that comes along and allows any combination of people to reproduce together, by taking a simple cheek swab—thus eliminating genealogical bewilderment.

The real enemy is selfishness and self-centeredness. A lack of humility. A posture that desires to control the world and especially to use human beings as instruments for one's own personal gratification. The ways in which selfishness expresses itself will look different in different eras. For Alex Haley and Malcolm X's ancestors it was slavery. For the Baby-Boomers it was divorce. For the Boomer's children it is the dehumanisation of children as lifestyle choices and accessories.

I read stories from people who are products of donor-conception and surrogacy—as well as their parents—on a nearly daily basis. One story I have yet to read is where a child expresses to a parent their grief over their missing biological mother or father—and the custodial parent *apologises*.

"Mom, I need you to recognise my loss. Knowing and having a relationship with my biological father was something I needed and deserved, and it was wrong of you to deny me that."

"You're right honey. You suffered because of decisions I made. I don't regret you, but I do regret that you didn't have your father in your life. Can you forgive me?"

Such a scene is fiction. I have never read it anywhere. Commissioning parents have a habit of framing their children's woes in terms of existence or non-existence. If we express any critique over the means of our conception, the response is "but would you rather not be alive?"

There is a third way, but for some reason it doesn't occur to our parents. That is to love your child's other parent. I don't mean love in the sense of maintaining an emotional state of butterflies, lust or affection. I mean love as a willingness to suffer for them—a sense of duty to keep them in community even when one doesn't necessarily like their company, or want their involvement.

As the child of same-sex parents, it appears to me that our parents' greatest sin is that they worshipped pleasure above all other goods. Many of the authors in this section talk about how they longed for normal families. If I may suggest … the nuclear family of our popular imagination is not entirely natural—it requires sacrifice. It requires going against what Christians sometimes call *the natural man*. It means the male must sacrifice multiple sex partners and pour his resources into the children his wife bears by him, staying with her as she ages or loses charm.

Likewise the woman sacrifices her body and self in profound ways through pregnancy, labour, delivery, and nursing. She may well prefer to have other sexual partners herself, but remains loyal to this man, her children's father, because there are ideals and goods she finds more important than pleasure and sexual gratification—like family stability. She might sacrifice professional goals and interests to be an emotionally available spouse and parent. No "normal" nuclear family exists without a willingness to sacrifice on behalf of the good of the other.

In this way sexuality of the monogamous heterosexual male-female duo works to build community like no other sexually intimate bond can. They literally create new members of the human community together: children, siblings, cousins, nieces, nephews, and grandchildren. And their demonstration of self-sacrifice, commitment, and reverence for values beyond pleasure builds trust within the family unit.

Those of us who were not raised in this "normal" family type lack trust. The virtues that enable trust to flourish were not modelled. Pleasure and service of the self were put first, and the authors in this section—in all their diversity—are collectively voicing their feelings about this particular missing virtue: love, rightly understood as the willingness to suffer and sacrifice for the good of the other.

Our portraits, plots, settings, characters and circumstances all varied dramatically. But pride and selfishness recur as the central conflict in all of our stories.

Notes

[1] Alex Haley, *Roots* (New York: Doubleday, 1976).

[2] Alex Haley, *Autobiography of Malcolm X as Told to Alex Haley* (New York: Ballantine Books, 1987).

Chapter One

The Call of the Child

Robert Oscar Lopez

I believe in being called. Whatever greater force people believe in, be it God or fate, most have to believe that individual lives have purposes. For most of my life, I struggled to find mine.

"What am I supposed to do?" was a question writ large in my mind, going all the way back to my crazy childhood. I was an extraordinarily awkward boy, friendless and socially inept. For some reason I liked learning Romance languages. I learned Spanish from my mother's Puerto Rican family, and French when I was sent briefly to live on the border of Québec and Maine. Then I acquired the other Romance languages on my own through obsessive self-instruction.

From Caribbean Spanish I inherited an unfortunate lisp that spilled over into all the languages I spoke, including English. The polyglot spirit made things worse for me; even in cursory interactions with peers in English, I developed an incomprehensible accent and often spoke in a mélange of cognates that didn't make sense to people, especially in blue-collar Buffalo where I grew up. Given that I was sexually confused, the grating lisp made things more painful.

During my early teen years, when I wasn't being tormented by boys in school or seduced by men three times my age, I studied Latin, Portuguese, and Italian. Sometimes I all but disregarded the homework I was supposed to be doing, to barrage myself with hand-written flash cards until the wee hours of the morning. The language obsession was one of many, many inexplicable things that happened in my life: Yale. Prostitution. Working in children's television while living a seedy double life as a gay night crawler. Calling myself "gay" but then waking up next to a woman who just took my virginity. Protesting against the invasion of Iraq but then serving in the Army Reserves. Einstein could be forgiven for not being able to make sense of such a chronology of human experience.

I was fluent in Portuguese and Italian at the age of eighteen without having gone to Brazil or Italy, and having ancestors in neither place. I lost seventy pounds in one year and then scored a 282/300 on the army physical fitness test. I was 39 years old and training alongside 18-year-olds; this was when I had a PhD and had once been a complete pacifist. Such quirks puzzled people. The fact that I was always puzzling to everyone puzzled me more.

Few people around me, other than my wife, have ever had patience with my manic freakishness. My twenties and thirties came and went, with no relieving maturation point, where I could finally say I "grew up" and found some way to exist in my skin and in the world at the same time. Peers who wondered "what could my life possibly be meant to accomplish?" usually looked to their childhood for answers, especially if they were in therapy. Therapists, I am told, love to ask patients about their childhoods. I was never one to share my thoughts with psychologists, since few could possibly hope to understand someone as unusual as I. My biological parents, with whom I'd had many struggles, were both psychiatrists, so I wasn't eager to go to shrinks. Not only would they remind me of my mom and dad; they were also likely professional associates of both. The last thing I wanted to do was to 'out' my mother's sexuality to people who might have viewed her with professional respect.

Hence, as I turned forty, I had never found the common factor to pull together the dizzying fragments of my inexplicable life. My early childhood never suggested itself as an omnibus cause for all the madness. My early childhood was something I had avoided thinking about, for decades. To be truthful, I was a terrible drifter in my twenties and lost all photographs I had of my childhood. As the youngest of my mother's children, I had not been photographed much anyway.

My high school yearbooks disappeared at some point after I had to leave Yale in 1990. Memories of growing up were spotty after that year, which was the year of my mother's death at the age of 53. In 1997, when I worked at MTV Networks and got assigned to Nickelodeon International, the training facilitators asked us to sniff crayons and remember who we were when we were eight years old. Maybe I never even played with crayons. My mind drew a blank.

What a fateful coincidence I faced in 2012! At the age of forty-one, I saw a landmark sociological study on "new family structures" by Mark Regnerus in *Social-Science Research*.[1] It rendered relevant my life experience, up until then an anomaly of little interest to people. I was still socially inept and utterly puzzling to everyone who met me. In all the past moments when I'd wondered what my life meant, I had never given much thought to the possible effect on me of being raised by a lesbian with the help of her lifelong female partner, to the exclusion of my father, between my toddler years and the age of nineteen. I had never considered whether my life was strange because adults who made unusual decisions *created*, for me, a strange life, and my strangeness was not actually my fault (or perhaps anyone's) but rather the consequence of having been thrown into incomprehensible and bizarre life conditions at an age too young to have any say in the matter.

When I was a toddler, I was wandering through the wilderness of same-sex parenting; it was the 1970s and nobody, least of all the gay community at that time, took seriously the concept of two women raising a child together and seeing the child as a common "son".

It may be hard for people to realise this now, but in the 1970s and 1980s, the predominant camps of the gay community did not like to think about children raised by same-sex couples. We reminded them of bisexual life histories, divorce, and the fact that many such children were born to homosexuals in times of confusion and secrecy. Moreover, many such early "gay families" were headed by divorced people who didn't think of themselves as gay households; they thought of themselves first and foremost as divorced parents who owed it to their children to stay in contact with the parent of the opposite sex. Their goal was often to keep the children out of whatever rows might arise as a result of their new gay relationships. My mother's partner, for instance, was meticulous about maintaining lines of contact open between her children and their father and stepmother. (My mother, less so.) Since both women's primary concern was to relieve their children of unnecessary stress, they didn't see it as necessary to pretend that their love had "created" the six children they had between them. These realities, which shaped our childhoods, were not things that interested advocates of gay families.

Heather Has Two Mommies changed everything.[2] It was published in 1989, a year before my mother died. Had she ever read the book, I am sure she would have slammed it shut and thrown it out with the harshest of condemnations. To drag one's children into political controversies about sex—can you imagine? The thought of it was anathema to how my mom and her lover lived their lives. My mom and she had separate houses in town and spent weekends together with me in a camper, in a park, hidden deep in the Allegany region of New York State.

When I met with an ambassador of a very conservative nation at the United Nations recently, he asked me, "you were raised by lesbians but you seem so accomplished and normal. You even went to Yale. Why do you oppose this so much?" My answer to him was that I suffered from not having contact with my father *but* I benefited greatly from my mother and her partner's decision to raise us without officialising us as "children of same-sex couples". Our context differed from the way modern children of same-sex couples were being exploited for political gain.

This difference is why the 2013 Doug Allen study found that children raised by same-sex couples in Canada had such awful academic problems, only graduating from high school at 65% the rate of heterosexual married couples' children.[3] The new generation of lesbians' kids has been thrust into more public controversy than I had to endure. Though it might have been painful, at least I had the option to withdraw into my foreign languages to escape from public-opinion warfare.

Since everyone in my childhood pretended that what was happening wasn't really happening, I'd spent all my childhood pretending I didn't know my mother was a lesbian, even though I had passed hours upon hours reading her stacks of hidden books about homosexuality in the basement, books such as the 1973 *Male and Female Homosexuality: A Comprehensive Investigation*.[4] I am sure I could be drawn and quartered by the gay press for hypothesising as much, but it is certainly not impossible that I got the idea in my head that *I* was gay from reading my mother's secret stash of books about homosexuality. Perhaps my self-doubt was even a way of reclaiming some sense of clarity about all the unclarified homosexuality going on, by convincing myself that

I, not my mom, was the homosexual causing so many odd homosexual-related things.

A sensible way to interpret the strange life I'd led would have been to say: "His household was full of contradictions, secrets, and confusion, so Bobby busied himself with endless obsessions and distractions, from teaching himself four Romance languages to engaging in compulsive sex with older homosexuals and then not telling anyone about it". I had never been able to connect the dots.

But then came 2012, and the landmark publication of Mark Regnerus's study. When I saw the study for the first time, I did a double take. Up until that point the plethora of studies claimed that children of same-sex couples were perfectly normal. These claims made me feel all the more abnormal, since I couldn't even attribute how weird I was to the obvious fact that my household was unusual. Regnerus's study produced data that fit in with my own experience. According to the Regnerus study, children raised by same-sex couples miss out on something and end up struggling to function as adults. They have more trouble at work and school, more difficulty staying in marriages, more likelihood of turning to drugs or public assistance to avoid facing the doldrums of life.

Reading about the study in the *Chronicle of Higher Education* jolted me. I posted some comments online.[5] Not long afterwards, I was contacted by people who Googled me and wanted me to write up my experiences. I received an email from someone named Ryan Anderson, who suggested I send the essay to a journal I'd never heard of, called *The Public Discourse*.

I wrote the essay "Growing Up with Two Moms" and sent it off.[6] It got published, and suddenly I got slaughtered by the pro-gay media. The vilification was relentless. *Queerty*, *The New Civil Rights Movement*, *ThinkProgress*, *Equality Matters*, GLAAD, Pink Grit, *Towle Road*, Human Rights Campaign, Right Wing Watch, *Raw Story*, and *OnTopMag* published hostile statements. Yet if there was one thing that I inherited from a brusque, fearless lesbian mother of the 1970s, it was the right to fight back. The more I got blitzed by vicious gay writers, the more I shot back with harsh words of my own on *American Thinker*,[7] and eventually *English Manif*. Decades immersed in gay culture will tend to make a person verbally fearless – or "bitchy," as the vulgar would put it – and I was no slouch.

God gives us contradictory events side by side. It suddenly dawned on me that I'd spent so much of my life as someone incomprehensible to others because of a household that was untranslatable to almost any peers. That is why God inspired me to learn those other languages and become an internationally curious person. If I had not gone through such bizarreness in the 1970s and 1980s, I wouldn't exist to offer an adult's educated and sober analysis of what it's like to be raised by homosexuals, at a time in the 2010s when such an analysis is pertinent. And at a point when the debate in the United States had become most landlocked and stalemated, I found myself, in 2012, presented with *the dictate of fate* to engage in the conversation. Not only was same-sex parenting being foisted upon the United States and Canada by a Gay Lobby determined to pretend that there were no drawbacks to the practice. It was also being exported all over the globe.

Most notably, in France. As I was flying to Princeton, New Jersey, to speak at the Love and Fidelity Network conference days after Barack Obama's re-election, something was stirring across the Atlantic. Frigide Barjot, Laurence Tcheng, and Xavier Bongibault were assembling hundreds of thousands of people to storm Paris to protest against gay adoption.

The Grand Rabbi of France, Gilles Bernheim, had published a pamphlet explaining the Jewish case against same-sex marriage,[8] and some of the key leaders of the marriage movement in the United States sent me the brochure, asking that I translate it into English. As I researched the same-sex parenting debate in France, the French language awakened inside me with a vengeance. French was the language in which I'd found emotional shelter, back in 1986, when problems at home led my mother to send me away to Maine for a time, close to the border of Québec. There, in Maine, I had become involved with a Francophone boy a few years older than I, in a love that tested the boundaries between platonic and sexual romance. French was my language, unlike Spanish, which my mother spoke, or English, which her partner spoke. I kept my diaries in French from 1986 on. Now, in December 2012, it was suddenly useful to people far beyond myself.

Once I completed a translation of Gilles Bernheim's work, a Franco-

American activist living in New Jersey encouraged me to broadcast my story to the people of France. I recorded a YouTube testimonial in French, on a whim, to get away from the nastiness in the United States. I posted it one Sunday, a few days after the massive mobilisation in France on January 13. It quickly reached over 50,000 viewers in Europe.[9] I launched *English Manif* at that point, as a storehouse for all my translations of breaking news. It rapidly became a hub for international readers, getting over 20,000 hits in the first month and reaching 700,000 hits before I decided, in December 2014, to archive the 2,000 essays by me and some twenty-five correspondents.[10]

Laurence Tcheng is a Franco-Chinese socialist who was involved with the French movement for traditional marriage. She contacted me and let me know that the French leaders wanted to meet me. They were interested in having me speak before the protestors for an event on March 24, 2013. By coincidence, I had submitted a proposal for a conference paper to be presented in Lille, France, on March 22, 2013, so I was scheduled to be in France two days before that!

When I arrived in Paris in March, I was interviewed by a number of press outlets. Frigide Barjot asked to meet with me in a coffee shop a few blocks from the Eiffel Tower. I had watched the videos of her and never imagined I would meet her face to face. She was passionate and gorgeous in person. She told me that she was interested in having me speak not only in Paris, but also in some other cities. The next day, she asked me to come with her to Brussels, to speak before delegates in the European Parliament. We rode a train from France to Belgium with a crew of French cameramen surrounding us. There, in Brussels, some allies led us through a maze of stairways and elevators, so we could meet with a secret council of European diplomats concerned about the expansion of same-sex parenting in Europe. They came from Portugal, Italy, Hungary, Poland, Croatia, Slovenia, Slovakia, Ukraine, Holland, Belgium, Ireland, Spain, Germany, Sweden, Luxembourg, Austria, Romania, Bulgaria, the Czech Republic, and Ghana.

"Please translate for us," Frigide suddenly asked. There, in that chamber, I felt a warm sensation. God was whispering something to me as I turned on my microphone and started transferring the tidal waves of words among French, English, Spanish, Portuguese, and Italian.

"All those years," I heard ringing in my ear, "when you were alone and confused and wondered why, this is what was planned for you."

In Brussels, we were driven from the Parliament to a venue where we were supposed to deliver speeches. The discussants included: me, a Swede, Frigide, Xavier, a spokeswoman for French Muslims, and a Belgian philosopher from the renowned University of Leuven.

A mob of protestors awaited us, because someone had blogged to Belgian activists that we had set out from Paris earlier that day. Xavier Bongibault was assaulted with a pie. Frigide Barjot held my arm, seeking to stabilise herself as she walked from the car, surrounded by hired bodyguards from Eastern Europe, facing the barricades, behind which a crowd of screaming leftists frothed with hatred.

After we gave our speeches, we survived that night. We were spirited away along a secret route through a Brussels park, in order to avoid the protestors installed at various checkpoints in the city. Days later, I found myself in Paris, watching the tear gas sail through the air, reminded that my time in the Army wasn't entirely wasted. I had been gassed dozens of times in training and could easily recover from tear gas. That skill came in handy, as I blinked out the pain and mounted the stage set up below the Arc of Triomphe, staring at a crowd that wasn't the 50,000 or 60,000 I'd expected. It was a crowd of over a million.

Returning from France on March 26, 2013, I had to leave behind the exhilaration of Europe and face the annoyances of my tenure case at California State University in Los Angeles. Outside gay groups were pressuring people within the university to sabotage my promotion and have me dismissed for daring to break with gay orthodoxy. Amid the annoyances, I found a new strength, because I knew what my life was made for. The mysteries of my strange life, my untranslatable life, my "puzzling" and "jarring" language and behaviours, finally came together.

All along, there had been a reason for it--to defend the one being forgotten in all the whirling debate about gay issues. The child. "The child" is not merely the human being who is little and helpless, existing as a miniature person between the ages of infancy and adolescence.

"The child" is something far different, far more meaningful. The child is all of us. Children's rights are human rights. We all have a right to know where we came from. We all have a right to be raised by our mother and father, where possible; and if it isn't possible, to have at the very least a mother and a father to love, if a living parent of each sex is available, or to remember, if one has passed away. We all have a right to be born free, not bought, sold, or manufactured.

Nobody, gay or otherwise, has the right to deprive us of those rights. Nobody has a "right" to *us*. To believe that people can have a "right" to another person is to believe in slavery.

When children's rights are violated, human rights are violated, *in perpetuity*, because even as adults, human beings have been violated if they must contend with memories of being bought or sold for adult whims, uprooted from their heritage, denied the love of both sexes (and therefore all of what makes humanity human), or denied a legacy. The crime against humanity that occurs when an adult violates one of these basic children's rights is a lasting intergenerational crime. It is a violence against the family tree to which another human being is entitled by the eternal life cycle that unites all of us.

I do not presume to speak as a prophet, but I know now the importance of finding one's calling. I was called to this fight, because I am one of very few people who can understand, explain, and translate what all of this means and why children's rights can never be overridden by adult whims.

Many gays and lesbians may never have intended to intrude upon these sacred rights. They may never have wanted their cause of "liberation" to spread so quickly around the world, becoming a threat to human rights everywhere. They have been called, as well, to practice self-critique, to disavow selfishness, to show restraint, to sacrifice some of their dreams so that the full entitlements of the more vulnerable among us are not cast aside.

God is calling to them too. Perhaps this is why Jo Jordan, the open lesbian in Hawaii's legislature, voted against same-sex marriage.[11] She has heard the whisper and been inspired to answer the call from the universe. I hope that others will be called, will hear their calling, and find communion with the higher force that calls us each to our tasks in this world.

The children's rights manifesto

Below is an editorial I placed in the *Irish Rover* on July 29, 2014, as a follow-up to a lecture I gave to Notre Dame's Students for Child-Oriented Policy. This summarises as succinctly as possible the belief system that took shape upon my return from Europe.

The Children Need A Club That's Just About Them

I followed, with interest, the debate surrounding the Students for Child-Oriented Policy (SCOP). The outcome of that debate was disappointing. Administrators at the University of Notre Dame accepted poorly conceived allegations lodged by a group representing LGBT interests against a group representing "children's" interests. As a result SCOP was denied recognition as a student group.

As the queer son of a lesbian, who was raised by a lesbian couple between the ages of two and 19, I see Notre Dame's action against SCOP as a slap in the face—not, as you might presume, an act in defense of LGBT people. LGBT activists across the globe have repeatedly claimed that their demands should be met in the name of, and for the good of, children in their custody. These children are, in 100 percent of such instances, not actually related to both adults in the gay household. Think about that: Gay activists look at a household where two same-sex adults have control of someone else's child, and instead of worrying about the child's loss or the child's grievances, their first instinct is to make sure that the two same-sex adults get even more benefits and privileges.

Is this really for the good of those children? No. The anti-SCOP group referred to social-science research that has ostensibly shown positive "outcomes" for children raised by same-sex couples but those "outcomes" are really just measurements of what adults want from children so the adults look good: Does the child have good grades? Does the child look happy in photographs that we can send to the Huffington Post? Is the child well-adjusted, healthy, a good athlete, well liked by his peers, likely to get married and have a stable family too? In other words, all that research has really asked a central question that has little to do with the child's humanity: *Do children in same-sex couples' homes turn out the way gay people want them to, so that gay people look good to straight people?*

Over the years I have worked with many adults who were raised by same-sex couples. I have collaborated with them, interviewed them, heard their stories, recorded their testimonials. I encourage you to go to English Manif, the website I edit, where these are archived. They are their own people. They are not extensions of gay people. They are not trophies or laboratory mice to study and inject with experimental drugs. Generally they are respectful and grateful to the adults who raised them, but they are also keenly aware of the extent to which such adults may have used, abused, and manipulated them for their own selfish purposes. They can love and feel fondness for a guardian and still know the person was self-absorbed and callous to their personal hurt. And many of them are mad about what happened.

Many do not care if the adults raising them are married or not, or receive proper respect from the world at large. They have peers raised by single mothers, grandparents, or divorced parents and do not see such peers as any less worthy simply because their guardians are not in a legally recognised sexual relationship. If the gay adults get married, it will mean that children will simply have more pressure from the legal system to obey the commands and meet the emotional needs of one or two people who aren't really their parents.

Every child has a mother and father. Those two people are human beings with a face, a name, and a heritage; even if the parent was simply a sperm donor, a gestational carrier, someone who abandoned the child, or someone who was thrown out of the house by the other parent. Making gay marriage legal changes none of that. And we know it.

The beauty of SCOP is that it is not strictly focused on same-sex parenting. The group asked me to deliver a keynote at their April 3 conference. The gay students who expressed outrage over SCOP did not come to my talk, as far as I know. I have placed the slide show online so that people who could not attend that event can understand that children's rights isn't about gay people, because it isn't about what adults want from children.

Children raised by gay people have a great deal in common

with adoptees, children of divorce, abandoned children, abused children, orphans, and children conceived through third-party reproduction. Sometimes the transfer of the child's custody to a non-parent was justifiable, but in many cases it wasn't, and in all cases it was hard for the child.

In all of these situations, helpless human beings are robbed of half or all their heritage, when they are too young to consent to such a loss, or even understand it. Sometimes the emotional violence of being severed from a mother, or father, or both, results primarily from the malfeasance or neglect of the lost parent(s), and sometimes it results from the selfishness and contrivances of the replacement "parent(s)." Sometimes, in the worst of cases, this emotional violence is the result of both. For instance, in surrogacy contracts, one mother sells her child to a couple that buys her child. The child must contend with having been sold by his own mother, who is absent, and then raised by the two people who engaged in human trafficking and chattel slavery.

Did you get a chill up your spine when you read the word "slavery"? Harsh words like that get adults on the defensive. People think of "slavery" as whippings, racism, and physical deprivation. But let us engage in an imaginary exercise. What if the myriad societies that practiced slavery in world history barred slave owners from whipping their charges, made sure race was not a factor in identifying human chattel, and forced estates to feed and clothe their subjects well? *It would still be slavery. Slavery* is the problem with slavery, not all the other terrible ills that are symptoms of the main crime.

The violation of three pillars of a child's humanity—the child's right to be born free rather than sold, the child's right to a mother and father, and the child's right to origins—is a serious human rights issue. It could escalate into something as ugly as slavery, even if right now it does not seem that bad to us yet. How would mankind have benefited if, in the 1490s, when Christopher Columbus landed on a new continent, there were groups that formed with the strict goal of advocating for the rights of people who were being treated like chattel, instead of advocating for the rights of the people treating them like chattel?

Recently both the Vatican and the United Nations Human Rights Council convened to discuss family and the rights of children, revisiting earlier declarations in order to update them and safeguard children against the abuses fostered by trafficking, bad adoption practices, abandonment, divorce, same-sex parenting, and third-party reproduction.

Largely launched in France, "children's rights" is a new human-rights movement bridging the concerns of adoptees, children of divorce, children of same-sex couples, orphans, abused children, and children conceived by third-party reproduction. This summer some of my comrades from the US, the UK, Ireland, France, Belgium, Italy, Canada, and China are launching the International Children's Rights Institute, in order to give children's rights a real home on American soil. Notre Dame would be on the cutting edge if the university acknowledged SCOP. It would make the campus a leader in a new field of human rights rather than a dupe of powerful lobbies that have turned children into products. The choice is up to you.[12]

Notes

[1] Mark Regnerus, "How different are the adult children of parents who have same-sex relationships? Findings from the New Family Structures Study", *Social-Science Research* 41, no. 4 (July 2012), 752-770.

[2] Leslea Newman, *Heather Has Two Mommies*, 10th anniversary edition (Los Angeles: Alyson Publications, 2000).

[3] Douglas W. Allen, "High school graduation rates among children of same-sex households", *Review of Economics of the Household* 11, no. 4 (December 2013), 635-658.

[4] Marcel T. Saghir M.D. and Eli Robins M.D., *Male and Female Homosexuality: A Comprehensive Investigation* (Baltimore: William & Wilkins, 1973).

[5] Peter Wood, "The Regnerus Affair at UT Austin", *Chronicle of Higher Education*, Innovations (July 16, 2012), http://chronicle.com (Accessed December 27, 2014).

[6] Robert Oscar Lopez, "Growing up with Two Moms", *Public Discourse* (August 6, 2012) www.thepublicdiscourse.com (Accessed December 27, 2014).

[7] See Robert Oscar Lopez, "The Soul-Crushing Scorched-Earth Battle for Gay Marriage", *American Thinker* (August 11, 2012) www.americanthinker.com (Accessed December 27, 2014).

[8] Gilles Bernheim Grand Rabbin de France, "Mariage homosexuel, homoparentalité et adoption: Ce que l'on oublie souvent de dire", published by Gilles Bernheim (2012) www.scribd.com (Accessed December 27, 2014). See translation in *First Things:* Gilles Bernheim, "Homosexual Marriage, Parenting, and Adoption", *First Things* (March 2013) www.firstthings.com (Accessed December 27, 2014). A scandal broke later on,

because the Grand Rabbi had actually plagiarised parts of this essay from Beatrice Bourges, among others.

[9] *Nouvelles de France*, "Un Américain élevé par deux lesbiennes demande à rencontrer Najat Vallaud-Belkacem (en français)", Poing de Vue (January 22, 2013) *www.ndf.fr/ poing-de-vue* (Accessed December 27, 2014).

[10] To understand the situation that led me to archive and take down the 2,000 articles, this article is helpful: Robert Oscar Lopez, "Here's What You Should Know to Take on Big Gay", *The Federalist*, Culture, (January 7, 2015) www.thefederalist.com (Accessed January 18, 2015). Below is a section of that piece:

Big Gay has a large staff of "social media experts." They love free blogs because left-wing "watchdog groups" cut them checks to sit at home and scan your postings for words to clip out of context. It became clear to me by 2014 that there were handlers assigned to me in particular. *Ad hominem* is their game; Google is where they play to win. Their mode of operations is to compile a dossier of quotes with a high Google ranking. They hope journalists will drop these nuggets into articles and attribute them to you, even if quotes are completely misleading, you have deleted them, or the vast majority of what you write is temperate and logical. GLAAD's profile on me was composed entirely of out-of-context lines clipped from my blog; my public speeches and widely read publications gave GLAAD's hit men very little ammunition. None of the money quotes reflect the full range of their original blog posts, and the vast majority of them are no longer even online anymore. Trolls have a short attention span and are often eager to get back to their porn; if you run a personal blog, they can do a quick search, cut and paste a few things, and then report to their employer that they were doing a heckuva job fighting against anti-gay hate. Don't give them free stuff. Don't blog. Don't do Twitter or Facebook or Instagram. At best, have a mild and innocuous LinkedIn profile. Remember that Big Gay is making money by demonising you. They are raising money by positioning your misquoted words to their funders. Meanwhile, nobody is compensating you. Publish your stuff in places that have good editors. Don't publish on your own. Work on a book or something that can come out in print and isn't free fodder for lazy guttersnipes doing a simple Command+Shift+F search on your document.

[11] Diane Lee, Interviewer, "Exclusive: Why Rep. Jo Jordan voted against Marriage Equality", *Honolulu* (November 2013), www.honolulumagazine.com (Accessed December 27, 2014).

[12] Robert Oscar Lopez, "The Children Need a Club that's Just About Them", *Irish Rover*, Web Exclusives (July 29, 2014) www.irishrover.net (Accessed January 19, 2015).

Chapter Two

AN ADOPTEE'S MANIFESTO

Benoît Talleu
(Translated by Robert Oscar Lopez)

I am publishing here the manifesto written by Benoît Talleu, the Franco-Vietnamese youth who made history in January 2013 by delivering a rousing speech before 700,000 people in Paris. I translated that speech from French into English a year ago and was honoured when it went viral, even in Asia. It remains the fifth most popular post on English Manif.

The topic of Benoît Talleu's original speech was ostensibly an argument against homosexual adoption by an adoptee. Few who listened to Talleu's speech could fail to see that there was a much deeper message in his words, reflecting on the emotional dilemmas of adoption itself, and of course, transracial adoption. Talleu's famous line, "we are not a medication for you", was not only relevant to the problematic tendency of gay activists to objectify children as a means of advancing an image of LGBT normalcy. In a deeper sense, Talleu's statement was a clarion call against all forms of objectifying children in order to satisfy adult desires for parenthood.

I interviewed Benoît in May 2013, because I wanted to use part of my interview with him for a presentation at the American Literature Association conference in Boston. I was presenting before the Asian American Studies group of the ALA. By then, it became clear to me that Talleu's talent for emotionally moving people, and his eloquence, needed to be given attention outside of the contentious debate about gay marriage or gay adoption.

When I went to Paris on February 2, 2014, to speak for another Manif pour Tous, I set aside time to interview Benoît in person, and in depth. He is now studying international law in Lille and wants to dedicate himself to the advocacy of children's rights. Even now, he is still recognised by passers-by in France who remember his speech from the grand January manif (demonstration) in the Champ de Mars, just below the Eiffel Tower.

I urged him to become a writer, to give voice to the complex emotions of trans-racial adoptees in France. In the English-speaking world, there has arisen a rich array of voices commenting on trans-racial adoption, but Benoît, I felt, could provide a window into the lesser known experiences of Francophone adoptees. Benoît would be embarking on the genre of adoptee literature from a fascinating position as someone who had already become a public figure as a teenager.

The result of my meeting with Benoît on February 2 is this opening framework for his theory of adoptee experience, his "paradigm," if you will, of three sufferings converging into a form of healing. It was my honour to translate this into English.

The new manifesto of Benoit Talleu
Two friends have a talk.

– Tell me; your family, is it your true family?

– Why would you ask that?

– Well, because you are adopted. So what's up with that? Is it not so hard for you?

– Why do you ask that?

– As for my part, I don't know what's … can you explain it to me?

– Adoption is a happiness that is born of several sufferings meeting one another …

In 1995, in Vietnam, a woman takes up with a man; they make love and conceive a child from their love; this child is me … When the man learns that my mother is pregnant, he is overcome with fear. With the courage one is familiar with in men, he flees. He leaves behind mother and child in the poverty and shame that are often attributed to young, unmarried Vietnamese mothers.

What can a weak, lonely woman do, rejected and abandoned by her parents, as well as her friends, and even the man by whom she thought she was loved?

The methods widely used in our Western nations, *soi-disant* « developed and civilised » would call for the existence of the child to be solved pure and simple ... that is, he would disappear, be forgotten in silence and in the long muffled cry that he exerts at the moment of « medical » intervention ...

Those who aren't informed but who convince themselves of their own generosity (often Westerners) and who are so far from the reality of the real misery that grinds down countries classified as « emerging nations, » might think that these women, weak and just as indifferent as they are, leave their children before church doors before running away and disappearing or, better yet, leaving them in a floating bread basket and trusting them to the currents of a river.

Perhaps that is the case sometimes, but it isn't the case for this child I am telling you about. It isn't the case for this woman, who is a mother and has a maternal conscience. Therefore what ought this poor mother do?

Well, she will make the most generous and giving choice available to her: she entrusts her child to an adoption center, with the hope that he will have a father, the father she couldn't give him, and a mother, the mother she must refuse to become.

Therein lies the first suffering.

The first suffering belongs to the biological mother, alone and abandoned; who has the courage to give her child the life and love of a mother who may also provide him with the love of a father. It is a suffering that I believe is the greatest and which is certainly the longest. It is a suffering that is born from the deepest maternal love.

Anonymous entrusting of a newborn to the state (*l'accouchement sous X*), is therefore now a done deal. This woman gives birth and hopes that someone will provide parents to the child.

The child is born, without a name or history ... but so that he will have a name, they baptise him Nguyen Hien Hòa.

Hien Hòa finds himself, just like other children, in the orphanage, and like all children, he has one sole desire: to be able to have the fortune of saying, « Dad, Mom, I love you. »

But what can he do? Nothing.

He awaits, hopefully, the moment for a father and mother to love him, this same hope that allowed his biological mother to entrust him to the adoption system, the same hope she harbors still today, in saying to herself, « I hope he is happy with *his* father and *his* mother. » He says to himself: « I hope to be happy with *my* mother and *my* father. » But he must wait.

Therein lies the second suffering.

This is the suffering of a child who is orphaned. It is certainly the hardest of the sufferings, when one accounts for the weakness of the child who has just been born ...

Finally, a French couple appears. The couple learns that they will not be able to conceive children together. Before anything, they must accept the fact that the love that unites this couple will not allow them to claim a child of their own flesh and blood: it is a painful shock. Still, their status remains; they have the job of parenting children. They make the decision to sign up for adoption: they offer themselves as father and mother, loving parents, to a child who has none. While knowing that they cannot have a child of their flesh and blood, while knowing that they will watch a child grow who does not resemble them, and who will not give them grandchildren to mirror them ...

Therein lies the third suffering.

This is the suffering of a man and a woman who have the theoretical possibility of giving birth to a child, suddenly seeing that possibility nullified by sterility.

But it is important to wonder which suffering is the most important to fulfill: the loneliness of an orphaned child, the tragedy of an abandoned mother, or the anger of a couple that cannot understand why they cannot have a child? It is certain that one must place first the child. He is alone, weak, barely existing if it is not an existence in « Bụi đời » (the wretched dust of life) in the eyes of Vietnamese society. We cannot betray the suffering of the mother, her courage, and trust. Finally the couple offers itself. The father and mother by adoption offer themselves to the child and receive motherhood and fatherhood due to the faith of the woman who gave this to them.

Today, the couple has seven children and Nguyen Hien Hòa is named

Benoît TALLEU. He has a history, roots to which he has grafted more, in the process giving himself a name, a past, and a future. He returned to Vietnam where he saw his maternal ancestry, the orphanage ... He met as well women who, like his mother, have confided their motherhood, after Benoît's history was explained to them. One of these, moved, took him in her arms and cried over his young age, which he did not understand at first ... But today, he knows that it is the proof that these brave women ought not lose hope, because they can know that today, their child has for certain the chance to be loved, surrounded by a father and mother who love him as their own child because they know that this child could have been just like their own flesh and blood.

That is what adoption means. It is a constant yearning for the best possible in an ocean of tears, a long consolation for a triple suffering which looks, against great resistance, to be healed with sweetness, tenderness, and hope.

Chapter Three

CHILDREN OF GAY PARENTS (PART 1)

Brittany Klein (BK)
Robert Oscar Lopez (ROL)
Dawn Stefanowicz (DS)

ROL: I am here with two great guests. One of which is Dawn Stefanowicz, and the other of which is Brittany Klein. Among the three of us we are all adults who were raised by adults who were in same-sex relationships. We have a lot of shared experiences to talk about, and also, some differences. So let's start with the first question, which I will pose to Dawn and then to Brittany: We're hearing a lot in the popular media, that there is a consensus, from sociologists and psychologists and also groups like COLAGE (Children of Lesbians and Gays Everywhere) which represent children of lesbians and gays. The consensus is that there's no difference between growing up with a mom and a dad and growing up with same-sex couple. Dawn, what do you think of that? How does that consensus match your experience?

DS: I have to say that we are very rare to have grown up with same-sex couples. Because, if I could just mention, in the US, in the 2010 census, when they were looking at over 650,000 households,[1] which included two adults of the same gender, they found that only 1 in every 17 children of gay parents actually lived with a same-sex couple (based on the statistics). Now because of my own background, I never felt that I belonged. So I don't agree with COLAGE, I don't agree with the American Psychological Association (APA) saying that there's no difference for us when we grow up with parents involved in same-sex relationships. We're impacted long-term. But as children we don't realise this. It takes us often until the late 20s, early 30s, to realise or start realising the long-term impact. For me, I never felt that I belonged. I felt that there was this prolonged and unresolved grief, sadness, and depression in my life. And I had two brothers as well. And I saw that each one of us was very much affected by the environment that we grew up in. Ours wasn't just the home environment, it was also that we were taken regularly into the developing GLBT subcultures beginning when my twin brother and I were eight years old. We had quite an extensive background under the GLBT umbrella. Because for us it began in infancy when my father began bringing different men into the home.

ROL: Okay and what was that like when your father exposed you to gay culture?

DS: It's something where as a little girl growing up I didn't feel that my own femininity and womanhood was being affirmed, and valued, and loved, in that kind of environment. In fact, I felt that it was better to be a gay male, or even a transgender male, than it was to be a little girl growing up. I always felt that I really wasn't lovable because I did not see the men in my life loving women.

ROL: You know it's interesting because in the Doug Allen study, where he canvassed 20% of the Canadian census, he found that the worst performing combination is a woman being raised by two gay men. They only graduate at 15% the rate of children being raised by a mom and a dad.

DS: There's a lot of struggle academically and in employment because there's a lot of insecurities. I honestly felt that my personality was crushed. Now today you would look at me and think, "Well, no, I don't see any difference". We would have to look at not just the long-term impact but what I've done to overcome the challenges in my background. Even though I've overcome so much, there will be long-term challenges I will carry with me to the grave. Because I didn't grow up in a regular heterosexual environment that valued a married mother and father for children.

ROL: Right. Very good point. How about you, Brittany? What do you say?

BK: I'm going to have to agree with almost everything maybe for slightly different reasons in my experience. I glanced at what COLAGE is. It really honestly looked to me like more of the dog and pony show, the whole training. I could tell you that when my mother was not involved with somebody, she never showed up at the school. She didn't go to the PTA, she didn't go to anything. If she was involved with somebody, the second that notice came home, like for a science fair, she's like "oh, goody, look what we get to go to!" And that's why they went. It was a show put on for the teachers and the school to see how uncomfortable they could make them. And that obviously would put me in a terrible situation at school. I mean, I was an academic failure, I still am. Can't do multiplication, can't do any of those things.

ROL: But you write really great essays!

BK: I basically think APA is wrong. I don't know who they asked. I don't know what they asked. And I don't know how reliable, you know – you know, what were they judging? I read somewhere, and I can't remember where, where it said something like, growing up with same-sex parents is positive, because it makes the kids more sexually adventurous and it makes them more open-minded.

ROL: Yeah, I saw that, I think that was in Boston, it was a group of people who –

BK: And, who wants their kid to be sexually adventurous? What does that mean? That's one. And the other thing, the less bigoted and more open-minded, whatever it said, that was like a red flag to me, because, you know I could tell from that result that the question was manipulated. "What do you think of gay people?" "Oh, they're great, they're wonderful." Well, yeah, the two gay parents are sitting there with dagger eyes on you. You better say that.

ROL: Damn straight.

BK: But ask that same kid, what do you think of fundamentalist Christians? Bigotry only comes into play when it's someone you don't want to be bigoted against. Does that make sense?

ROL: No, yeah, I think you're making a great point. I think my response to the question is – you know, I looked really closely at the APA, and the American Statistical Association (ASA), and the foster care associations, and all of these associations are under massive pressure from the gay lobby. Any time you come up with any data that runs counter to it, you almost get fired. That's what happened to Mark Regnerus and Doug Allen and Loren Marks, and the people who published them, and me. So I don't trust any of the research. Also because I don't think statistics can capture what it means not to have a dad in your life.

BK: Well yeah – you don't have one biological parent in your life, and you have a whole troupe of people coming in with whatever whim they have in their head that day that you have to play to. And when everything hits the fan, there isn't plan B. If a kid knows, if everything hits the fan, I can go live with a grandparent. But there isn't a plan B there. Do you know what I'm saying?

ROL: Yeah, for me it was a little bit odd. I'm a little different from you guys because my mother was in the same relationship from the time I was two until the time I was nineteen and my mom died. So my mom's partner was a very stable presence in our life. They did not live in the same house which I think was the right thing to do. I think my mother made a good choice with that but even so I was very aware that she and her partner were a couple and that they both sort of had this authority and emotional connection to me. For me the problem was being a boy being raised by two lesbians and having a lisp, I struggled so much with a lisp. Partly because I inherited the Caribbean Spanish accent from my mother's family and partly because I was effeminate. But I just didn't have a dad there and aside from the problem of not being able to model behavior, for me the biggest problem was I didn't have a man there. I don't know if this is a fair reading of what happened to me but I really tried to fill that gap. And I filled that gap sexually. And from the age of 13 on, I was extremely promiscuous and sleeping with a lot of older men. And they would give me gifts and money, and I knew where to find them. You know, you go to the sauna at the YMCA or the parking lot outside the 24-hour supermarket; they were just everywhere. And partly this was because I had a heightened awareness of gay culture because my mom had so many gay friends and partly it was also the problem of not having a dad. So for me all those problems came together. Does that make sense?

DS: Well Bobby, you know, about 30% of us will become 2nd generation which is really high compared to, say 2% in the general population.

ROL: So 30% of us become gay or bi, right?

DS: Right. We become like our gay or lesbian parents, 30% of us. And I have to say that of all the adult children I've spoken to and had communication with, via email, almost all of us have had some level of sexuality confusion. Not that we came out and labeled ourselves. But we struggled. A number of us—I don't know about Brittany, but with myself, there was sexual abuse. There was sexual abuse with other adult children I have spoken to. So it's a very sexualised environment. Not just within the home but within the subculture that I was exposed to. And so for me it was frustrating because I was trying to find that father love affirmation so I began having boyfriends at age 12. Now I may have appeared to be promiscuous because I had all these boyfriends but really I was trying to fill that deep down need, to be affirmed as a daughter, from my father.

ROL: But that's interesting because you had a dad. That's fascinating to me.

DS: But his attention was always centered on the males in his life. There were three key males in my life growing up but there were also multiple partners that my father had and his partners had, that they were involved with sexually. So in some ways it wasn't always like a couple, it almost seemed polygamous at times because my father and his partners could be involved with 12 other men at the gay bars downtown.

ROL: Yeah, you know, this – Brittany, I don't know if you've had any exposure to this – but this matches the feedback I've gotten particularly from ex-wives who lost custody of children to gay husbands who came out of the closet. All of them express panic about the open relationships that their ex-husbands have and the fact that there's this parade of men in the house. One of the scenarios I hear again and again is that they leave their pornography around.

DS: Right, my brothers came across that.

ROL: Do you have any thoughts on that, Brittany?

BK: My mother had – there was some pornography, I thought most of it was supposed to be a joke. Because my mother was into gay culture for a time. I mean, in the heyday, the early 1970s, the gay men and the lesbians, everybody got along great. And then when the gay men noticed that the lesbians didn't have enough money to party it up, there was a switch.

ROL: Right.

BK: And the lesbians were kind of kicked to the curb. You know, "go live in your bad neighborhoods. We're going Dutch on this date." Right?

ROL: Yeah, Dawn had the same observations. I was talking to Dawn earlier and one of the things she was saying was that gay male culture was very kind of posh. Whereas I always thought of gay culture, because of my mother's experience, as being very blue collar.

BK: Well, yes, the gay men went to the really nice places for vacation and we went to the rustic bungalow park.

ROL: The RV park. That's where I spent all my time.

Chapter Four

CHILDREN OF GAY PARENTS (PART 2)

Brittany Klein
Robert Oscar Lopez
Dawn Stefanowicz

BK: For me, my mother, you know she had some of that pornography around and the books and stuff. What I found even more distressing than all that – I didn't realise then, but I realise now, she was very invested in trying to figure out what my sexuality was. A boy would be over and she'd be like, "you know, I think he wants to kiss you." And I'd be like, "yeah, well so what? He can go kiss a doorknob." I literally just completely closed down that way. I was just completely androgynous. I never flirted with a boy ever, in my life. And then, in a sense, the way I got married was sort of perfect. We were like, "do you want to live in this place or that place? Do you want to have this many kids or this many kids? Who's going to work and who's going to stay home? Okay, done deal. See you in four weeks, under the huppa."[1]

ROL: You had something to add, Dawn?

DS: Well it's interesting. You know, I had very low expectations of marriage. What I was looking for was stability in my marriage partner. My husband and I, now we've been married for almost 30 years.

ROL: Wow.

DS: And he's a very moral, good man. And we've never had a lot of money. But we've always had stability in our relationship and in our home. And I didn't see that growing up. My father had a lot of disposable income. We did travel to very nice vacation spots and I loved hotel swimming pools because I would have the whole pool to myself, while my father was off gallivanting with his partner in the gay cruising area nearby. We would actually switch hotels 50 miles out. It could've been Ft. Lauderdale. My father would find out about another gay cruising area, and we'd actually switch hotels 50 miles down the road. There there'd be a swimming pool so I could have that pool all to myself while my father was out again. So this is where our vacations were very interesting for my brothers and me; and I loved that pool looking up at the starry night sky. I didn't realise how lonely I felt inside at the time, how rejected and abandoned I felt inside. It wasn't until much later that I realised that my father had chosen very selfish vacation spots that would meet his needs. But you know, going to Disneyland, or going to beautiful gardens once, was great, but out of the whole vacation, a lot of it for me was spent alone.

ROL: It sounds like it was a by-product of the culture.

BK: Well I think there are two impulses in the culture. Dawn is hitting on one of them, you know, get in as much "gay fun" and gay sex as possible in four days, and then the other part of the culture was, "We're better than they are." And they could be – "They" was any heterosexual that walked by you. Which was everybody. "They" was the teacher, the librarian, and everybody else. You know, "we're better, we're smarter, we're more advanced, we're more honest". It was for a couple of years, a buzz, every woman's a lesbian. "You're really a lesbian. You just don't know it." And then there was the hierarchy with them, of lesbianism. Who's more of a lesbian, who's been a lesbian longer. Who cashed out and got married and did the hetero thing. There was status in certain things....

ROL: So you were saying there was a difference in the way they dealt with your brother versus the way they dealt with you and your sister.

BK: Yes, me and my sister. I mean, my sister was cute. She was a cute child and she's much younger. So she was also a trained dog, being cute and adorable and accepted. Because there was a point when the whole thing collided and merged into the hippie culture and the music culture. My mother got hooked up with some hippie people and also with some people in the music industry, you know, like the New York Dolls. I don't know if you've ever heard of the New York Dolls. But they all dressed in drag. She was really into the drag scene and having these guys over. Most of them were just mean and dumb. My sister and I were just invisible at one point. We just sort of didn't exist. And my brother was more gregarious. He would be the one to make the drinks and serve them to everyone. He learned very early how to please. But I think that what Dawn was saying is that no matter which way you slice it, whether it was the social or the political or the sexual, it was always about *them*. When you sent me the questions, I looked up some stuff. One thing I found was this tiny quote from this woman, somewhere in New England, some scholar in New England, and she says something to the effect of, "gay parents tend to be more motivated and committed than heterosexual parents, because they really want those kids". And I thought to myself, that just shows how this woman supposedly – I guess she's heterosexual, I don't know – this woman academic absorbs the gay community's hatred of women. Even the lesbians, in a weird way, hated heterosexual women.

ROL: I always felt that both gay men and lesbians had a similar misogyny. Because lesbians want to be more like men and then gay men want to be hypermasculine.

BK: So she said, they're going to be better parents because they want it. And what I saw her actually saying is that because heterosexuals can get pregnant by accident, or in the back of the car and they didn't mean it, that they didn't want those kids. To me, there's a huge aspect that they're missing in this picture, called sacrifice. You get pregnant in the back of the Chevy, and you have a baby, that's a sacrifice. That's where parenting comes from and they didn't get that. They so did not get any of that. Their research shows and their statements show even now, that they don't get it. Everything – there was no concept of childhood. There cannot be a concept of child or childhood when the only identity is sexual.

DS: Can I add something, Bobby?

ROL: Yeah, sure, go ahead.

DS: For me the environment was very sexualised from infancy forward. A lot of sexual experimentation was going on in the home. In the sub-cultures where I was taken to, my father was involved in all different aspects of experimentation. I wouldn't limit it to just "gay." When I say the GLBT umbrella, I am including every form of sexual experimentation you could fit in there. He was into Craig Russell big time by the time I was 8 or 9 years old. Everything was about Craig Russell.

ROL: Who's Craig Russell?

DS: Pornography, you know, these kind of underground men's magazines. Where they'd be pornographic but you could be wearing scantily clad underwear. My father was actually an underground male model for underwear in a community magazine. So what I picked up was that he and his partner also had an affinity for underage boys. I have to say this –

ROL: You know, I have to jump in and say something. You know, I saw that so much in the gay male culture. You get *viciously attacked* by GLAAD and by HRC when you even allude to it. But I think that finally with this issue of Tom Daley, that diver, the 19-year-old who got preyed on by that 39-year-old screenwriter, and then –

BK: After his father died.

ROL: Yeah, and then the *Huffington Post* defended it. I think finally the gay community can't deny it anymore.

ROL: Well, you sent me that thing that Apple has a new app for twelve-year-olds to find sex.

DS: Yes, Bobby, what my father was afraid of. Whenever he brought other gay men to the home, he had a fear that any one of his gay friends could hit on my brothers. And so he was a bit guarded when he found out, he would come from working late, and he was wondering why one of his partners was sitting at the kitchen table playing cards with my brothers and I. He was very upset about it.

ROL: Well at least he had a fatherly impulse.

DS: He did. The other thing, I was afraid to bring boyfriends home, even in my young teens because my dad would hit on the good-looking ones.

ROL: Are you serious?

DS: He would actually – he and his partner at the time actually hit on a very good-looking boy I brought home that was about fourteen or fifteen. And they wanted three-way sex with him up in the bedroom. This all happened right before my eyes; I couldn't believe it. Even though I'd seen so much already, I would still be stunned by there being no boundaries around sexuality, around the number of partners, around age, around various types of sexual practices. There were no limits.

ROL: Right, and you know, they just broke another story from Alabama with the same thing.

Note
[1] *Huppa* is a special canape used in traditional Jewish weddings.

Chapter Five

CHILDREN OF GAY PARENTS (PART 3)

Brittany Klein
Robert Oscar Lopez
Dawn Stefanowicz

ROL: What do you guys feel? This obscure thing that we went through, in the 1970s and 1980s, is all over the news. What do you think?

BK: It's that if AIDS hadn't happened it was on its way to where it is now. If AIDS hadn't happened, we would've been here in 1983.

ROL: Okay, that's a good point.

BK: That's what I think.

ROL: What do you think, Dawn?

DS: Well, my father died of AIDS in 1991. And at that point, I mean, people treated you like you had cooties if you told them that you had a close family member that died of AIDS. Even in the culture of the 70s, 80s, and early 90s, I think there was a lot of ignorance about children growing up in this environment. It was not talked about. I did not grow up seeing children in the subcultures. It was kind of rare that my brothers and I were on a nudist beach at Hamlin's Point, Toronto Island. Canada. We were the only kids there amongst all these gay males. But there would be a few females that were topless who were female models but they were surrounded by 14 or 16 gay males. So it was a very interesting background that I have. But really the culture at the time, I don't think was ready. Until very recently. I know there's been a lot of marketing efforts in the 80s and the 90s. And now the television sitcoms are just full of gay characters. I don't know if it's 50% but it seems like almost every program or 2nd program has at least one gay character in it. And so it's very front and center. But I feel that the right messaging, the truth about how it impacts children, is not being heard in the living rooms in North America or in Western civilisation.

ROL: Well, it seems to me that's what's happening, because my experience was that even the gay community in the 80s and even to a certain extent in the 90s, was very uncomfortable when I would tell them, you know, my mom was a lesbian. They did not want to deal with that because—

BK: Right, exactly, because they don't want to know from you.

ROL: Because they didn't want to hear the truth. I think they suspect in their heart of hearts, they know the kids have a lot of very dark stories to tell. Their relationship to us is very strained. It was even more strained back then. They looked upon us as a mark of shame. It meant that there were gay people who got involved in heterosexual relationships before they came out as gay. And so there was a mark on me. It's been difficult to have this all of a sudden catapulted to public awareness and to go from having to keep my mother's sexuality secret to protect her, to now keeping secret the fact that it was so hard for me....

DS: I didn't go public until about 20 years ago. And I didn't come out with my book *Out from Under* until 2007. It took me that long because it was such a bold step to even go public to that degree. They were such vulnerable, intimate details of my upbringing. I knew that everyday people with their heads in the sand would have a very hard time understanding what it was like for me to grow up in this environment. And they don't want to hear that. They wanted to hear the rhetoric, and see the nice fun sitcoms on TV, making everything seem all happy and gay. They didn't want to know the reality that this was extremely difficult and painful. And traumatising for me as a child growing up.

ROL: Brittany, you had something to say too?

BK: I grew up with a lot of, I don't know what to call it – gay media? – they thought it was very subversive and humorous. The killing of Sister George or them obsessing about Batman and Robin and seeing gay codes. You know, just like religious fanatics with Bible Codes. They would see gay things coded in every soap opera they watched, little messages just to them. I did also find that hostility in the gay culture. They didn't want to know from us. You know we're not going to be their long-lost children in any way. But I distinctly remember meetings and things in the late 70s, of them saying, "we have buying power; we can put pressure on this company or that company". All of that was in the works then. It came together more recently. The AIDS thing... I think the way it's framed has changed, but the essential nature of it hasn't changed. The way they present it to the rest of the world has changed, but the essential nature of the whole thing has not changed. If that makes any sense. Back then, who wanted to get married? "Married" was like, "who needs the piece of paper? Why do we have to prove anything to anyone?" It was the counterculture. Marriage was a bad institution. Now they want a tax break. What's her name? You know, that very rich Jewish[*] lady who went to the Supreme Court.

ROL: Oh, Edie Windsor?

BK: Yes! Yes, I mean, she's a nice old Jewish lady. I wish her well, but that was about taxes.

ROL: Yeah, it was $3.5 million and that wasn't enough. She wanted $360,000 more.

BK: That's the thing. I do remember about the marriage thing. While it was much more fluid and changing partners, I do remember they wanted their relationships respected and treated the same as heterosexual relationships. I mean, you're never going to find a lesbian who goes any place by herself. No, no, that does not happen. They have to go to the supermarket? They're going together. And make sure everybody knows about it. And so, I think, it has been marketed in a way that tries to make it look all "same-y," you know, "we're just like you," but it isn't the same. I mean, that kid – what was his name? The Boy Scout.

ROL: Oh, Zach Wahls.

BK: Yeah, I mean, that he was a Boy Scout. That just tells me – He's another one, exactly like my brother was. Exactly. What does it take to be a Boy Scout and good at it? Conformity.

ROL: Right, yeah, well that's the opposite end of the difficult

---

[*] Brittany is herself Jewish and means nothing disparaging with this remark [-ROL.]

experiences for kids of same-sex couples. This leads to my last question. Which is, whether kids of same-sex couples have it better now. I actually think that they have it a lot harder.

BK: I think so too.

ROL: Because it's so politicised. When I was growing up, I had the option of going into my cubby, and not dealing with this at all. But the kids of same-sex couples now, they just don't. Their parents send Christmas cards to the governor with their pictures on it, they bring them to the Easter egg hunt, and they throw them in the middle of all these political battles. *And they just don't stop.* They're so pushy with their kids. I just think it's a lot harder for them. I don't know what you guys think....

DS: I think they've been used as guinea pigs to present a particular political agenda. You know if you talk about gay marriage; Canada has already – that's an old hat now. It's been legalised in Canada. If you read the gay magazines here in Canada, the truth is, the majority never wanted marriage. Never wanted anything that would have ever been close to heterosexual monogamy. In fact, they like the freedom of being involved with whomever they want, whenever they want. That was more the reality –

[Break]

ROL: So Dawn, you were talking about how you feel like a lot of these kids are being used now. Like guinea pigs.

DS: Yes, I don't feel that we are allowed to be honest. We have to hold a lot of secrets inside for a very long time, which creates a lot of stress for us. We have to pretend that this is okay to have a gay parent and his or her partners in our home, and be involved in the subcultures. We have to smile and be happy and say this is all okay. We're still dependents. But when we're no longer dependents, and we have developed a sense of independence and distance from our family of origin, and have some strength ourselves, to be able to speak, we can now be honest and say this is going to be very difficult for us, not only to tell you what the actual reality is, for us to grow up in this kind of situation, but it's also going to impact us for the rest of our lives and as we come together with other adult children who have also grown up in a same-sex couple's relationship – now, when I say a couple, I want to use that loosely, because often, especially in my father's situation and I noticed among gay males, they often have open relationships, with multiple sexual partners,— "couple" makes it almost sound like it's monogamous, when it was absolutely not. I really feel that we need a voice to express to the public, to – you know, whether that be through the media or an academic environment, we need to let our politicians know that there are adult children like us, who are no longer dependent. We're not worried about whether our college or university education will be sponsored by some GLBT group. We're independent, we're grown up. We have a voice and we're saying, this has negative outcomes for us long-term.

BK: One thing that scares me now is, you know, nobody said anything or did anything for years and years. We could've been starving but – finally, something happened and somebody dropped a dime and called Children's Social Services, off to foster care, and there we went... Now, I'm afraid, I know for a fact, nobody in the gay community is going to turn anybody in.

ROL: Nobody. I totally agree with you. I've seen that. Not only that but even people who are gay-friendly, who have gay friends, they will see horrible things going on between the gay parents and the children and they won't say –

BK: And that's what scares me. Even the heterosexual community is so cowed right now that they will not do it either.

Chapter Six

CHILDREN OF GAY PARENTS (PART 4)
Brittany Klein
Robert Oscar Lopez
Dawn Stefanowicz

BK: ... I mean [snitching] saved us... We were sent back after a while but it saved us. You could, you know – Maybe the nasty little Christian spinster down the street would be a real witch and drop a dime and call Child Social Services. But now? I don't know. I think it's worse. I think these kids are in much worse situations than we were in.

ROL: Well, the documented cases we've gotten in the press all attest to that. You have the case of that Australian couple that went – that horrible case where they conceived the child with a surrogate and they came back to Australia and nobody wanted to say anything. They even profiled them as two great dads while they were sick.

BK: I read that. The journalist that profiled them as two great dads wrote another article if you can find it, where she said that she does not feel badly that she profiled them as two great dads because homophobia is worse.

ROL: Yeah, that's terrifying. That's terrifying.

BK: I mean, as if – really? My mother did have partners at times who were saner and more mature than she was. And they left.

ROL: Right.

BK: You know. They left, they ran. I remember just standing in the driveway when one of them was leaving, the only one who actually put plates on a table, with a glass, with food on the plate. And you know, she was a schoolteacher and she was like, now we're going to eat. Try to do things normally. And I remember she was leaving, and I was like in the driveway, saying, "Don't go." And she literally said to me, she said, "In a few years you'll be able to get out of here." I was in sixth grade. It was a long few years.

DS: Wow.

ROL: Wow.

DS: Bobby, you know, I agree, because I did not feel that any of my father's partners were really there in the home for me. I felt like my brothers and I were neglected. Our needs were not met. I don't remember any one of my father's partners reaching out and saying, "Dawn, how are you feeling? How was your day?" And really really caring about me. But what I did feel was, I was being criticised about my appearance. That I had to go out and get something more fashionable. Or wear Chanel No. 5. Or get my hair done.

ROL: Oh my God, that sounds like the worst gay male nightmare.

DS: My heart was in the basement at that point....

ROL: That's what Rupert Everett said in England; he said there's nothing worse than being raised in that environment. Because the assault on your ego would be constant... I have to admit, my situation was a little bit different because my mom's partner was really the source of so much comfort for me, and she was sort of the good cop. [Break] My mother's partner was definitely the good cop in the good cop-bad cop situation, and she was so stable and showed me so much care. That's why it was so hard when my mom passed away. Because my siblings did not see my mother's partner as a second mother. They saw our father as their father. But I was conceived with that in mind; my mother intended to raise me with her partner, so it was a little bit different....

BK: I did not get along with most of my mother's partners. The last one I absolutely did not get along with. But she was – She had a notion of integrity, that much I'd give her. She wouldn't – They would all be sort of planning, and manipulating, and lying, and thinking of things, and my mother's partner would say, I don't think this is such a good idea. She was also humourless. And incredibly, really masculine. I mean, she got mis-gendered every minute.

DS: My father's partners were always ten years younger than he was. And always more submissive males, almost taking on wifely like roles.

ROL: Interesting.

DS: My father was more macho. The more masculine type of gay male. And you know, if I can say this, it's hard to use the term 'gay' for me, because I look at someone's attraction as being a bit more flexible and leaning toward heterosexual as we age. But when we use the term 'gay,' it's often a social political term, because it's where our parents affiliated most. My father affiliated almost all of the time with the gay subcultures. But of course we had the GLBT subcultures—even though everyone was separate under that umbrella, there were times when we would see each other. The transgendered males were often there—I had a hard time figuring out if they were gay males dressed up in drag, or they were men that actually thought of themselves as females. I had a very hard time understanding the nuances of transgenderism as an 8-year-old girl.

ROL: Oh my God, that's a whole other, that's a whole other ball of wax....

BK: Somebody like RuPaul is a gay man. A really gay man. I think most people who say they are transgender are heterosexual males who have a cross-dressing fetish. Which is another thing that's really upsetting about GBL—whatever they're calling themselves this week. If you do a breakdown of who it is, it's mostly men. It is a gay, it is a male organisation.

ROL: And as you and I have both pointed out, we saw it from the ground up; gay men used lesbians at certain times and then asked them to make a quick exit. When it wasn't valuable to them.

BK: Right, and they're still doing it. The lesbians are put out there first, you know, why they do it, if you want to talk feminism or anything, what they call POV, I only got one POV going on. In my life. I mean, these women have all these guys, and I think in a weird way they are so dangerous to children, you have the children growing up in it who are at risk, and then you have them bringing to bear, saying, oh, um, "gay is passé, we have transgender now," so let's sterilise your 8-year-old son. And castrate him too while we're at it.

ROL: I know, it's really sick.

BK: It's insanity and I don't understand how people are going along with this.

ROL: Well there's a lot to talk about. I think I have to wrap it up right now.

Chapter Seven

ROLL-CALL OF CHILDREN RAISED
BY SAME-SEX COUPLES

Ed. Anonymous

The following are brief contributions from adults and children who were raised by gay and lesbian parents. They offer counter-narratives to the consensus on same-sex parenting. They have been compiled by several volunteers who wish not to be named, out of fear of retaliation by gay organisations. ROL

Jean-Dominique Bunel
Raised by lesbians
"It was not the taboo of homosexuality that made me suffer, but same-sex parenting. Homosexuals should naturally be greeted with brotherhood. They enrich humanity and if necessary, of course, give them as much as possible the same rights as heterosexuals but this equality obviously cannot apply to a 'right to the child' which exists nowhere and is not found in any text. This is indeed what cannot be: gay parenting. ... I oppose this bill because in the name of a fight against inequalities and discrimination, we would refuse a child one of its most sacred rights, upon which a universal, millenia-old tradition rests, that of being raised by a father and a mother. You see, two rights collide: the right to a child for gays, and the right of a child to a mother and father. The international convention on the rights of the child stipulates in effect that 'the highest interest of the child should be a primary consideration'

(article 3, section 1). Here this 'higher interest' leaves no doubt. But it is the wounded man who concludes: 'If two women who raised me had been married prior to the adoption of such a bill, I would have jumped into the fray and would have brought a complaint before the French state and before the European Court of the rights of man, for the violation of my right to a mom and a dad.'"[1]

Dawn Stefanowicz
Raised by gay father

"I ... grew up in a homosexual household. My mother was quite ill. I attended school, community and church programmes like most children. However, from my infancy my father was involved in homosexuality, inside and outside of the home. My mental and physical health was jeopardised as I was exposed to my father's and his partners' lifestyle choices, leaving me traumatised. I was at high risk of exposure to particular pathogens, including hepatitis. I was aware of polygamous relationships, experimentation with gender and varying sexuality, and grieved suicides and the treatment of discarded (ex) partners. Laws around public sex were often ignored in the sub-cultures and I saw precious few heterosexual couples. By thirty years old, I was deeply grieved as my father had died of AIDS and many of his (ex) partners were either dead or dying. ... I too had my 'days of silence' as my father threatened me. He used me as bait to attract sexual partners. Though I was deeply disappointed with my father and his partners' sexual behaviours, I couldn't say anything negative about my dad or the homosexual lifestyle. For a time, I coped by being performance oriented and denying the influences around me, pretending I could rise above everything."[2]

Katy Faust
Daughter of a mother who loves women

"In addition to the distinct and complimentary ways that men and women parent, children need both sexes in their immediate world as they develop their own gender identity. It's strongly held within the social sciences that beginning as early as age three, children can (and should) identify with their same sex parent. Boys begin to gravitate toward dads who should actively seek to include their sons in their world. This gives incredible confidence to their boys and communicates, 'You are like me.' Girls begin to imitate mom and mothers should encourage strength and femininity within their daughters. This identification tells our girls 'I'm on my way to womanhood and it's beautiful.'"[3] ... "If love between adults was the only important factor in child rearing, then step-parents would be interchangeable with biological parents. While there are situations where the blended family improves a child's situation, this is generally not the case. Research shows that stepfathers spend less time with their spouse's children than do biological fathers. On average, remarried mothers spend less time with their own children (often because stepfathers and children compete for mom's attention). In a home with both biological parents, the father loving the children is usually viewed by mom as an act of love toward her and vice-versa. Some object that not every marriage produces children and therefore children are not a significant component of marriage. This is indicative of the myopic view that marriage is an adult-centered institution. Flip this around- not every marriage produces children, but every child had a father and a mother. Our definition of the family unit should reflect this biological reality and developmental necessity."[4]

Brittany Klein
Raised by lesbians
"You can't shame anybody. I saw that too. My mother would have all these gay guys come over. There was one guy, his name was Joe, who was supposedly a travel agent. And every time he came over there was another boy he brought. Not a little boy. Maybe 14, 15, 16. I don't know exactly. They were always very thuggish. You know, monosyllabic. Like street kids. You know, always with a Bronx accent. Petulant, surly, street kids. And he'd buy them a new pair of sneakers, and everything was Quaaludes and Nebutol. And those popper things. And it wasn't until years later that the dime dropped in my head about what was going on, 'cause I was like eleven, maybe. And I realised what was going on and I said to my mother – because she let my brother go off with him, I said to her, 'how could you have done that? How could you have let him go off with him?' And my mother said, completely, without batting an eye, she said, 'your brother was seven then. He only likes twelve and

71

up.' Like this is okay? And it was a fixed like, twelve and up, not six, not five, not three not four. Twelve and up."[5]

Robert Oscar Lopez
Raised by lesbians

"Quite simply, growing up with gay parents was very difficult, and not because of prejudice from neighbors. People in our community didn't really know what was going on in the house. To most outside observers, I was a well-raised, high-achieving child, finishing high school with straight A's. Inside, however, I was confused. When your home life is so drastically different from everyone around you, in a fundamental way striking at basic physical relations, you grow up weird. I have no mental health disorders or biological conditions. I just grew up in a house so unusual that I was destined to exist as a social outcast. My peers learned all the unwritten rules of decorum and body language in their homes; they understood what was appropriate to say in certain settings and what wasn't; they learned both traditionally masculine and traditionally feminine social mechanisms. Even if my peers' parents were divorced, and many of them were, they still grew up seeing male and female social models. They learned, typically, how to be bold and unflinching from male figures and how to write thank-you cards and be sensitive from female figures. These are stereotypes, of course, but stereotypes come in handy when you inevitably leave the safety of your lesbian mom's trailer and have to work and survive in a world where everybody thinks in stereotypical terms, even gays. I had no male figure at all to follow, and my mother and her partner were both unlike traditional fathers or traditional mothers. As a result, I had very few recognisable social cues to offer potential male or female friends, since I was neither confident nor sensitive to others. Thus I befriended people rarely and alienated others easily. Gay people who grew up in straight parents' households may have struggled with their sexual orientation; but when it came to the vast social universe of adaptations not dealing with sexuality—how to act, how to speak, how to behave—they had the advantage of learning at home. Many gays don't realise what a blessing it was to be reared in a traditional home."[6]

Lee Taylor
Raised by gay father

"Looking back over the past sixty-five years of my life, I have come to understand late in life that child abuse is not about parents who consciously want to do irreparable damage to their children. It's not as if they plan ahead to turn their children's world into a living hell. That comes quite naturally and predictably as they do their very best to give what is truly theirs to give, all of the unconscious toxins which motivate their blinded lives, and it is only through becoming aware of their own childhood hell that this process will ever end. Their feelings of shame, guilt, worthlessness, abandonment, rage, and a host of other debilitating feelings, have all been well preserved and carefully hidden in that dark underground of their psyche where they prowl as demons awaiting the first opportunity to strike at a most convenient victim, a totally vulnerable and willing victim, their baby, their child. There is not even the slightest doubt in my mind that my parents consciously wanted the very best in life for me and my brothers and sisters. There is also not the slightest doubt in my mind that they were among the most dangerous and destructive parents that any child could survive. Their lack of conscious awareness of their own psychic demons did nothing to assuage the pain and suffering of my physical, emotional, spiritual and sexual abuse. It would've been no less painful if they'd planned it."[7]

Debbie Smith
Raised by gay father

"In addition, my dad didn't change his lifestyle. Actually, it worsened. His drinking made him more irritable and undependable. In addition, he finally gave in to his desires to seek sexual relationships with males. Having several failed relationships with women after my mother died, Dad decided that perhaps it was time to do what he had always desired – join the gay subculture. In all likelihood, Dad was out with his 'gay' friends the night of the fire. In many ways, I suppose I was fortunate. The gay community in the 1970s was not as bold and flamboyant as it is now. Gay pride parades were not the norm and most gay communities were located in urban areas such as the one that Dad eventually chose to live in after forcing my brother to move out to Dupont Circle in

Washington, D.C. Other aspects of the 'lifestyle' affected my life. How is a young woman supposed to deal with homosexual pornography that she finds in her father's closet? Is this something that one talks about in private conversations? I never talked about it until I got into counseling years later. Or what does one do when dear old Dad asks you to type up some things that he's written, and it turns out to be pornographic in nature? The desire to please and obey parents is overridden by the disgust felt upon reading this trash. How can your own father think like this? It is difficult not to feel polluted by the experience and wonder if, somehow, you are not damaged goods because of the corruption of your father's mind. What about the lack of positive feedback regarding females and femininity? As I look back, even when my brother and I were young, there was little interaction between my father and I. There were few compliments about the way I dressed or acted in ways that were affirming. Expressions of emotion were rare, unless they were angry rants about his job, his relationships or other challenges in his life."[8]

Mitzy Lancaster
Raised by lesbian mother
"Soon after my father and brother moved out a 'friend' of my mother's moved in. I was uncomfortable with her sharing the room my father and mother had been in before her. She wasn't with us very long. My mother seemed dissatisfied with her for what seemed to me to be strange reasons. Then my mother and I took an apartment in a questionable neighborhood and into our lives came Sandy, her new friend. Needless to say, things were not the same. Mom seemed very stressed and remote. Over the years I became accustomed to the coming and leaving of my mother's partners. I'm not writing this as some kind of revenge against my mother. Nor am I writing this to shame her. I have a good relationship with my mother and I love her very much. I am writing this because of the growing glamourisation of homosexuality. We can't watch anything on television or in the movies without some sort of reference to someone choosing an alternative lifestyle. More often than not it is portrayed as something normal, or as if they are the underdog, or making it seem fun and exciting. I have watched to many times how the media has taken a less than acceptable behaviour and desensitised society towards it by

adding humor to it. If we can laugh about it, if it makes us feel happy, then it can't be all bad. Heck, we might even experiment with it to see if we can arouse that same humor first hand. Whether it be adultery, getting drunk, robbery, insults or. . .homosexuality. A spoonfull of sugar helps the conditioning go down."[9]

Dolores Oliveira
Raised by lesbian mother
"I want to make the case against gay and lesbian marriage based on my own very personal and painful experiences ... Mom disliked straight people, which was particularly mean when it came to going to school functions, meeting parents of my friends, and so on. I felt on the outside of normal most of the time growing up. She would whine to me, 'I don't like those kind of people.' I found out in my independence at age 23 that I liked squares, her name for Straights. I amazed and delighted myself at how great straight people were! I felt safe because I didn't sense they were hiding a dark secret from me. My husband's parents were living simple lives and, God help me, I loved that! (One Christmas, Mom met us there and she was so uncomfortable she was practically squirming. ... Again, she had to 'get away' and I took her on a long drive into town so we could shop.) I missed out on a healthy and stable family life. I wasn't aware of how deeply sad my life with my mom was until I had my own child. My goal is to provide a stable and healthy home life, no lying, no secrets, and we live as far away from the lesbian community as we could get within the city boundaries. My mom died alone, friendless, still coping with her choices. Her last live-in lover, a woman my age, went straight and left my mom. Mom made several attempts to contact her by phone but this woman just dropped off the planet."[10]

Jeremy Deck
Raised by gay father
"After my parents' separation, my sister and I began spending every other weekend with my father in the city. He shared a condo with a man who had also left his wife and children. The man's two daughters seemed to have adjusted to the situation. It was as if everything was 'normal.' But I felt anything but normal. It was as if I had fallen asleep and woken

up in a bizarre alternate reality. At the end of the day, my father would not walk into the bedroom with my mom, like he had done only weeks before. Instead, he headed off to bed with a man I had met only days before. Those weekends were a nightmare for my sister and me. Not only were we forced to leave our mother and friends, but we were placed in a culture we knew nothing about. It was not just a foreign culture; it was one which was anathema to the community in which we were raised. How could my father, who once reigned over our Eden, suddenly become a supporter of what we had seen as the enemy? It is this side of the story that I feel compelled to tell. Children of homosexuals have a unique vantage point on the complexities of the issue. Homosexuals are often able to surround themselves with like-minded individuals in the thriving gay culture. Spouses, parents, or siblings of homosexuals do not usually immerse themselves in a homosexual environment once their loved ones 'come out'. Children, however, are in a sense forced to live a lifestyle they have not chosen. My father has never made me go with him to gay sections of town, but as a child you are emotionally dependent on your parents and do not often feel the right to tell your parent. ... When I visit my dad I begin to truly understand what it's like to live as a homosexual. My dad does not take me bar-hopping to gay taverns at night, but I am basically surrounded by homosexuals. It's a strange feeling to be standing on a street corner watching a gay rights parade while your dad laughs hysterically at the 'Dykes on Bikes' — something that, only a few years earlier, you would have been punished for viewing. This transition has made me leery of putting trust in anyone. As a child, I had placed uncompromising trust in my parents. But since that trust was violated, I've found it difficult to put that much faith in anyone's word, or in their character. Even when all is going well, I constantly guard myself against being too happy, aware that at any second my life could be dismantled again."[11]

Jakii Edwards
Raised by lesbians

"Dear Massachusetts legislators, Life with my mother was not an easy one by any stretch of the imagination! She was openly gay in a time and era when it was almost unheard of for a young lady to graduate from high school and not get married shortly thereafter. ... The scene you just read about took place when I was 12 years old, but when I was fourteen, I walked in on her and a lover in the throes of having sex. I was so scared, that I turned and ran as far as I could and as fast as I could in an attempt to obliterate the sound and images I had just witnessed. ... From that night on I realised that the bad dreams and nightmares I had experienced were real. It became obvious to me that I had been awakened before by those noises and I would force myself to go back to sleep thinking that it was just the sounds of the wind outside our house or my aunt or uncle playing tricks on me. ... It was not often that my mom's lovers would be happy about her dragging two brats along with her when she came over to spend the night. The only bed I was offered was the floor or a sofa and that offer was never made with kindness but with a lukewarm smile of 'intolerance.'"[12]

Denise Shick
Raised by transgender gay father

"My dad was a cross dresser when I was a child. This made me feel very uncomfortable around him growing up. This confused me with his role of a father in my childhood. I just wanted him to be my 'dad'. I learned after his passing that he was in a homosexual relationship. This was another dilemma for me to deal with. Even though he had passed on, it seemed like another chapter of his life was revealed to me. I had questioned this to myself growing up. I never told anyone about myself questioning 'if he was gay'. Now the truth was there on pen and paper. There are many of us going though this situation. There are many of us out there. Don't think the Gender Identity Disorder does not exist or hurt people. It is not as funny as the T.V. programs portray. I can know what it is like living with someone who was hurting deep inside with the Gender Identity Disorder. I lived to experience and know the emotional pain within my father and my family. I found a letter from my dad after he passed away. His words read 'Don't throw me away'. I believe in my heart I am involved in this out of respect and love from those words that my dad wrote."[13]

Adult male – name withheld

"I ... stand with traditional families, being raised by a lesbian mother, I know first-hand the damage it does to a child and society. It is not the Supreme Court or any Government body to re-define marriage or any Religious Ceremony according to the United States Constitution- 1st Amendment for Religious Freedom. Marriage is a covenant between a man, a women and God (Yahweh)."[14]

Charles Mitchell
Adopted by gay men

As reported in *National Catholic Register:*

> Charles Mitchell and two brothers were adopted as infants by two men. He called same-sex adoption "a tragic social experiment" and said, "homosexuality destroyed a normal way of life for us." Often, the homosexual parents shown in the media are straight-laced, responsible men. Mitchell said that his "dad" and "uncle" weren't unlike that. But "it's not just the two people involved; it's the environment" Both he and his two adopted brothers were sexually molested by friends of his "dad" and his "uncle." To this day it is difficult for him to trust men, he said on a March 14 "Straight Talk Radio" broadcast.[15]

Suzanne Cook
Raised by gay father

As reported in *Connection:*

> Suzanne Cook, who was raised in part by her divorced father living with his gay lover. "But it takes more than love to raise children in an appropriate and healthy way. We shouldn't be experimenting on another generation." ... Cook, a resident of Fort Worth, Texas, has an insider's perspective on homosexual parenting. Cook said that when she was seven years old her father left the family to pursue a homosexual relationship. Three years later, her parents divorced but shared custody. Cook and her younger brother spent every other weekend at the apartment of her father's partner. "They did not refrain from having sex when we were there", Cook says. "They

didn't come out of the bedroom until noon". ... Cook says her father's partner molested her brother for the next several years. "I had to deal with keeping my brother safe", Cook says. "I had to put on the role of a parent as a little kid. I felt the whole world on my shoulders." (Cook's father declined comment) ... Confused about her sexuality as a young teenager, Cook supposed the only way to have a relationship with a man was to offer sex. Even her mother encouraged her to have sexual relations outside marriage so that she would not mistakenly wed a homosexual.[16]

wow

Nathan Bell
Raised by gay father
As published in 1999 by Love in Action:

"Kids," Dad said to us, "after much thought and consideration, I have come to the place where I need to tell you something. I believe in my heart that I want to live the rest of my life with men rather than women."

The news brought me to the edge of my seat and I blurted out, "You're gay?!" My Dad looked at me, nodded, and responded softly, "I'm gay." I felt goose bumps up and down the back of my neck. My attempts to rationalise my dream had been viciously crushed by Dad's words. Responding to my tears, my parents explained that the dream I'd had two years earlier was given to me the very evening my Dad revealed his secret to my Mom. The sharp tone she used in her response was a cover-up to hide her shock. To her, the dream and the timing involved were more than coincidental.

My Dad's words to my mother two years before reflected his commitment to a specific destiny. He was making a purposeful statement, declaring that he no longer was going to combat his fleshly yearnings. His was a conscious calculation of the consequences with a conclusion: for him, the freedom to have sex with men was worth any price. Whatever the cost, my Dad had chosen to surrender his life to homosexuality and it meant that soon, certain people would have to hear about it. Specifically, it meant that someday there would come a time when he would tell his children.[17]

Bronagh Cassidy
Raised by lesbian mother
As reported in *Townhall:*

But Cassidy knows better: She is one of the first generation of "gayby boom" babies, raised by two moms. Adult children of same-sex parents are rare. I recently came across Cassidy's story by accident, after she e-mailed a friend of mine who is a family scholar. Back in 1976, Cassidy's mom had a religious ceremony with a woman named Pat. To make Cassidy, they did artificial insemination at home, mixing the sperm of two gay friends "to make sure nobody would ever know who the father was," says Cassidy. (That was in the days before widespread DNA testing.) The two women stayed together for 16 years, until Pat died. Three years later, Cassidy's mother married a man. ... What was it like for Cassidy being raised by two women she called "Mom" and "My Pat"? ... "When growing up, I always had the feeling of being something unnatural," Cassidy says. "I came out of an unnatural relationship; it was something like I shouldn't be there. On a daily basis, it was something I was conflicted with. I used to wish, honestly that Pat wasn't there." ... Why does she oppose same-sex marriage? "It's not something that a seal of approval should be stamped on: We shouldn't say it is a great and wonderful thing and then you have all these kids who later in life will turn around and realise they've been cheated. The adults choose to have that lifestyle and then have a kid. They are fulfilling their emotional needs — they want to have a child — and they are not taking into account how that's going to feel to the child; there's a clear difference between having same-sex parents and a mom and a dad." ...Some people will say if Cassidy's mom and "my Pat" had been legally married, everything would have been fine. Cassidy doesn't think so. "Even if society were open to it, there's just the whole issue of your self-identity. I always had the feeling I was in a lab experiment." She feels driven to do something, say something to protect other children like her. "Whenever I see it on TV, something inside of me says NO. I don't think it's fair that the kids are being put in this situation. They don't have a choice about it." Do any other adult children with same-sex parents feel the same way? Will we allow any space in this intense debate between adult combatants for something as simple as one child's feelings?[18]

Meg
Raised by lesbians

"My relationship with my 'other mom' was awkward. She helped raise me through my most formative years and I cannot recall life without her. I have many fond memories with her, but what I mostly remember is how awkward and uncomfortable our relationship felt. I had a mom, a dad whom I ached for, and then I had her. I hated the times she would try to parent me by offering me comfort or discipline. I accepted her only as my mom's partner, not as a parent. Later, when she and my mom split up I felt relieved. I felt sad for my mom but I didn't miss my 'other mom' despite the fact that she raised me as her own daughter. ... As a child growing up within the gay community, I was exposed to a lot of inappropriate things very early on. From the adult toys and pornographic magnets in the local gay and lesbian bookstore, to the men who parade around in S&M costumes at gay pride festivals. My interaction with and exposure to these parts of the larger gay culture and my missing father created the perfect storm that led to my early sexualisation. As I got older, I used attention from boys to try to fill the wound my missing father left. I found myself in two abusive relationships in college because I was looking for the love and approval of a man but I had no idea how a good man should treat me. I accepted almost anyone who would "love" me. ... Do I wish my mom lived a miserable life married to a man she didn't love? No. I want my mom to be happy. But I also wish that she and my dad did love each other and that somehow it could have worked out. Her happiness cost me a great deal. We have to recognise that all children of same-sex parents are being raised in brokenness. Something precious and irreplaceable has been taken from us. Two loving moms, or two dads, can never replace the lost parent. In my case, and in many like mine, I was raised by same-sex parents because I was intentionally separated from my other biological parent and then told that 'all that matters is love' and 'love makes a family.' Love matters, but accepting and promoting same-sex parenting promotes the destruction of families, not the building of families."[19]

Manuel Half
Raised by gay father

"You stand up for the idea of a father without a mother, which is, without a mother, no father at all, but something else. And it, that mother, you say, matters for nothing—don't think of her at all: And don't look for her among people made from fathers and mothers, since you say they suffer with their fathers and mothers. ... And you say that I am the example and model that proves your full and healthy wholeness, which you built at the cost of my full and healthy wholeness. ... I am Manuel Half, half a man."[20]

Anonymous girl
Raised by lesbians

"I have gay parents. I spend most of my time at my best friend's house. I hang out with her Dad cos I never had one and he is this awesome guy. My friend's Dad is a lot like Charlie from Twilight! I cried when I read about Bella's father in the books and in all his scenes in the movies. Mostly at my friend's house it feels like I can just be myself. Someone has to say it cos I don't hear it but gay parents are selfish in a way. They don't think what it's going to be like for me to live in their world. ... Am I the only one who feels this way? Am I a bad daughter because I wish I had a Dad? Is there anyone else who has 2 Moms or 2 Dads who wonders what it would be like if they were born into a normal family? Is there anyone else who wants to be able to use the word normal without getting a lecture on what is normal??? ... I don't know my real father and never will. It's weird but I miss him. I miss this man I will never know. Is it wrong for me to long for a father like my friends have? She has two brothers I play basketball with all the time. It feels so amazing to be included in their family. When I am there I think this is what it's like to be in a family that has a Mom and a Dad. Then I have to go home to my own world. I just don't fit in it anymore."[21]

Anonymous
Son of gay father

"I hate my dads so much...WHY didn't they just adopt some baby instead use ovum donor and surrogate mother? Don't you think gay people who want to get a baby by ovum donor and surrogate mother are horrible? I think they are horrible as hell [...] am I a bad person to feel this way? What should I do...? I'm still so young but everyone wants me to accept everything that I can't and don't want..."[22]

Anonymous
Raised by gay father

"I'm 14 and live with my father. He always told me that my mom died when I was very young. Recently I was going through some files and found out that I was actually born by a person who donated their egg and I was born through a surrogate mother in [--------]. This led me to believe that my father was never married. I'm also very sure my dad was never married because I discovered that he is gay. Why would my dad keep this all from me?"[23]

Anonymous
Raised by lesbians

"Reading half of these stories has really saddened me. I have the most amazing mums, who couldn't have done a better job with me and my 2 younger sisters. We all have the same donor dad and the same mother. And I don't need nor want a father, but I do have a lot of curiosity about my 'bio dad'; ... What does he look like? ... What is he in to? ... Is he tall? ... Short? ... Wide? ... Slim? ... Does he even know that me and my sisters exist? ... However, if I do ever manage to find him, I have no intent on building a relationship with him. He's not my dad, he just helped 2 amazing women bring 3 very happy girls into the world. Another reason I would like to find him is due to some medical mysteries, if not for that I doubt I would even bother looking!! ... I mean my mums really have done an amazing job with me and my sisters, me and my youngest suffer from quite severe dyslexia (so struggled immensely throughout school) whilst my other sister has ASD (Autistic Spectrum Disorder, for those who aren't aware). So they did and do indeed have their work cut out and with very little support from their families, who still to this day, despite the successes me and my sisters have become, believe gay couples cannot raise children. ... I love my mums & am incredibly grateful for everything they have done & put up with for the sake of me and my sisters. … And if I do manage to find my 'bio dad' then great, if not then no big deal."[24]

Anonymous
Raised by lesbians
"I am a Donor conceived person. My parents were great but since they were lesbian they couldn't have kids. Also my parents were too old to have kids (45). But my Mum desperately wanted kids so My twin brother and I where donor conceived. I just happened to get ethnic donors. The sperm donor was half Arab and British. The egg donor was half Italian and white (with areas of French). My twin brother and I looked NOTHING like our parents. They have blond, blue eyes. I am tan skin, very dark brown hair, big amber eyes and slender, the complete opposite to my parents. The thing is, I looked hugely Arabic. My brother, on the other hand, has dark brown hair, light tan skin, and sea-foam eyes, more Italian, but quite white. This was hard as I always got questions on my ethnicity. I did know my donors actually. But the huge question I got was, when I told them my ethnicity, they told me to speak the language! But of course I couldn't. Isn't it hard explaining to people everything. Especially to your homophobic Muslim friend ."[25]

Pseudonymous commenter
Raised by lesbians
"Congrats to them both and the baby. I am the daughter (not biological) of two mom's. I love them both sooo sooo much but there is not a day that goes by that I didn't wish I had a dad. It is very hard for kids like me that are different. No matter how accepting society is. I have men in my life – my moms' friends but it is not the same. Please, please don't get me wrong, I really love them both but I guess I'm just saying it is not the same."[26]

Anonymous
Raised by lesbians
"I have two wonderful moms that have split up and are about 55 and 60 years old. My mom who had me was too old to have a baby so my mom had to get a sperm donor and egg donor. My mom was pregnant

with my twin brother and me. He came out first through 'c' section
.... and then me. Everything was great until I was about 5. My moms
started to fight so badly..... I was really sad. My moms were also very
old for average mothers. When I was 5 or 6 I realised something was
wrong with my family... I got really shy and to this day I still am. My
moms broke up. There was a huge case going about who would look
after my brother and me. We are ending up swapping each week. One
of my moms was always the meanest. We are having so much trouble
at home. I only have peace when I come to my other mom's house.
When I'm at my mean mom's house she has a new partner who is so
mean and rude to me. I always cry everyday when I'm there. My mom
says "Why don't you invite any of your friends over not just your best
friend." I love Sarah I tell her everything. I can't bring any of my other
friends over because most of them feel uncomfortable around gays. I
feel so sad and angry that I'm so different. I love my nice mom so much
but it's so hard sometimes when I go to my other house. Thank you for
reading this.... I know this is not relevant, but the *Frozen* song, 'Let it
go' is exactly what I feel like and did. I pretended I was okay. I didn't
care. I keep things. I have a really complicated life that no one, NO ONE
knows about. I keep it to myself. Because I keep things bottled up I can
be really moody and at school it's helped me get in a huge amount of
trouble. I don't get sad, I get angry. I don't cry."[27]

Anonymous
Raised by lesbians
"I have forgiven my moms for lying. I suppose they were trying to
protect me in their own way but really I was cut off from a lot of people
who just wanted to love me. I have learned we don't have to approve
of each others' sexuality to form communities in the world. I spent a
year working on green co-op farms and it didn't matter. I am still drawn
to older men, fatherly types. Still searching for the Daddy I will never
know. You cannot just donate your sperm and walk away because there
is so much more to you than a biological contribution. When you walked
away you denied me the chance of ever knowing you and loving you,
and you denied yourself the chance to know and love your child. If
you donated sperm about 18-20 years ago to two gay women, I could

be your daughter. The movie *Delivery Man* with Vince Vaugh is about a man who meets his sperm donor children as adults. I cried and cried and cried. It was sort of a healing but it also brought the pain up to the surface again. I know he is out there, I can feel the pull. What am I supposed to do with that?"[28]

Examples of abuse (selected excerpts)

1. 'Mary Rowles, mother of the children, and Alice Jenkins, Rowles' live-in partner, had already pleaded guilty to dozens of crimes against the children. Before handing down her sentence, Judge Patricia Cosgrove heard testimony on the abuse, which included pictures that showed for the first time the infamous urine soaked closet where some of the kids were kept for extended periods of time until breaking out and being found walking the streets in the middle of the night. 'In that closet, you can see the plaster broken off the wall from a child banging his head against the wall,' said prosecutor Mary Ann Kovach. 'Three kids in a closet less than three-by-five where they can't sleep because there's not enough room to lie down and stretch out.' The oldest child also testified."[29]

2. "Frank Lombard is an associate director at Duke University's Global Health Institute and a homosexual who was charged last week with the molestation of his adopted 5-year-old black son and actively trying to sell him for sex on the internet. The 40 words above are 40 more than the Main Stream Media has said on this horrible story. In nearly a week since Lombard was arrested, not one national broadcast or cable television news show has picked up the story. Compare this to the weeks on end of sensational coverage of the white male lacrosse players of the same university charged with rape several years ago."[30]

3. "A boy sexually abused by his adoptive father and his gay partner was labelled an 'unruly child' by social workers who ignored his complaints for years, a damning report has revealed. They sent Andy Cannon, now 23, back to the couple's home despite his protests of abuse, praising the gay man who adopted him as a 'very caring parent'. The report accuses Wakefield social services, in Yorkshire, of 'folly and gross misjudgment'. Mr Cannon, who was wrongly diagnosed with mental disorders and prescribed anti-psychotic drugs, believes he would have been listened to sooner if his adoptive father wasn't gay."[31]

4. "The magistrate criticised Hanelie for failing to report Jandre's abuse at the hands of her lover to the social workers monitoring Jandre's progress, after she had gained custody of him during a lengthy court battle with her ex-husband. She also failed to report the abuse to her ex-husband. The boy's father became aware of Jandre's abuse only on the day of his death, June 12, 2003. De Nysschen contacted him and said Jandre had fallen earlier in the day and had died."[32]

5. "With no previous convictions, they came across as respectable men who simply wanted to help boys with a variety of problems. In reality, they were paedophiles, who repeatedly abused the children in their care. Even when the mother of two of the children reported her suspicions to the council, officials accepted the men's explanations and did nothing. … The children's charity Kidscape said those in charge of overseeing the safety of children in the care of Faunch and Wathey had allowed political correctness to override common sense."[33]

6. "The case of a same-sex Connecticut couple accused of repeatedly raping and abusing two of their nine adopted boys is headed for trial. Married couple George Harasz and Douglas Wirth of Glastonbury were supposed to be sentenced Friday in Hartford Superior Court under a plea deal, but instead withdrew from their agreement with prosecutors."[34]

7. "A 5-year-old Los Angeles boy is fighting for his life after police say he was severely tortured with burns and food deprivation by his lesbian mother and her live-in girlfriend. Officials say the child has countless cigarette burns all over his body, including his genitals, and can't open his hands because he was forced to put them flat on a hot stove."[35]

8. "Serenity Richardson was visiting Erica Mae Butts, her godmother and her mother's best friend, and Shanita Latrice Cunningham, who was Butts's lover, for two weeks at their home in Summerville, South Carolina when the abuse took place. 'It is nearly impossible for words to accurately describe what these women did to that poor little girl', said Elizabeth Gordon, assistant managing solicitor for Charleston County. 'They beat her repeatedly both with a belt and with plastic coat hangers. You can see the outlines of the strikes on this child's body. There is not one area of this child's body that was unharmed except for the soles of her feet.'"[36]

9. "Domestic partners Suzette Stevenson, 45, and Jamie Lynn Martin, 26, have been charged with aggravated child abuse after a 7-year-old boy illegally in their care escaped from the two women after they allegedly drugged him and left him in a car as they shopped for a Florida timeshare. The boy, who is not a biological child to either woman, was allegedly tied by his wrists and made to stand in an upright position for hours at a time, forced to drink shampoo, was burned with cigarettes and had to urinate and defecate in a closet, according the Baker County Sheriff's Office documents. The boy was born in 2000 in California. After his mother became involved in drugs, he was taken away from the mother and given to his father, Baker County Sheriff Joey Dobson told ABC News. The father, who allegedly did not want to care for the child, gave him to an aunt, who was in a relationship with Stevenson."[37]

10. "Cardiff Crown Court was told how Carol Stokes, 32, became pregnant by a friend after she and her lover, Colleen O'Neill, with whom she lived, decided they wanted a child together. But she allegedly drowned 16-month-old Lewis in a bath just a week after Miss O'Neill walked out on her."[38]

11. "A Harlem lesbian beat the toddler son of her female lover to death – fracturing three ribs and rupturing his liver – simply because he soiled himself, law enforcement sources said yesterday. Carmen Molina, 32, and the mother, Zahira Matos, 20, were charged with second-degree murder in the death of tiny Yovany Tellez Jr. who had 60 bruises all over his body – and face a maximum penalty of life without parole."[39]

12. "The lesbian parents of an 11-year-old boy who is undergoing the process of becoming a girl last night defended the decision, claiming it was better for a child to have a sex change when young. Thomas Lobel, who now calls himself Tammy, is undergoing controversial hormone blocking treatment in Berkeley, California to stop him [from] going through puberty as a boy. But Pauline Moreno and Debra Lobel warn that children with gender identity disorder forced to postpone transitioning could face a higher risk of suicide."[40]

13. "Eraca Dwan Craig, 31, and Christian Jessica Deana, 44, were both arrested at the scene on suspicion of felony child cruelty, false imprisonment and other charges. The women, who are domestic partners, do not appear to have criminal records in Monterey County. … Investigators found little food inside the home, which was cluttered and dirty, according to reports. The girl and the older boy were adopted children, and the younger boy is the biological son of one of the women, Miller said."[41]

14. "On Friday, Mark J. Newton, 42, was sentenced to 40 years in prison and was ordered to pay $400,000 in restitution to the child. His boyfriend, Peter Truong, 36, pleaded guilty and is awaiting sentencing. The couple bought the child from his Russian mother for $8,000 in 2005. Investigators say Newton and Truong flew the boy between Australia, the United States, France and Germany to record at least eight other paedophiles sexually abuse him."[42]

15. "[Carl] Herold and Charles Dunnavant are charged with sodomy, aggravated child abuse and sexual torture. Authorities said the victim is Herold's son and Dunnavant's stepson."[43]

16. "Some of the relatives viewed a photo of the boy's body. His lips were swollen. There were bruises all over his body and there was a gash under his left eye. There appeared to be cigarette burn marks between his eyebrows. … Wade has a lengthy rap sheet with 13 arrests. The most recent was in September 2012 — a month before ACS gave him custody of Myls. King, a transgendered woman originally born Christopher King, has a sealed rape arrest on her record. A woman suffered a fractured jaw in the attack, sources told The News. It appears King was arrested as a teenage boy and not convicted."[44]

17. "Cindy Close and Marvin McMurrey III differ on whether they planned to co-parent the children or whether Close would simply carry the children as a surrogate for McMurrey and his [homosexual] partner, assuming no role in the children's upbringing.   They did not put their agreement in writing, and Close gave birth to the twins in July 2012. McMurrey sued her two weeks later, seeking a declaration that he is the child's father and that Close was 'surrogate or gestational carrier' without parental rights."[45]

18. "Douglasville Police Department investigators say a local mom and her girlfriend put a 6-year-old boy in a small dog cage for hours, poured syrup and cat litter on him and made him hold a brick over his head."[46]

19. "Sarah Bray, who last week claimed that she had been banned from visiting her same-sex partner in an Indianapolis hospital, is now facing battery and criminal confinement charges … 'She is an amazing mother to those two boys,' Bray said. 'And I just want to be able to know that I can be with the person I love more than anything.' But Jennifer Clemmer's statements as well as witnesses' statements to detectives portrayed a more tumultuous relationship."[47]

20. "A woman accused of killing her ex-girlfriend's 2-year-old girl and trying to kill her 10-year-old brother drugged the boy and tried to drug his sister, who was found submerged in a bathtub Monday, according to Jupiter police. According to a Jupiter police report, Kymberley Dawn Lucas was babysitting the boy and his baby sister at an Abacoa apartment when Lucas came to him and said she had a pill for him to take that would make him grow faster. She said the pill was too big, so she crushed it and put it into a cup of coffee with sugar and cream. The boy drank it."[48]

21. "David Tutera, the host of the TV show *My Fair Wedding*, is embroiled in a nasty split from his longtime [gay] partner with whom he is currently expecting twins. The couple, together as domestic partners for a decade, split in January and are due to become parents in July. Both have filed legal papers seeking full custody of the babies."[49]

22. "Miller gave birth to Isabella via artificial insemination in 2002, but she and her partner, Janet Jenkins, dissolved their Vermont civil union two years later. Miller then moved to Virginia, where she became a born-again Christian who renounced homosexuality. Miller decided she did not want Isabella to see Jenkins and sued for sole custody in the state, according to *The New York Times*. But in 2006, after several years of custody battles, a Virginia appeals court finally sided with Jenkins, ruling that under the Parental Kidnapping Prevention Act, Virginia had to defer to Vermont courts, granting Jenkins visitation rights."[50]

23. "Twin five-year-old girls who effectively have three mothers are at the centre of a fierce custody battle between the two lesbians who brought them into the world. The children live with their birth mother but were conceived from eggs donated by her ex-partner – and later adopted by her current partner. Under the Human Fertilisation and Embryology Act

2008, the egg donor has no legal status as a parent."[51]

24. "A Florida judge has approved the adoption of a 22-month-old baby girl that will list three people as parents on her birth certificate—a married lesbian couple and a gay man. The decision ends a two-year paternity fight between the couple and a friend of the women who donated his sperm to father the child but later sought a larger role in the girl's life."[52]

25. "A Kansas man who donated sperm to a lesbian couple said Thursday he would appeal a judge's ruling that he is the 'presumptive father' of the mother's 4-year-old daughter, which makes him potentially liable for child support. In her ruling Wednesday, Shawnee County District Court Judge Mary Mattivi decided that William Marotta, of Topeka, did not qualify for sperm-donor protection under Kansas law because a licensed physician did not perform the artificial insemination."[53]

26. "Doll, Kitten and Brynn, from Massachusetts, were joined together in a marriage-style ceremony last August and are expecting a daughter in July. Kitten, 27, is pregnant after undergoing IVF treatment using an anonymous donor, and the women say they eventually plan to have three children – one for each of them. Their plan is that Kitten will bear all the children, but they are open to other options, such as adoption. Brynn, 34, says: 'The hope is to have three kids altogether. We always joke that the children should never outnumber the parents.'"[54]

27. "There are some 65 cases of babies stuck in Thailand that were conceived by homosexual Israeli couples and birthed, or are about to be birthed, by surrogate Thai women, according to the group 'Help Us Bring the Babies Home'. The group formed a Facebook page last week that has already garnered some 14,000 'Likes' and the support of Gal Uchovsky, a prominent Tel Aviv LGBTQ activist and journalist. The babies were conceived and born, or will be born, through the arrangements of Israeli couples, but are unable to come to Israel because the Interior Ministry has not granted Israeli citizenship to the infants, according to an advocacy group formed around the issue. The ministry maintains that bureaucracy is snagged on Thai regulations that now require surrogate mothers to legally surrender their rights as a parent of the baby, a situation that complicates bringing the newborns to Israel."[55]

28. "A female resident of Peruwelz, around 20 years old, gave birth to a little boy. Nothing exceptional here, except that Sonia (her code name) sold her uterus, pregnancy, and her biological son to a gay male couple in Paris for 5,000 euros."[56]

29. "He said surrogates were being exploited and agencies were ready and willing to cash in on them and the future parents. The journalist interviewed one Australian couple whose daughter was born to a surrogate as well as women at the centre of this lucrative industry. The couple, James and Mikey, told Abboud they travelled to Thailand after exhausting all other options for parenthood."[57]

30. "Thomsen, who is 6-feet-3 and weighs 280 pounds, was arrested last Friday after he was accused of putting the hands of nine different children on his genitals over his clothing between May 27 and June 4, according to a criminal complaint. He also allegedly pressed the head of a tenth victim against his clothed genitals and rubbed the buttocks of three other children the same way, the complaint said. The alleged victims were boys and girls, either 4 or 5 years old. ... Thomsen's parents, lesbian couple Brigitte Thomsen and Marianne Larsen, who have since separated, flew in from Denmark to support their son."[58]

31. "About a decade ago, Barbara Cough adopted two girls from China, Kimberly and Catie. Barbara and her partner, Marilyn Thomas, are raising the children in Portland, Me. I filmed the family last year when the girls (who are not biological sisters) were ages 9 and 11. More than 80,000 girls have been adopted from China by Americans since 1991. In recent years, China has made adoptions by same-sex couples, already difficult, nearly impossible. But at the time the girls were adopted, in 2003 and 2004, Barbara and Marilyn felt that adopting girls from China afforded them more protections as parents than domestic adoptions would have, given the complex rules around birth parents' rights in America."[59]

32. "Leo Felton's parents didn't stay married long. They divorced when he was 2 years old, and Leo, born in 1970, was the only child they had together. His father had previously been married to a black woman, so Leo had five black half-brothers and two black half-sisters. After his parents' divorce, Leo's mother became a lesbian. Leo and his mother moved in with her girlfriend, a feminist author, and her children, thus creating perhaps the only family in the comfortable, mostly white suburb of Gaithersburg, Md., that had two white mothers, two white daughters and a biracial son. ... The story of Felton's institutionalisation, as described in the court psychologist's report, is a disturbing one. He spent most of the next four years in various hospitals and residential homes. According to Leo, after a few months, each institution tried to discharge him, but each time his mother was able to convince the people in charge that Leo needed to stay, sometimes over the objections of his father. When state school administrators concluded that Felton did not need further residential treatment, his mother hired an attorney, sued and got the decision reversed."[60]

33. "The baby [who died after being left in a car] was placed with Jackson and his partner by a contracting firm that lost a competitive bid to renew its license last year but which was still allowed to sponsor licensed foster homes as a subcontractor. The State Children and Families [office] has opened an investigation and instructed two other licensed contractors to inspect all foster homes associated with the firm, Secretary Phyllis Gilmore said. In the meantime, all future placements with the firm have been suspended. Neighbours described Jackson and his partner as doting parents. 'They are two of the most kind-hearted guys that I have ever met. And I hate that there's so much controversy right now with babies being left in the car, because I truly don't feel from the bottom of my heart they would ever do this on purpose,' said Lindey TenEyck, who lives across the street. A mother of two, TenEyck realised something was amiss when fire trucks, police cars and ambulances converged on her street. When she went outside, Jackson was on the ground near the silver Dodge Charger, practically in the foetal position. 'He was mentally breaking down. He was hysterical. There is no doubt in my mind he will suffer for the rest of his life in his mind,' she said. 'It's very heartbreaking on all accounts.'"[61]

34. "Our two young children were wilfully and intentionally thrust into a world of strife and combative beliefs, lifestyles, and values, all in the name of 'gay rights.' Their father moved into his new partner's condo, which is in a complex inhabited by sixteen gay men. One of the men has a 19-year-old male prostitute who comes to service him. Another man, who functions as the father figure of this community, is in his late sixties and has a boyfriend in his twenties. My children are brought to gay parties where they are the only children and where only alcoholic beverages are served. They are taken to transgender baseball games, gay rights fundraisers, and LGBT film festivals. ... Both of my children face identity issues, just like other children. Yet there are certain deep and unique problems that they will face as a direct result of my former husband's actions. My son is now a maturing teen, and he is very interested in girls. But how will he learn how to deal with that interest when he is surrounded by men who seek sexual gratification from other men? How will he learn to treat girls with care and respect when his father has rejected them and devalues them? How will he embrace his developing masculinity without seeing his father live out authentic manhood by treating his wife and family with love, honoring his marriage vows even when it's hard? ... My daughter suffers too. She needs a dad who will encourage her to embrace her femininity and beauty, but these qualities are parodied and distorted in her father's world. Her dad wears make-up and sex bondage straps for Halloween. She is often exposed to men dressing as women. The walls in his condo are adorned with large framed pictures of women in provocative positions. What is my little girl to believe about her own femininity and beauty? Her father should be protecting her sexuality. Instead, he is warping it. ... Without the guidance of both their mother and their father, how can my children navigate their developing identities and sexuality? I ache to see my children struggle, desperately trying to make sense of their world. ... My children and I have suffered great losses because of my former husband's decision to identify as a gay man and throw away his life with us. Time is revealing the depth of those wounds, but I will not allow them to destroy me and my children. I refuse to lose my faith and hope. I believe so much more passionately in the power of the marriage covenant between one man and one woman today than when I was married. There is another way for those with same-sex attractions. Destruction is not the only option—it cannot be. Our children deserve far better from us."[62]

35. As reported by Robert Stacy McCain: "Way to go, [lesbian moms]! Except that your 'sensitive' son seems to have some issues with ... *lesbians*:

An Open Letter to Jennifer Meyer and Kate Hill...
My name is Cathy Brennan, and I am a lesbian activist in Baltimore, Maryland. ... I want to ask you to do something now that will also take amazing courage — please tell your [transgender son who wants to be a] daughter, Tobi Hill-Meyer, to stop terrorising lesbians.... Tobi has taken it upon herself to tell lesbians that we are bigots for shunning penis. Perhaps you don't know this? She also has perpetuated the myth that lesbians as a group secretly crave penetration by males – because some lesbians use dildos. And Tobi, aided and abetted by would-be helpers who think they are waging a noble battle against 'bigotry,' willfully violates the boundary established by Females for Female-only space. . . .

Guess what? Tobi Hill-Meyer is now working in that ultimate expression of 'emotion and sensitivity', *the porn industry*:

Why do I make porn: I came of age in sex positive communities where I saw people's sexuality being celebrated in amazing and positive ways — but it was always a cis person or sometimes a trans guy. Trans women were tolerated in my communities, but not really expected to participate on that level. I wanted so badly to see someone like me being celebrated for being sexual, and although I couldn't have that when I needed it most, I realised I could be that for someone else. So after getting the boot from mainstream porn because my body won't ejaculate, I set out to make my own and create opportunities for trans women to represent ourselves in ways we actually wanted to be represented.

She-male porn produced by a she-male! I'm sure Tobi's lesbian feminist mother is proud that her emotional and sensitive son grew up to be a 'daughter' who still has a penis but who has been effectively neutered by hormonal treatments so that his/ 'her' genitalia is so completely dysfunctional he/ 'she' can't work in 'mainstream' she-male porn. ... Feminists everywhere must applaud this kind of parenting 'success.'"[63]

36. "An Ohio mom and her same-sex partner are suing a Chicago-area fertility clinic for sending sperm from a black donor instead of the white donor's sperm that she ordered. ... Thirty-six-year-old Jennifer Cramblett of Uniontown, Ohio, said that, as a lesbian, she knows what discrimination feels like. She doesn't want her mixed-race daughter, Payton, to feel the same pain because of the color of her skin. ... According to court documents, the 2-year-old girl is already facing racial prejudice in Uniontown, a community of 3,300 people — 97 percent of whom are white. ... The lawsuit was filed Monday against Midwest Sperm Bank for wrongful birth and breach of warranty, citing emotional and economic damage. ... After poring over pages of donor histories from Midwest Sperm Bank three years ago, Cramblett and her partner, 29-year-old Amanda Zinkon, selected donor No. 380, who was white. Cramblett used the sperm to get pregnant and, months later, the two decided to reserve more sperm from that donor so Zinkon could one day have a child related to the one Cramblett was carrying. ... During that process, the couple learned the truth: An employee at the fertility clinic allegedly misread a handwritten order — and Cramblett had been inseminated by donor No. 330, who was black."[64]

37. "Dan Savage has gone around advertising the fact that he and Terry, his husband, have an open relationship with other people. That involves instability, increased risk for infections, distrust, competition, and turmoil. Think of the added risks imposed because of the unknowns related to the outside male partners themselves. Rarely could two gay husbands have had enough time to get to know these additional flings well. They might sexually assault or get violent with one of the husbands, or burrow into their lives and then turn abusive eyes toward the children, perhaps out of jealousy. The world is a dangerous place full of dangerous people. The whole point of marriage is that you only expose yourself to danger when you've gotten to know the other person, a process that hasn't taken place between the cheating gay husband and the cuckold. The adoption agency that placed a child in such a home violated the sacred rule that the best interests of the child hold sway over the adults' desires."[65]

38. "When the child begins to ask, 'why don't I have a mom?' or 'why don't I have a dad?' the abuse grows, for the gay 'parents' will likely respond with an answer that protects *them* from criticism but disallows the child's recognition of hurt feelings. ... Consider what Rob Watson wrote in the *Huffington Post* in an open letter to Justice Anthony Kennedy:

If you come, you will meet my 10-year-old sons, who will likely impress you, given how personable, articulate, polite and bright they are. You might ask, as many people we meet do, if they are twins. The answer will be, 'They are 'almost-twins': Their birthdays are four months apart.' That will bring a 'huh, come again?' look, and I will explain how I adopted them as babies from different drug-addicted birth mothers through foster care.

If Watson's standard routine in explaining his situation to strangers is to highlight the fact that his two ten-year-olds came from 'drug-addicted birth mothers,' it is possible that he has been explaining it this way to his own sons for years. He wouldn't be the first gay dad I've heard say to an adoptee, 'you don't have a mom because your moms were drug addicts and I was the only one who wanted you'. That's emotional abuse at its worst. ... Watson's glib narrative is reflective of the larger genre of same-sex parenting manifestoes. For a movement like the LGBT lobby, which grew out of a desire for openness, the silences imposed on children of same-sex couples are criminally hypocritical. Kids have a clear, specific script to follow when outsiders ask where they come from—don't mention the sperm bank, don't mention the woman who sold you, don't talk about the ugly divorce from five years ago, don't ....*Just don't talk. Just shut up and smile. Say you like this.* Otherwise, bad things will happen. You'll go back to being an unloved being with nobody willing to put up with you any more."[66]

39. "Megan Hofner, who carried twins for a gay couple in Australia, now claims the surrogacy agency has stiffed her to the tune of $90,000 for unpaid hospital bills. Her complaint includes blistering and sometimes vulgar emails sent by the Drewitt-Barlows. ... One email said, 'I advised your Ips (Intended Parents) NOT to pay you anything at all because you are a crazy bitch who deserves to be locked up! Your Ips will not be paying you one more penny! I am so happy that they ran from you!' ... Another said, 'You should be ashamed of yourself you utterly selfish cow! You are just trailer trash woman and I want nothing more to do with you! I will dig up all your dirt including all the lawyers you p****d off on this case! You will not get one more penny, let's face it your contract will not stand up in any court in Brazil! Lol.'"[67]

40. "The grandparents of two children given to a gay couple for adoption have been denied access to them for three years. ... They claimed they had been barred from looking after the youngsters because they were deemed 'too old' to care for them, although the council refutes this. ... The couple, who raised seven children of their own and cared for their eldest daughter's children until the boy was five and his sister was four, claim promises of contact were broken. ... The 64-year-old grandfather has since suffered a stroke – and now fears he may die without seeing them again."[68]

41. "The dissent rests primarily on the personal vignettes of the cherry-picked litigants. Rather predictable, gold star lesbian moms. Women play better than men in these cases. The plaintiffs in *DeBoer v. Snyder* are a lesbian couple with three adopted children. The main argument for same-sex marriage is a version of 'for the sake of the children' and taps into old prejudices against children born out of wedlock—irresponsible women. In this case, the story of this family contains a residue of a wider cultural misogyny and weighted by classism and I suspect racism. ... Judge Daughtry's dissent pays special attention to the biographical specifics of these children:

> N was born ... to a biological mother who was homeless, had psychological impairments, was unable to care for N, and subsequently surrendered her legal rights to N. The plaintiffs volunteered to care for the boy, brought him into their home following his birth...

Judge Daughtry is sure to note of the biological mother, 'She surrendered her legal rights.' ... How did the birth mother do this if she was 'impaired'? ... The unstable and impoverished mother is a useful trope in misogynistic and classist discourse. I wonder what was done to find this biological mother housing so she could in fact leave the hospital with her son. It is likely that few if any good-faith attempts were made to keep 'N' with his mother, let alone find his father and enforce child support or at least compel some kind of connection so that 'N' could know his origins. ... Rather than a story of an abusive system ripping a child away from where he came from, it is presented as a tale of sacrifice and heroism on the part of the women who adopted the infants. Equally disturbing is the fact that this is expressed with no regard to the child's future feelings, only as it serves to make the couple appear worthy and deserving. This begs the question as whether or not this 'biological mother' had the mental capacity to surrender her rights. Could the adoptive 'mothers' have had legal counsel, while the birth mother was without any support or help navigating the often-hostile legal maze? When these stories go public, these details are hidden, seemingly by design ..."[69]

42. Lesbian couples raised two girls who both ended up girlfriends of Matthew Shepard's killers. Check this out: "[A]t the time of the murder both [killer's girlfriend] Kristen Price's mother and the mother of [other killer] Russell Henderson's twenty-year-old girlfriend, Chastity Pasley, were in lesbian relationships and 'there was no evidence whatsoever of Aaron or Russell expressing anti-gay feelings'. ... 'Aaron lived in the same house with Kristen's mother for months and they never had a problem,' Bill recalled". Hence the most famous case of anti-gay violence in recent history—the cause célèbre of Matthew Shepard—involved not one, but two lesbian couples producing daughters drawn to cold-blooded murderers of gays.[70]

Notes

[1] Jean-Marie Guénois, "J'ai été élevé par deux femmes", *Le Figaro*, Mon-Figaro (January 9, 2013) http://lefigaro.fr (Accessed December 28, 2014). Translated by Robert Oscar Lopez for *English Manif.*

[2] Dawn Stefanowicz, Public Testimony before Connecticut General Assembly's Judiciary Committee (March 26, 2007), www.dawnstefanowicz.org/docs/R000326-DawnTMY.pdf (Accessed December 28, 2014).

[3] Askme, "You're only against gay marriage because of your religion. Part 3 Gender Identity", *asktheBigot: a place where ideas, not people, are under assault* (August 20, 2012), www.askthebigot.com (Accessed December 28, 2014).

[4] Askme, "You're only against gay marriage because of your religion. Part 4- Biology Matters", *asktheBigot: a place where ideas, not people, are under assault* (August 20, 2012), www.askthebigot.com (Accessed December 28, 2014).

[5] Interview with Dawn Stefanowicz and Robert Oscar Lopez, first published in March 2014 on *English Manif.*

[6] Robert Oscar Lopez, "Growing Up with Two Moms: the Untold Children's View", *Public Discourse* (August 6, 2012) http://thepublicdiscourse.com (Accessed December 28, 2014).

[7] Lee Taylor, "Religion: The Fifth Column of Child Abuse", *dawnstefanowicz.org* (Undated), www.dawnstefanowicz.org/pdfs/LeeTaylorSonofHomosexualEvangelistExperiencesRitualAbuse.pdf

[8] Debbie Smith, "A Daughter's Reflections of a Gay Father", *dawnstefanowicz.org*

(Undated) www.dawnstefanowicz.org/pdfs/DebbieSmith'sAUTOBIOGRAPHY.pdf

[9] Mitzy Lancaster, "Closet Children of Closet Parents", *dawnstefanowicz.org* (Undated), www.dawnstefanowicz.org/mitzylancastertestimony.htm (Accessed December 28, 2014).

[10] Dolores Oliveira, "Straight Daughter of a Lesbian: Why I Defend the Marriage Amendment", *dawnstefanowicz.org* (Undated) www.dawnstefanowicz.org/dolores.htm (Accessed December 28, 2014).

[11] Jeremy Deck, "My Father's Closet", *Boundless* (Undated) www.boundless.org (Accessed December 28, 2014 via web.archive.org).

[12] Jakii Edwards, Testimony before the Massachusetts Judiciary Committee (April 28, 2003) www.mafamily.org (Accessed December 28, 2014 via web.archive.org).

[13] Denise Shick, "Denise's Story", Help4Families.com (Undated) www.help4families.com (Accessed December 28, 2014 via web.archive.org).

[14] Email statement forwarded March 29, 2013, to Robert Oscar Lopez. This individual conducted several interviews with Lopez during the summer of 2014 but then chose to return to a low profile.

[15] *National Catholic Register*, "Adopting chaos", *Catholic Online*, Views on the News (April 6, 2006) http://www.catholic.org (Accessed December 28, 2014 via web.archive.org).

[16] John W. Kennedy, "Gay Parenting on Trial", *Connection* (August 2002), www.connectionmagazine.org (Accessed December 28, 2014).

[17] Nathan Bell, "A Son's Journey", (Memphis: Love in Action, 1999). Excerpted by Exodus International. http://exodus.to (Accessed December 28, 2014 via web.archive.org).

[18] Maggie Gallagher, "Adult children speak out about same-sex parents", *Townhall* (July 7, 2004) www.townhall.com (Accessed December 28, 2014).

[19] Meg, "A Casualty of Love: the daughter of two moms speaks out. (Guest Post)", *asktheBigot: A place where ideas, not people, are under assault* (December 19, 2014) www.askthebigot.com (Accessed December 28, 2014).

[20] Manuel Half, "Manifesto of Manuel Half", trans. Robert Oscar Lopez, published in this book for first time.

[21] Anonymous, "Child of Lesbian Parents", *AnonymousUs.org*, Stories (July 17, 2013) www.anonymousus.org (Accessed December 28, 2014).

[22] These are fragments of an anonymous submission sent to a donor-conceived discussion website, but it was taken down shortly after it appeared. Only small snippets here are included.

[23] Anonymous, "What I've found out at 14", *AnonymousUs.org*, Partners/Friends/Others (December 9, 2014) www.anonymousus.org (Accessed December 28, 2014).

[24] Anonymous, "Curiosity", *AnonymousUs.org*, Donor-Conceived (January 9, 2014) www.anonymousus.org (Accessed December 28, 2014).

[25] Anonymous, "My Story!", *AnonymousUs.org*, Donor-conceived (January 11, 2014) www.anonymousus.org (Accessed December 28, 2014).

[26] Leila, "Should Children Sit Down and Shut Up?" *Little Catholic Bubble* (June 30, 2013) http://littlecatholicbubble.blogspot.com/2013/06/should-children-sit-down-and-shut-up.html (Accessed December 28, 2014).

[27] Anonymous, "my story J", *AnonymousUs.org*, Donor-conceived (June 22, 2014) www.anonymousus.org (Accessed December 28, 2014).

[28] Anonymous, "Love is Hate", *AnonymousUs.org,* Donor-Conceived (July 13, 2014) www.anonymousus.org (Accessed December 28, 2014).

[29] WKYC, "Kenmore couple gets 30 years each for abusing children", Akron-Canton News (January 14, 2004) http://archive.wkyc.com (accessed December 26, 2014).

[30] Zoe Ortiz, "Gay Duke U. Official Attempts to Sell Black 5-Year-Old Son for Sex: MSM Out to Lunch", *NewsBusters* (June 29, 2009), http://newsbusters.org (Accessed December 26, 2014).

[31] Steve Robson, "My adoptive dad abused me for years but social workers ignored my complaints because he's gay", *Daily Mail* (March 28, 2013) www.dailymail.co.uk (Accessed December 26, 2014).

[32] Baldwin Ndaba, "Lesbian Couple Guilty of Gruesome Murder", IOL News (March 26, 2006), www.iol.co.za (Accessed December 26, 2014).

[33] Paul Sims, "Gay couple left free to abuse boys—because social workers feared being branded homophobic", *Daily Mail,* News (September 5, 2007), www.dailymail.co.uk (Accessed December 26, 2014).

[34] Erik Ortiz, "Gay Connecticut Couple Accused of Raping Adopted Children Will Face Trial", *New York Daily News,* News (April 7, 2013) www.nydailynews.com (Accessed December 26, 2014).

[35] World Net Daily, "Police Arrest Lesbians for Torturing Boy, 5", *World Net Daily,* Archives (June 15, 2008) www.wnd.com (Accessed December 26, 2014).

[36] BelleNews, "South Carolina: lesbian couple collapsed in court when heard the life sentence for killing a toddler", *BelleNews,* US News (November 6, 2011), www.bellenews.com (Accessed December 26, 2014).

[37] David Schoetz, "Sheriff: Women Drugged, Starved Boy", ABC News, US (November 21, 2007), http://abcnews.go.com (Accessed December 26, 2014).

[38] *Independent,* "Mother killed baby after split from lesbian", *Independent,* News (March 7, 1998) www.independent.co.uk (Accessed December 26, 2014).

[39] Murray Weiss, "Monster Moms—Lesbians Kill Potty-Tot: Cops", *New York Post,* News (September 21, 2004) www.nypost.com (Accessed December 26, 2014).

[40] Daily Mail Reporter, "The little boy who started a sex change aged eight because he (and his lesbian parents) knew he always wanted to be a girl", *Daily Mail,* News (September 30, 2011) www.dailymail.co.uk (Accessed December 26, 2014).

[41] Associated Press, "3 children found starving, 1 chained to floor in California home", *Fox News,* Crime & Courts (March 22, 2014), www.foxnews.com (Accessed December 26, 2014).

[42] Michael Walsh, "Australian pair in L.A. convicted for making child porn with 'adopted son' from Russia", *New York Daily News,* Crime (June 29, 2013) www.nydailynews.com (Accessed December 26, 2014).

[43] WaayTV, "Prosecutors ask for continuance in Carl Herold's child sex case", WaayTV, News/Local (July 23, 2014), www.waaytv.com (Accessed December 26, 2014).

[44] Barbara Ross, "Baby-sitter starved, beat 4-year-old Myls Dobson, then watched him 'completely shut down': prosecutors", *New York Daily News,* NYC-Crime (January 11, 2014) www.nydailynews.com (Accessed December 26, 2014).

[45] Jeff D. Gorman, "Surrogate Claim Won't Stick to Mother of Twins", *Courthouse News Service* (April 17, 2014) www.courthousenews.com (Accessed December 26, 2014).

[46] Amanda Thomas, "Police: Mom locked 6-year-old boy in dog cage", *Douglas County Sentinel,* Local News (April 24, 2014) www.douglascountysentinel.com (Accessed

December 26, 2014).

[47] Kristine Guerra, "Lesbian who claimed hospital ban faces assault charges", *Detroit Free Press*, Archives (*USAToday*) (November 21, 2013) http://archive.freep.com/ (Accessed December 26, 2014).

[48] Scott Smith, "Ex-girlfriend kills toddler, drugs 10-year-old brother in Jupiter's Abacoa neighborhood, police say", *CBS12 News* (May 2014) www.cbs12.com (Accessed December 26, 2014).

[49] Greg Hernandez, "TV's David Tutera and husband involved in ugly public split involving unborn twins", *Gay Star News* (May 2, 2013) www.gaystarnews.com (Accessed December 26, 2014).

[50] Meredith Bennett-Smith, "Peter Sprigg, FRC Fellow, Suggests Gay Parents Shouldn't Be Protected From Parental Kidnappings", *Huffington Post*, Gay Voices (March 11, 2013) www.huffingtonpost.com (Accessed December 26, 2014).

[51] Louis Eccles, "Custody battle over five-year-old twins with THREE mothers: Fears for children as love-split lesbians fight it out", *Daily Mail*, News (May 2, 2014) www.dailymail.co.uk (Accessed December 26, 2014).

[52] Kevin Gray, "Florida judge approves birth certificate listing three parents", Reuters (February 7, 2013) www.reuters.com (Accessed December 26, 2014).

[53] Michael Winter, "Kansas sperm donor to appeal ruling over child support" *USA Today*, News-Nation (January 24, 2014) www.usatoday.com (Accessed December 26, 2014).

[54] *PCMD Gazette*, "The 'Redefining' continues – lesbian trio now 'married' and expecting this", *PCMD Gazette* (April 23, 2014) www.thepcmdgazette.com (Accessed December 26, 2014).

[55] Stuart Winer, "Efforts underway to bring surrogate babies from Thailand", *Times of Israel*, Israel Inside (January 19, 2014) www.timesofisrael.com (Accessed December 26, 2014).

[56] F.P., "Péruwelz: Sonia a offert son ventre à un couple homosexuel vivant à Paris contre... 5.000 euros", *SudInfo.be*, Régions>Tournai>Actualité (January 25, 2013) www.sudinfo.be (Accessed December 27, 2014). Translated by R.O. Lopez.

[57] News.com.au, "SBS journalist Patrick Abboud investigates the dark side of commercial surrogacy in Thailand", *News.com.au*, Lifestyle (October 28, 2013) www.news.com.au (Accessed December 26, 2014).

[58] Shayne Jacobs and Ginger Adams Otis, "Intern at Midtown preschool arrested for sexually abusing 13 children: officials", *New York Daily News*, NYC-Crime (July 3, 2014) www.nydailynews.com (Accessed December 27, 2014).

[59] Liz Mak, "Chinese, on the Inside", *New York Times*, Opinion (March 3, 2014) www.nytimes.com (Accessed December 27, 2014). Editor's Note: note the fact that this lesbian couple purposefully undertook an adoption in a foreign country in violation of that country's rules, in order to avoid having to be bound by the child's rights under domestic adoption.

[60] Paul Tough, "The Black White Supremacist", *New York Times*, Magazine Archives (May 25, 2003) www.nytimes.com (Accessed December 27, 2014).

[61] Tracy Connor and Jim Doblin, "Wichita Foster Dad of Baby who Died in Hot Car 'Wants to Die'", NBC News Storyline (July 25, 2014) www.nbcnews.com (Accessed December 26, 2014).

[62] Janna Darnelle, "Breaking the Silence: Redefining Marriage Hurts Women Like Me— and Our Children", *Public Discourse* (September 22, 2014) www.thepublicdiscourse.

com (Accessed December 29, 2014).

[63] Robert Stacy McCain, "Another Feminist 'Success' Story", *The Other McCain* (October 28, 2014) http://theothermccain.com (Accessed January 2, 2014).

[64] Lindsey Bever, "White woman sues sperm bank after she mistakenly gets black donor's sperm", *Washington Post,* Morning Mix (October 2, 2014) www.washingtonpost.com (Accessed January 19, 2015).

[65] English Manif, "More studies about what 'monogamy' means for gay male couples – and more proof gay men should not adopt", *English Manif* (June 26, 2014) http://englishmanif.blogspot.com (Accessed December 1, 2014). Based on several other articles, including: Matthew Tharett, "WATCH: Dan Savage Explains the Pros and Cons of a 'Monogamish' Relationship", *Queerty,* Do This Not That (July 2, 2013) www.queerty.com (Accessed January 19, 2015). Also based on: Daniel Reynolds, "A Majority of Gay Couples Have 'Arrangements' for Outside Sex", *HIV Plus,* Sex & Dating (May 31, 2014) www.hivplusmag.com (Accessed January 19, 2015). Here is an excerpt of the original *English Manif* post:

> Plus, there is a deeper problem here. There is virtually no way for family court, adoption agencies, or other professionals – the folks devoted to determining "the best interests of the child" – to certify that the two men residing in the home with this child are actually in a sexually exclusive relationship. The two men may say they are exclusive in order to get custody, but the gay male community is a culture that grew out of dealing with being closeted and lying about the truth of their sex lives. Regardless of what the men say to authorities, we have substantial research that shows that the chances are high that the two men who are asking for a child to be placed in their custody, whether they are married are not, are involved sexually with other parties. Read this excerpt [from Reynolds]:
>
> Though many gay couples are monogamous, and Bob and John asked to remain unidentified because of the stigma of open relationships, their experience is not unheard of. According to a study by the University of Michigan, a slight majority of gay couples—57 percent—have "ground rules" like theirs that lay out the guidelines for sexual behavior with others, including provisions for acceptable sex acts, honesty about encounters, and when they need to use protection like condoms. But, the study finds, too often agreements about how to handle sex outside of a relationship go loosely defined or develop without a real conversation to settle the terms, which may then fuel the spread of HIV. The findings, published last year in *The Journal of Sex Research,* came after researchers polled 361 couples and discovered that 207 had such a sexual agreement. However, the rules weren't always clearly communicated between partners, many of whom reported discrepancies in what they believed they could or couldn't do. The couples had all responded to ads about the survey on Facebook. "Among these couples, 58 percent said that they explicitly discussed the agreement, 84 percent concurred about having the same type of agreement, and 54 percent of the couples had both men adhering to it," the study noted. The researchers concluded that if little over half actually followed their own agreed-upon rules, that meant there was a lack of communication about acceptable behaviors.

This magazine, which caters to gay male readers, is soft-pedalling the data. Most studies find even higher rates of infidelity. Even the University of Michigan sets at 57% *only*

103

those gay male couples who agree to an open relationship, meaning that it does not say anything about how many of the remaining 43% include gay male partners who are cheating without permission. Throw those in the mix, and you are in the danger zone. Essentially, there is about a 3 in 4 chance that two gay men in a long-term relationship who show up to court asking for custody of a child are going to be raising that child in a home that's sexually compromised.

66 Robert Oscar Lopez, "Same-Sex Parenting: Child Abuse?", *Public Discourse* (July 8, 2013) www.thepublicdiscourse.com (Accessed January 19, 2015). Quoted within excerpt: Rob Watson, "A Gay Dad's Invitation to a Supreme Court Justice: Come to Dinner with My Family", *Huffington Post,* HuffPost Live (February 7, 2013) www. huffingtonpost.com (Accessed January 19, 2015).

67 Austin Ruse, "Gay 'Poster Boys' for Surrogacy in Britain Condemned by US Critics", *Breitbart,* Big Government (January 6, 2015) www.breitbart.com (Accessed January 19, 2015).

68 Marcello Mega and Graham Grant, "Grandparents of children given to gay couple for adoption are denied access for three years", *Daily Mail,* News (September 6, 2012) www.dailymail.co.uk (Accessed January 19, 2015).

69 Brittany Klein, "LGBT Demands for Other People's Children Are Misogynistic", *Federalist* (February 3, 2015) www.thefederalist.com (Accessed February 9, 2015).

70 Stephen Jimenez, *The Book of Matt* (Hanover, New Hampshire: Steerforth Press, 2013), 48.

Chapter Eight

MOTHER'S DAY FOR
A GAY MAN'S SON

Robert Oscar Lopez

Manuel Half's "A Candle for My Mother," is a short but beautiful piece of prose poetry. Unfortunately, it cannot be republished here but the story that prompted it is worth retelling. On May 6, 2014, just before Mother's Day, a news site called Unione Cristiani Cattolici Razionali (UCCR) ran the article below, commenting on a dramatic argument taking place between Giuseppina La Delfa and me in Italy, largely due to the ripple effects of Pope Francis's declaration that children had a natural right to a mother and father. Below is the text of the UCCR article that prompted Manuel Half to respond with a beautiful ode to mothers, from the perspective of a boy raised by a homosexual father without a mother. The footnotes within the text have been added by the editors of **Jephthah's Children** *to give readers outside Italy more context. The final footnote provides the publication information for the column itself.*

UCCR Article

In order to assure that the place for child-raising be suitable, not only does it not matter whether the parents are a homosexual couple. Even more radically, "it doesn't matter whether they're raised by one, two, or eighteen parents."

Even 18 homosexual fathers therefore are just swell. So says Giuseppina La Delfa, who is convinced of these ideas. She is president of Italy's "Rainbow Families".

Recently, showing all of her characteristic tolerance, she has made a public response to none other than Pope Francis.[1] Francis, you may recall, dared to support and defend "the right of children to grow up in a family, with a dad and a mom capable of creating a suitable environment for development and emotional maturation. They need to mature in relation to masculinity and to femininity, of a father and a mother."[2]

Scandalised, the leader of the mysterious organisation called "Famiglie Arcobaleno" or "Rainbow Families" (already an oxymoron according to the Italian Constitution, which defines "family" as "the natural social unit founded on marriage"), retorted by writing, "a child has no right to live in a family with a father and a mother... A child has a right to grow up in a suitable environment for development, yes, this is true."[3] ...

La Delfa proceeded to venture into familiar territory, citing for her part whatever points came to mind: science, psychology, anthropology, pediatric psychiatry, sociology, law, and jurisprudence. "They all say the same thing," she wrote, which is that the father and mother are useless. The suitable place for raising children, Giuseppina La Delfa commented in response to Pope Francis, is just about anywhere, "regardless of who the parents are, of which sex, or of which sexual orientation, no matter whether they number one, two, or eighteen. But one thing matters: responsibility, care, presence, establishing limits, ... or as we can state in two words: support and attention."[4]

It is worth noting that in order to demonstrate the adequacy of homosexual couples to adopt a child, the president of "Rainbow Families" came up with the notion that even eighteen parents would be fine. So why not 69? Or even 241? Statistically, this would indicate that the child would receive even more "support and attention" compared to having *only* 18 parents.

If these are therefore the bases by which a place is deemed suitable for raising a child, then it is easy to point out that even an orphanage offers just as suitable an environment. But this then flies in the face of the rhetorical argument posed by people who support LGBT adoption: "better a gay couple than an orphanage".

If biological parents are not important, if no importance is paid to the sex, or orientation, or number of parents, who can argue that the directors of an orphanage aren't able to provide "responsibility, care, presence, setting limits, and cradling, all summed up in two words: support and attention"? After finishing up a cumbersome piece of work, La Delfa concluded her "reply" asking for children to be liberated from all forms of religious education. She considers religious upbringing to be mere superstition and educational manipulation, especially if it comes at the hands of the Church, which she likens to a dictatorship. As a consequence, she has attacked whoever has been religiously raised, or follows a faith, accusing them all of being manipulated and lacking any critical sense. Including, of course, Pope Francis.

The Spanish [sic] professor Robert Oscar Lopez, who was raised with gay parents, sent by way of the "Tempi Foundation" a letter responding to La Delfa.[5] The letter was blocked first by Lucia Annunziata, the editor of the Huffington Post. Robert Oscar Lopez explained about having experienced the challenges of growing up with two lesbian moms: "Can Giuseppina La Delfa look me in the eyes and tell me that I lost nothing? That I suffered not at all? Do I not have any right to love my father *as* my father, simply for the fact that he is my father?"[6] So he wrote what he had already in passing described as the problems that go along with such arrangements: "I ask you to apologize to all children—to all humanity in fact—to have stated such an atrocious thing: the notion that people do not have the right to a father and a mother."[7]

"The most dangerous enemies of Italian gays are, often, gays themselves," wrote a while back Domenico Naso.[8] Especially for their reasoning, as is obvious after this umpteenth article-salvo from Giuseppina La Delfa.[9]

"A candle for my mother"

The dogfight between Giuseppina La Delfa and me raised a Mother's Day firestorm in Italy. Manuel Half was close to being pulled into the middle of it. I delivered remarks at Lombardy's county seat on April 1, 2014. Pope Francis's declaration of a child's right to mother and father came ten days later. With the Pope in one backyard and a clanging gay lobby in another, the aftermath of my appearance caused many to beckon Manuel into the debate. He responded with graceful dignity, saying that there must be some well of humanity hidden inside La Delfa to help her understand why boys want to know their mothers on Mother's Day. He lit a candle in the window of his urban apartment and said to his mother—whoever and wherever she was—that he hoped she might pass and see the flame to know that he was okay.

Notes

[1] Giuseppina La Delfa, "Diritto naturale e famiglie di fatto: lettera aperta al sig. Bergoglio", *L'Huffington Post* (April 14, 2014) www.huffingtonpost.it (Accessed December 28, 2014).

[2] Pope Francis, "Discorso del Santo Padre Francesco alla Delegazione dell'Ufficio Internazionale Cattolico dell'Infanzia (BICE)", Official Vatican Website (April 11, 2014) http://w2.vatican.va (Accessed December 28, 2014).

[3] Giuseppina La Delfa, Ibid.

[4] Giuseppina La Delfa, Ibid.

[5] Robert Oscar Lopez, «Care Famiglie Arcobaleno, sono stato cresciuto da lesbiche, ma è offensivo dire che i bambini non hanno diritto a mamma e papà», *Tempi*, Società (April 22, 2014) www.tempi.it (Accessed December 28, 2014). Translation into English by author:

> I am writing this to respond to the assertion that children "do not have a right to be raised by a mother and father." The argument put forward by the author (Giuseppina La Delfa) is that a different "right" – the right to be raised in conditions that sociologists and experts consider ideal – supersedes and actually erases the right of a child to a mom and dad. This argument is deeply offensive, especially coming from someone who claims to represent gay rights. The entire rationale behind gay marriage and gay parenting is that homosexuals have rights that they do not need to justify to other people. Despite the fact that copious statistics show that homosexual relationships have higher rates of instability, domestic violence, and emotional abuse, advocates for gay marriage still claim that they should have a right to marry because it is an entitlement that isn't subject to the approval or endorsement of other people, even experts. Yet what is the attitude shown toward kids who are forced to live in same-sex couple homes? The key word is "forced," because no child ends up in a gay home unless adults have taken extraordinary measures to place the child under the power of at least one, and possibly two, people

who are not biologically related to him and therefore have no genetic or conceptual relationship to it. Suddenly when children are involved, gay advocates say, "you don't get to have legal recognition of your relationship to the father and mother who gave you your identity, who made you who you are, because we have scientists who have proven that it's good enough for you to live the way we want you to live, and to love the guardians that we say you ought to love." If such an attitude represents the way we give rights to people's relationships, then why are we arguing about marriage? We should say, "you don't have the right to marry the same sex. You don't have the right to marry the person you love. You only have the right to be in a relationship that sociologists say is healthy for you, which would be, statistically speaking, a relationship with the opposite sex." Obviously the statement above is offensive to a gay marriage advocate. So why is the statement about kids not having a right to mom and dad not offensive to me? I was raised by a lesbian and her lifelong partner, and my father was not in the picture. Can the author look me in the eyes and tell me I lost nothing? I suffered nothing? I have no right now to want to love my father as my father, because he is my father? There are two "offensive" positions in conflict here. We have the gay adult who is offended to hear that he or she can't love the person they prefer and have a family with children at the same time. We have the child who is offended to hear that he or she can't love at least one of the two people who gave the child an identity and life. Between these two people, the child takes precedence, because: 1) The child's loss of a parent is not consensual, unlike the gay adults, who are old enough to choose their relationships already. 2) The child's loss is of something universal. Not all people marry but all people have a mother and father. 3) The child's loss is permanent. Two gay adults can get divorced. A child cannot undo the decisions made about removing half of his or her heritage. For these reasons, I ask that your newspaper apologize to children everywhere – to humanity, in fact – for saying such an atrocious thing as "people do not have a right to mother and father." Sincerely, Robert Oscar Lopez.

[6] Robert Oscar Lopez, Ibid.

[7] Robert Oscar Lopez, Ibid.

[8] Domenico Naso, "Caso Barilla: cari gay, è il momento de crescere", *Fatto Quotidiano*, Diritti (September 27, 2013) www.ilfattoquotidiano.it (Accessed December 28, 2014). Trans. Robert Oscar Lopez.

[9] Editorial Staff, Unione Cristiani Cattolici Razionali, "La 'Famiglie arcobaleno': vanno bene anche 18 genitori", *uccronline.it* (May 6, 2014) www.uccronline.it (Accessed December 28, 2014).

Chapter Nine

FATHER'S DAY FOR A LESBIAN'S SON

Robert Oscar Lopez

I waited until the night of Father's Day to write this, because I couldn't bear to post it in the midst of all the winsome father's day specials everywhere—odes to the mentorship, paternal fealty, male role modeling, and caring that everyone attributes to fathers.

I do not want to be covetous, so I am genuinely happy for everyone who has fathers to celebrate and commemorate on this day.

I have a close relationship with my father. I had to go out of my way to build that from scratch when I was in my late twenties. Some of this is not the fault of my lesbian mother. None of this is really the fault of her partner. Some fault lies in my own reaction to things growing up, my curling up and withdrawing from what was such a confusing arrangement of custodian figures and role models and parental units that I had to protect and shield, when I was still a child who just wanted to be protected and shielded.

Father's Day isn't a day when one should be finding fault. One should be cherishing one's father. And I have one now, so I cherish him and love him. But Father's Day is always painful because it is on this day that everyone around me shares stories and tells tales about this person in their lives, most often involving the tender years of childhood and adolescence. I have a father but I don't have those stories to tell, so I am torn. Instead of narratives about being taught how to pitch a baseball or pep talks to stick up for myself against bullies, I have maudlin and pathetic stories about being a teenage freak, getting beat up, having nobody to turn to and defend me, feeling abandoned and alone, finding solace in male prostitution and hookups with lecherous gay men.

My father became my father when I was twenty-seven.

By that time I was already a New York City professional, working at MTV Networks. The time had passed for me to learn how to be a man. Lost were the rites of passage or masculine guidance. I had arrived at my late twenties not knowing how to be a man, and making it up as I went along, replacing the missing father with the collective nurturing but ultimately unhealthy guidance of the gay male community. I'd looked for and found countless proxy father figures who ended up dying of AIDS or disappearing. I'd been accustomed to having a huge void where my father should have been, which I filled with a lot of self-medicating behaviors: compulsive sex, drinking, obsessive careerism, recklessness.

I had cancer in January 1998. I ignored the pain as the growth hardened and worsened, convincing myself nothing was wrong. I had no reason to believe I had cancer. The thought never crossed my mind. But then on a cold winter day, the doctor told me that he'd received a report on my blood works. My tumor markers were hundreds of times the normal rate and the growth was likely to metastasise. He said he had to operate immediately.

My brother took the train up from Manhattan to help me prepare for the surgery as I rushed into Montefiore Hospital's ambulatory care unit. The Harlem River seemed to separate me and my brother, like a continuing symbol of the gulf that had always divided me from him in the same family. I'd looked up to him as an older sibling, but we'd never been close. I had almost no memories of him and me doing anything together in the house where we grew up. He was always close with a family down the street that had three sons, one daughter, and an all-American Mom and Pop business they ran as a clan. In some ways it seemed as though they adopted him as an honorary Polish American when we were kids. He was always over at their house, leaving me to deal with the crazy lesbian melodrama of our nutty Puerto Rican asylum.

I didn't feel right leaning on my brother in the middle of the crisis. I was living with an HIV+ cross-dresser who I worried might shock and discomfort him, so I was wary of having my brother come over to my house. Little white lies aren't so bad, right? I told my brother I'd be fine and didn't need his help, so he could go back to his place off of 125th Street. Then when he left, I felt terribly alone. It wasn't just the pain, it was also the knowledge that something as serious as cancer was real and happening to me. It was the fact that the ultimate consequence of the disease was still an unknown. I needed someone there, someone of my flesh and blood. My mother had been gone for eight years, but I knew that her partner would come to New York if I called her.

I picked up the phone. Something snapped in my head, and instead of calling her, I called Dad. His voice was calm and unruffled over the phone as I told him about what was happening. There was some surprise, but he was never one to get hysterical in a crisis. The fact that we were speaking to each other was a shock in itself, for I'd grown accustomed, over the years, to communicating to him only by leaving messages with his receptionist. I drummed up the courage to ask if he would come and help me through the operation.

Each second felt like an hour as I waited to see what he would say. My first guess was that he'd say he had too many appointments. His business partners would need him to be away on business, or else he didn't know how his presence would help. But then came the big surprise: He said without hesitation he would fly down.

Things sped along in the next day or two. I was rolled into surgery and someone miscalculated the anesthesia, so it wore off in the middle of the procedure. The pain I felt being cut open and sewed shut was something that defied description. Perhaps the worst part of the surgery itself was that I felt truly alone surrounded by doctors and nurses I didn't know if I could trust. They put me to sleep with some injection then rolled me into a basement hallway to recover next to stabbing victims and junkies going cold turkey.

When I came to, my father was there. "You're my father", I said. "I'm your son". That was all I could really say, but it said everything that needed to be said.

In the two years that followed, I embarked on a recovery that went far beyond overcoming cancer (I ended up going into complete remission and being fine, eventually). The aftermath of cancer turned out to be more focused on my father, this mysterious man who'd hovered over me like a question mark, and less about oncology.

Perhaps on a rash whim, I quit my job at MTV Networks and moved into my father's house in Buffalo. The doctors transferred my care from Montefiore to Roswell Park Cancer Institute, skipping over the doctor's recommendation that I go to Sloan-Kettering. To outsiders, the next years might look creepy or distorted: I regressed to the emotional state of a nine-year-old, wanting to relive my childhood, but now with my father there. I enrolled in graduate school at SUNY Buffalo down the street and got a scholarship that allowed me to focus on my studies. Other than my studies, I was largely concentrated on learning how to be a son. I helped take care of my father's ailing mother, who was in her nineties. I did chores around the house. I invited myself to his parties to drink beer alongside his buddies. We went to football games. I watched all his favorite James Bond films and his beloved documentaries about World War II. In 1999, we went to the Philippines together and he was proud of my fluency in Spanish, which allowed me to translate the nineteenth-century baptismal certificates of Dad's ancestors and build his long-lost family tree.

The fact that my father was proud of me, that I wasn't something to be kept secret or feel ashamed about, meant the world to me. It really did. Some of my friends mocked what was going on, because they couldn't believe that a grown man with a career in television would willingly move in with his dad and act like a teenage boy begging his pop to play catch in the backyard. But for strange reasons, I didn't care that it was weird. The point was, I had lived my whole life never having these Dad-and-son things. My life had brought me to a point where I was convinced that I deserved them and shouldn't shy away from taking them back.

Did my reunion with my father make up for lost time? No. It wasn't lost time. It was new time. It was a relationship that became something profoundly important for me, even transformative, something that allowed me to understand all of who I was and why I had to turn away from the hurtful self-medicating behaviours that had filled the void in the past.

Though I love what my relationship with my Dad has become, the void wasn't really filled. It's still a void for those first 27 years, when there was no dad, because my mom was a lesbian and she didn't really want a dad in her life—or rather, in mine. She was actually very close to her own father.

Therein lies the rub for the boy raised by lesbians. You grow up seeing a loving relationship between two women who have defined themselves against what you are, and against the man who gave you life. Father's Day becomes a black hole of time, a day you get through, trying to listen to everyone's stories about their dads without rolling your eyes. The happy ending that concluded my journey through a fatherless life is something I treasure and am grateful for. But I grieve for the many boys raised by lesbians who will never have the fortuitous twists that allowed me to reunite with Dad: the cancer, the empty room in his house, graduate school, my own inexplicable decision to send my brother home and call Dad instead.

If there is any day on which I feel the importance of opposing same-sex parenting, it's Father's Day by far. Lesbian moms have done something cruel by forcing kids to grow up with a gaping void that their peers never feel. There are children whose fathers die, of course, but most often, these children have a tombstone to visit and their widowed mothers will sit them down and tell them sentimental tales about what their father was like. That's not like having a lesbian mom who can't bear the thought of your dad, the reflection of you as a male, sharing your home and actually being part of your life.

I used to be timid about criticising lesbian moms, but not anymore. People have been too reserved about telling them to their faces that their families are abusive and their decision to deprive children of fathers a gross crime. Father's Day is a time of love but also a time of honesty. Honesty can be affirming, but it can also hurt. Every child has a father. The lesbian couple raising a child has simply decided to steal the child from his father and to steal the father from his child. That's wrong. And this would be the day to take a break from the charming stories, to be frank.

Chapter Ten

BIRTH CERTIFICATES

Robert Oscar Lopez

An open letter to Governor Brown & Jimmy Gomez

Dear Governor Brown,

I work for you. I am an Associate Professor of English and Classics at California State University, Northridge.

I know that a bill, AB 1951, sponsored by Jimmy Gomez of Los Angeles, may reach your desk for signature soon.[1] It will allow for birth certificates to be issued, which indicate gay men as "mother" and lesbians as "father". I would like you to veto it and please begin the process of reversing California's destructive trend toward same-sex parenting homes. While you may have been led to believe that children raised by gay couples are delighted with their lives and view their guardians uncritically, the hidden truth is that many of us who were raised by gay couples are hurting and feel that our rights have been violated.

Rather than compound California's problem – *too many kids growing up in gay homes* – you need to veto this legislation and begin to reverse the process by phasing out third-party reproduction and ending gay adoption. What I am saying may seem infeasible, even shocking, but the reality is that gay parenting is a problem, not a solution. Like past social experiments, such as Lebensborn or mass adoption of Native American children, the drawbacks to this current fashion of custody are impossible to see for many people who are so immersed in the issue that they cannot take a broad view. The innovation is still new, there is so much pressure to view it favorably, and the people who want it to proliferate are powerful. Rather than exemplifying "the right side of history", this situation mirrors the conditions that led to gross injustices in the past.

I am asking you to see beyond the here and now and look at gay parenting through a historically informed, humanitarian lens, so you can see that it is a bad idea and something that should be abated and then ceased, rather then encouraged.

I know that will take a long time but it is urgent that you do this because these gay homes, despite all the ways they have been romanticized in the press, are often abusive and destructive.

They are abusive, first of all, because having a mom and having a dad are powerful, culturally significant parts of the human experience – impossible to quantify or attach a price tag to – and gay couples are being allowed to strip children of this universal entitlement simply to pursue their own dreams of the perfect alternative family.

We hear that gay couples have loving homes and they love their children. I don't buy that because I think love means you sacrifice for the other person rather than expect the other person to sacrifice for you. If you are gay and love a child, you either sacrifice your gayness and raise the child in a home with both mother and father, or you sacrifice your dream of parenthood so the child can be adopted by a home with a mother and father. If the child is an orphan or a special-needs child or an abandoned ward of the state, the child needs a mom and dad more than anybody else, for they need stability and normalcy in the wake of trauma. You don't ask your child to sacrifice something as important and universal as having a mother and father for your sake.

The "love" of a gay couple for children is coercive, because the child is being forced into an emotional relationship with at least one person who isn't a biological parent, whether the child wants this or not. Like most Cinderellas, the child will often not want the emotional relationship but the gay couple emboldened by state endorsement will force it on him or her anyway.

To be the child forced to live someone else's dream, and to have nobody to honor or commemorate on days as important as Father's Day and Mother's Day, are not small pains. They are profound emotional wounds, worsened by the fact that the State of California has inscribed into law the notion that our losses are meaningless, our pains non-existent, our missing fathers and missing mothers nothing to cry over. We are told to be grateful and smile for the cameras. That's wrong.

We shouldn't harass gay families that currently exist. Support them and please minimize the suffering of children in those homes, since it isn't their fault. They are very vulnerable to backlash from their parents. Most gay couples who have placed children in these situations have not had a chance to hear a frank, uncensored view of same-sex parenting from someone who grew up in such a home, reached adulthood, and now has the independence and hindsight to be objective. Many gay couples who raise children have been indoctrinated by an assimilationist agenda set by one part of the gay community. They don't realize that they can be beautiful people and live wonderful lives without having to pattern their relationship after a man and a woman who conceive children through lovemaking.

I have tried to speak for the many children of same-sex couples who don't like what was done to them, but I've been cowed into silence and blacklisted in California. My mother was a lesbian and was in a lifelong relationship with another woman for, basically, my entire childhood from my earliest memories until my mother's death. She died when I was nineteen. That was 24 years ago.

The explosion in same-sex parenting homes is neither something to take lightly, nor something to be proud of. At first I thought I was an outlier, or someone with an anomalous experience, not applicable as a general principle. The more I got in contact with other adults who had gay parents, and the more I got to speak to children living in gay homes, the more I realized that my experience is the rule, not the exception.

Over the last two years I have been studying the testimonials of other people who were raised by same-sex couples. Currently I have twenty-five that are available for the public, some drawn from the work of Dawn Stefanowicz, a woman who was raised by a gay father. Dozens of others have communicated with me but they are fearful about publishing any details, let alone their names, which might make it possible for same-sex marriage advocates to figure out who they are.

The same-sex parenting research has to be thrown out, since it has been carried out by biased scholars who handpicked examples of children raised in gay homes. The national climate is so hostile to children of gay couples who have negative feedback, even the best-intended researcher would find it impossible to record frank testimony from children raised in such homes.

I do not have time to recount the whole ugly tale of what gay parenting advocates, including many academic scholars, did to me in punishment for speaking against the supposed "no disadvantages" consensus. Once I came forward with a respectful critique of same-sex parenting based on negative outcomes in my life, I endured a brutal retaliation at my California State University job, orchestrated by powerful gay organizations such as GLAAD, the Human Rights Campaign, and the New Civil Rights Movement.[2] All three of these organizations became entangled with academic affairs.

GLAAD listed me on their "Commentator Accountability Project" list as someone who had supposedly made anti-gay statements. Their main complaint was that as a scholar of early American black literature I discussed the pain black slaves felt being bought and separated from their heritage. This allusion was to explain why it is no small thing to separate children like me from their heritage to make gay couples happy. They oversimplified this complex scholarly argument as "Robert Oscar Lopez equated same-sex marriage to slavery" and then wrote to Stanford University, urging them to block me from delivering a speech at a conference there on April 5, 2014.[3] Based on GLAAD's designation of me as anti-gay, a queer student group at Stanford succeeded in blocking funds to the Stanford Anscombe Society at both the undergraduate and graduate levels.[4]

The Human Rights Campaign maintains a list called the "Regnerus Fallout" page, designed to identify people who were behind Texas sociologist Mark Regnerus's article, which came out in July 2012 in *Social-Science Research*.[5] Mark Regnerus found that adults who had been raised by parents in same-sex relationships experienced lifelong difficulties. I had nothing to do with the study other than the fact that I wrote an article on August 6, 2012, describing my difficulties and pointing out that I could understand the Regnerus results in human terms.[6] For this, the Human Rights Campaign listed me, misleadingly, as someone "involved" in Regnerus's study; the Regnerus Fallout page also regurgitates GLAAD's oversimplified claim that I compared gay parents to slave-owners. The purpose of the Human Rights Campaign's list, like the GLAAD list, is to identify me and my existence in the academy, so that people know to block my publications, public speaking, or funding.

Long before I had even used my scholarship in African American literature as a comparison point to understand same-sex parenting, the New Civil Rights Movement had already waged a campaign of character assassination against me simply based on my honesty about negative experiences being raised by a lesbian and growing up in the gay community. The New Civil Rights Movement, in August 2012, had a writer named Scott Rosenzweig. He wrote over a dozen emails to my co-workers and bosses at Northridge, accusing me of bullying, gay-bashing, and hate speech because I recounted honestly my lifelong difficulties as the son of a lesbian.[7]

The Rosenzweig harassment was particularly threatening in late 2012 because he had already succeeded in forcing the University of Texas to open an investigation into Mark Regnerus. Laurie Essig, a Middlebury College professor and writer with the *Chronicle of Higher Education*, cited Scott Rosenzweig as if he were a serious authority on same-sex parenting (he is actually not a professor or scholar of any kind, being only a blogger).[8]

The actions by GLAAD, the Human Rights Campaign, and the New Civil Rights Movement demonstrate the extent to which political advocacy groups, flush with money, have interfered with academic research and retaliated against scholars who have contrary data. They have lashed out against children of same-sex couples who have scholarly credentials that enable them to articulate negative feedback. The fact that they have moved so blatantly to contain any challenges to the "consensus" on same-sex parenting proves the urgency in throwing that consensus out, since it is based on coercion and suppression of pertinent contrary information. Despite the highly public references to me by these three groups, no researcher in the field of same-sex parenting other than Mark Regnerus and Walter Schumm has ever contacted me or asked me for feedback on their scholarship. To them, apparently, I do not exist, which speaks volume about the illegitimacy of their research models.

Authorities in my college tried to block me from using grant money I'd received from outside donors. They approved a public records request, which allowed emails with sensitive information to be released to Scott Rosenzweig. They created a hostile work environment where I was constantly nagged about small details that my co-workers did not have to worry about.[9]

I am not going to say that the supporters of Proposition 8 handled the issue of gay parenting well. My view is that they should have stood up against gay adoption and third-party reproduction. They did not because they had a fixation with religious liberty arguments. They felt that marriage was more important than children's rights. It is possible that many traditional marriage supporters internalised some of the racist and classist assumptions about orphans or poor children. Perhaps they came to agree with gay advocacy organisations that a child raised in a wealthy gay home is better off than a child raised by struggling biological parents.

I am here to tell you that all the money and high-class living in the world cannot undo the pain and loss inflicted on a child forced to grow up without a mother and father. I grew up in a comfortable upper middle-class home and went to Yale, but I would have traded all that for a shack and gone to trade school, if I could have grown up with my father and mother and seen them love each other.

Being separated from half of your biological origins is always difficult, whether the people responsible for this separation were gay or straight. It just so happens that a small minority of heterosexual parents will decide to uproot children from their birth parents and place them in other parenting arrangements, yet one hundred percent of gay couples raising kids have made such decisions.

And then there is the reality that it isn't the same thing, growing up with two moms, two dads, or a mom and a dad. I needed a male parent to show me how to be a man. Lesbian moms who bring in "male role models" to teach this to their sons aren't cutting it. Those role models have no real authority over you and aren't truly a permanent or stable part of your life. The only way to make a father figure a stable part of your life would be for one of the lesbians to marry him and raise you as a family, which is precisely what the lesbians do not want to do. It is very difficult to learn how to be a man from men who are being actively excluded and minimized by two gay women.

As I was growing up, I also longed to connect with my father's roots; he was Filipino whereas my mother was Puerto Rican and her partner was white. There is an organization called the Filipino Intercollegiate Network for Dialogue, or FIND, based on the East Coast. It is still thriving today. I wrote the constitution for it and organized the inaugural gathering of the group in April 1991, in New Haven, Connecticut, bringing together over 120 students from thirty-three different colleges from Massachusetts down to Virginia. Anybody who was there at the very beginning knows that organisation was my project; I recruited all the original signatories and even drew the map of districts, complete with my original idea of a "district zero".

Even with all the trauma of watching my mother's health deteriorate until she died in 1990, I had had a passion about building some kind of Filipino social web so that people like me would have a way of connecting with the Philippines' culture. I couldn't explain to the other Filipino activists why this meant so much to me. I had to be mysterious about why I was half Filipino and had no childhood experience with the language or ethnic traditions associated with the community. How could I say, in 1990-1991, "my Puerto Rican mother and her white lesbian lover were my parental figures, but I want to find my roots?"

At the time, I did not even have a place to stay, but I started the work of launching this group before my mother died. It meant a lot to me to see the group get off the ground. Imagine how crushed I felt in 1991 when the rumors about my sexuality and the hidden truths about my Puerto Rican mother caused many of the Catholic Filipinos to feel nervous about associating my name with FIND. I had to drop out of Yale because of the problems with my mother's partner's status in the will; this added shame drove some of the adult funders and even a few students to scrub my name from the organization's history. If you go to the online history posted by FIND, you will see claims that the April 1991 event was just a "dinner" and that a group of Harvard students founded the organization in 1992. That was what it was like to be a child of a gay couple back then—your ethnic ties to any community were always strained and the urge of others was often to erase or minimize you.

Now, imagine the pain I felt in 2014 when I received an email from an old acquaintance of those days in the early 1990s. This friend said that some FIND alumni were embarrassed about my advocacy for traditional marriage and for a child's right to his or her original mother and father. The stigma has shifted—before, nobody wanted to be connected to gay families; now, to be seen as "anti-gay" is professional suicide. Not wanting to be tainted by an "anti-gay" persona, some were apparently seeking to make sure my name appeared nowhere in FIND's history. Yale's role in founding the organization seems to be progressively minimized each year. The myth that heterosexual "full-blooded" Harvard Filipinos founded the network can become "official history."

Having seen all that I've seen, I cannot accept the assurances that the children are going to be "resilient" and everything will be just fine when you erase biological roots and place children under the custody of gay people who aren't their parents. Maybe it seems like a safe idea to you as you sit in your governor's office; the child will have to reckon with all the mixed messages, contradictions, and broken promises. It is lonely living that way. On top of all these deprivations and confusions, there is the added reality that regardless of your parents' sexuality, the chances are overwhelmingly that you are going to grow up to be heterosexual. I call myself bisexual because I was involved with many men during the long period of sexual confusion, which lasted from the ages of thirteen to twenty-eight.

I lost my virginity to a woman at the age of twenty-eight and realized that I was really meant to couple with females. But it took me an extraordinarily long time to get up the courage to deal with a woman, because I grew up with no examples of men and women loving each other. I do not wish to disown my earlier past, so I call myself bisexual.

Gay culture is not the same as other ways of life. It is highly specific and fraught with problems. As statistics attest, gay adults have higher rates of depression, anxiety, eating disorders, sexually transmitted diseases including HIV/AIDS, domestic violence, sexual assault, and suicidal ideation. We need to help people who struggle with all these issues surrounding homosexuality.[10] By that I mean we must help them live as happy homosexuals; I am not calling for gay people to "change" if they really are gay.

Helping gay people live satisfying lives is an issue quite distinct from the best interests of a child whose well-being has been entrusted to your state. A child does not need to be exposed to all those problems. It does nobody any favors to pretend that gay people don't have a higher incidence of these problems and to feign equivalence between a gay home, where not one but two people come from this high-risk demographic, and a straight home, where the problems aren't so rampant.

Of course there are specific examples of terrible heterosexual homes. You will see carefully selected examples of highly functional, happy gay couples with kids, but as a governor you can't be naïve. Gay couples have a lot more hardship. Hardship rolls downhill and affects the kids, who are often expected to protect their parents when they should be the ones being protected.

If my father had died or if he'd abandoned me through some kind of tragedy beyond my parents' control, that would be one thing. I might have been able to deal with that. It didn't happen like that. Two lesbians valued their relationship with each other and dragged me into their romantic dynamics, cutting me off from my dad. I felt powerless and still do, when I think about it.

Overwhelmingly, the people who have spoken to me, who were raised by a biological parent and that parent's gay partner, did not want to be placed in an emotional relationship with the non-biological gay partner. They viewed that person as someone whom they had to adapt to, in order to have access to their biological parent, not someone whom they wanted the state's laws to impose on them as an added emotional burden. This dynamic is evident even in cases where the child came into the gay couple's home through sperm banking or through surrogacy. Even if the child has known nothing but the gay couple, the child generally does not want to have to deal with both gay adults as parents; they want one dad or one mom, and the added gay person in the adult pairing is a burdensome addition. Much of their longing and sadness in adolescence and adulthood focuses, moreover, on the vacuum left by the missing father or missing mother.

You will hear, from time to time, that same-sex couples need to be validated for their children's sake. This is false reasoning. Most kids being raised by same-sex couples didn't ask to be there and would probably not have dissolved their ties to their original mother and father, had they been given a chance to make an informed, independent, and mature choice. Many resent the implied threats from their gay parents when they feel dissatisfied with their state of deprivation. Gay parents do threaten their children when they hear kids saying things that remind them of homophobia. The problem is that often buzzwords or key phrases that remind gay parents of homophobia aren't signs that the child is bringing home outside prejudice; rather, it is a child crying out in pain because adults stole a mother or father from him or her, and the child knows it's unfair. The problem is that the unfairness was inflicted not by people who hated the child, but by the two people who claimed they loved the child most.

Up until now, the concerns and viewpoints I have expressed in this letter have been silenced and suppressed. In an incredibly undemocratic development, children have been forced to sever themselves from fathers or from mothers, because one political party wanted to please the gay lobby and the other political party decided we, the children, weren't worth fighting for. The media, the academy, the courts, politicians, and even many religious leaders have told us to shut up—even threatened us—because our gay parents have more power than we do. It is systematic child abuse, and your veto of this bill could be the first step in correcting it.

Please, Governor Brown, do the right thing.

POSTSCRIPT: This letter reached the governor but he signed the bill into law. The effect is that some California birth certificates are now fraudulent.

Notes

[1] See Matthew, "California Bill AB-1951: Official Statement of the ICRI", International Children's Rights Institute (Undated) www.internationalchildrensrights.com (Accessed December 28, 2014).

[2] See Robert Oscar Lopez, "A Tale of Targeting", *First Things*, Web Exclusives (October 21, 2014) www.firstthings.com (Accessed December 29, 2014).

[3] I confirmed that these communications were sent to the Stanford organisers when I met with the students who had organised the Anscombe Society conference eight months later, in December 2014, in Los Angeles.

[4] Kaitlyn Schallhorn, "Stanford student government upholds funding ban for pro-family group", *Campus Reform*, News (June 3, 2014) www.campusreform.org (Accessed December 29, 2014).

[5] Human Rights Campaign, "The Regnerus Fallout – Who was Involved?" *Regnerus Fallout* (2013) www.regnerusfallout.org (Accessed May 14, 2014).

[6] Robert Oscar Lopez, "Growing up with Two Moms".

[7] See Robert Oscar Lopez, "A Tale of Targeting".

[8] Laurie Essig, "The Big Lesson from Regnerus's Bad Gay-Parenting Study", *Chronicle of Higher Education*, Brainstorm (July 27, 2012) http://chronicle.com (Accessed December 29, 2014. Essig writes of Scott Rose, "On the same day that the internal audit was released, Scott Rose, an investigative journalist and a 'minorities anti-defamation professional,' released the evidence he will present to the University of Texas's Inquiry Panel on August 3." Contrary to the characterisation of Scott Rose as a journalist or professional, Mr. Rose seems to have no real credentials in the area of investigations or advocacy and is well known for excessive, malicious online badgering of people. See Brittany Klein, "This Lesbian's Daughter Has Had Enough", *American Thinker* (October 20, 2014) www.americanthinker.com (Accessed December 29, 2014). Also see *New York*, "Scott Rose in Full Bloom", *New York*, Daily Intelligencer (May 19, 2008) www.nymag.com (Accessed December 29, 2014). In the latter *New York* piece, the editors say: "Rose came to the attention of the editors after he left a staggering 736 comments over a span of six months, and last week, when his 734th comment caused a violent uprising from fellow readers, they decided to find out exactly who this guy was."

[9] Robert Oscar Lopez, "A Tale of Targeting". See also Robert Oscar Lopez, "The Devil Comes Home to Cal State Northridge", *American Thinker* (October 6, 2013) www.americanthinker.com (Accessed December 29, 2014).

[10] For hyperlinks to many studies backing these statistics, see Robert Oscar Lopez, "Gay Marriage and the Curse of Rumpelstiltskin", *American Thinker* (November 1, 2012) www.americanthinker.com (Accessed December 29, 2014).

Chapter Eleven

EUGENICS

Alana Newman

(First published in Public Discourse, November 10, 2014)

"Then how are gay people supposed to get kids?" asked a young woman from the audience. I had just given a presentation criticising donor-conception to 150 students at California State University, Northridge at the inaugural *Bonds That Matter* conference held by the International Children's Rights Institute.[1] I thought I had done a sufficient job of explaining that commodification of children and gamete donors dehumanises people into objects, property, chattel.

"But listen to yourself," I responded. "You just asked, 'how are they supposed to *get* kids?'"

Apparently, for my questioner, the idea of some people possessing others seemed neither frightful nor relevant.

I'd like to summarise my presentation here and reflect on what caused a small number of students to revolt after the conference—going so far as to harass its creator, Bobby Lopez.[2]

Are all technologies good?

I remember the first time I struggled to understand the ethics of a case involving reproductive technologies. I was five years old, folding clothes in my bedroom with my mom. She told me that my dad was not my biological father. My biological father was an anonymous sperm donor, whom we didn't know anything about.

I was told I was very loved and wanted, and this is simply what infertile couples must do to have kids. Our family was different, but we never did anything "wrong", so to speak.

After a wrenching divorce, I never again saw that "dad" of mine. My mother remarried, and I was given a new "dad". But neither the first nor the second man ever made me feel safe in my own home. It was clear to me that all men were evil and vile. I truly thought that either they lacked the capacity to love, or else there was something wrong with *me;* I was not worthy of love.

In art school, at the age of twenty, I sold my own eggs as a known donor. That was my way of improving the system: by removing anonymity, I was making things ever so slightly better. This experience gave me even more insight into donor conception and the fertility industry. I've been treated as an object many times by men in my life, but never so intensely as by the female fertility industry personnel who managed my egg harvest.

After founding the Anonymous Us Project nearly four years ago, I have read hundreds of stories from donor-conceived people, gamete donors, and involved parties.[3] I've become well acquainted with the issue from several angles. And here is what I'm worried about when it comes to the new ways in which we're bringing forth new life.

Stories of third-party reproduction gone wrong
Having children is currently our only legal path to achieving both genetic and memetic immortality.[4] Having kids isn't easy. You have to find a mate. You have to look outside yourself and into the eyes of another person and convince him or her of your decency, your desirability.

Third-party reproduction is not only used by the friendly, sympathetic infertile couples of our popular imagination. The cash-money market model of baby-making has opened the door to a broad consortium of terrifying players. Baby Gammy is just one example of how this new model serves predators first, children last.

Earlier this month, news broke about an Australian couple that, after commissioning a Thai surrogate in the creation of twins, *left* the male twin in Thailand due to his diagnosis of Down syndrome. According to the surrogate mother, when they got the diagnosis, they wanted her to abort, but she refused, carrying the child to term and naming him Gammy. They also demanded a refund. It has furthermore been revealed that the Australian father spent several years in jail for twenty-two convictions of child sex offenses. The little girl, baby Gammy's twin, is still in his care.[5]

There are many more. Mitsutoki Shigeta is a Japanese multi-millionaire who recently made international headlines for commissioning sixteen children born via Thai surrogates. He housed the surrogates, along with his children and nannies, in several condos that functioned as holding camps. He apparently has a great deal of sperm stored and was planning to commission at least a dozen pregnancies every year for as long as he could. A family member of one of the surrogates reported that in the surrogacy contract it was stipulated that if the woman were to bear an "imperfect" child, she would be required to pay $24,000 to *him*, Mr. Shigeta, and raise the baby herself. She would be paid just under $12,000 for carrying and giving birth to a healthy, normal child.[6]

Then there is Nadya Suleman, the infamous 'Octomom'. Nadya made headlines in 2009 after giving birth to octuplets born via sperm donation and IVF. Her story caused controversy, because Nadya already had six children and was living on public assistance at the time. She filed for bankruptcy in 2012, with over $1 million in personal debt. Around that same time, she released a porn video to help with her financial situation. In a June 2011 interview, Suleman purportedly told *In Touch Weekly*: "I hate babies, they disgust me . . . Obviously, I love them—but I absolutely wish I had not had them."[7]

Just one bad commissioning parent could mean tens—or potentially hundreds—of negatively impacted children.

Infertility and the industrialisation of parenthood

There are two categories of infertility: clinical and social. Clinical infertility arises from physical medical problems. Social infertility occurs when someone is unwilling or unable to attract someone of the opposite sex to procreate with.

Studies indicate that up to 15% of couples of childbearing age are clinically infertile. Much of this is due to our toxic environment, pollution, and unsafe chemicals, but there is also something to be said about our toxic behavior.[8] At least one quarter of female infertility is a direct result of sexually transmitted infections.

The sperm bank industry initially began as a mission in eugenics,[9] but ballooned due to our unspoken epidemic in low sperm count.[10] Clinically infertile heterosexual couples began quietly using donated sperm. After a while, they began to be open about using donated sperm and insisted that biology doesn't make a difference for the child's well-being.

Then lesbian couples began using sperm donors. They argued, if biology doesn't matter for a child's well-being, then why should a parent's gender? They declared that parenting is a set of tasks and obligations, and women can fulfill those tasks just as well as men can. Single-moms-by-choice followed, saying if biology and gender don't matter, why should the number of caretakers?

Fatherlessness invites a stark range of social ills. For instance, 90 percent of homeless and runaway youth come from fatherless homes, as do over 80 percent of rapists with anger problems. Now, those who promote fatherlessness via sperm donation are celebrating motherlessness via egg vending and surrogacy.[11]

Think motherhood is sacred? One surrogate pregnancy can generate $100-300,000. Today, the motherless child has become the fertility industry's most lucrative enterprise.

Third-party reproduction, human trafficking, and adoption

Because this is an industry, we shouldn't be surprised that fertility industry professionals are trying to *industrialise* the process and do things more efficiently. Surrogacy attorney Theresa Erickson was an "industry sweetheart" until she was convicted of baby-selling. Rather than waiting for commissioning parents to sign a contract before conception, Theresa expedited the process. She shopped for egg and sperm donors on her own and found surrogates to impregnate. Then, *after* the baby reached the second trimester, she would find parents, lie to them and tell them the original couple had backed out, and charge over $100,000 per child. She created more than a dozen babies this way.[12]

The only thing illegal about what Erickson did—the only reason she was put in jail for baby-selling—is that the paperwork was done *after* conception rather than before.

At a workshop where I once was on a panel with Theresa, she justified separating children from their parents by commenting that her mother was adopted, so what's the difference? Most people I speak to relate third-party reproduction to adoption just as she did.

We've accepted adoption as a good. Adoption can often be very good; it is an institution that finds parents for helpless children who desperately need a decent home. But, at some point, our concept of adoption slid. Many people now think of it primarily as a way of "getting" kids. We know that adoption is made possible by the fact that the relationship between biological parent and child has been severed. So if adoption is good, some reason, then the severing of that relationship must at least be neutral.

But it is not neutral. It's actually very sad.

Adoption is only morally sound as an institution that provides a loving home for *existing* children who—for some uncontrollable reason—cannot be raised by their biological parents. Third-party reproduction is inherently unethical, because it serves as a market to manufacture children for any adult who wants them, purposely severing the biological parent-child relationship for the sake of profit.

Disenfranchised grief and toxic shame

Children whose parents die are given the time, tools, and *permission* to grieve the loss of their missing parent. People whose parents are absent through sperm and egg donation do not have the luxury to grieve. The overwhelming majority of donor-conceived people do not have photos, video tapes, or letters from their missing parent. Yet we are told we should be grateful. We're told that if our biological parents had been forced to have a relationship with us, then they would never have agreed to give us life.

Since donor-conceived people are not allowed to grieve, we have few safe outlets for talking about our loss, and especially for talking about the inherent shame in how we were conceived. There is an ugly side to our conception: the masturbation, the anonymity, the *payment*. It's shameful to say, but my father was paid roughly $75 to promise to have nothing to do with me. My mother accepted semen from a total stranger into her body. It is an embarrassing and painful truth.

Well, hurt people hurt. As the 2009 *My Daddy's Name Is Donor* report states: "Donor offspring and those who were adopted are twice as likely as those raised by biological parents to report problems with the law before age 25."[13] I worry about how confused my donor-conceived peers are—and how confused I have been—regarding what qualifies as sacred versus commercial space. If our fathers were allowed to essentially pre-sell their own children, then what is off the table?

A tangled web

Growing up, donor-conception was sold to me as normal, even worth celebrating. There was a time in my life when I was enthusiastically in favor of commercial reproduction. After all, I wouldn't exist without it. I sold my own eggs at age twenty. Research has shown that donor-conceived people are twenty times more likely to sell their own sperm or eggs.[14]

Around the same time I sold my eggs, I was also volunteering at NARAL (the National Abortion and Reproductive Rights Action League), fighting for the legality of partial-birth abortion. That is the right to abort a baby who is fully developed and halfway out of the birth canal. After all, if it's okay to force a child into existence because it's so *wanted*, then why is it not okay to force a child out of existence because it is so *unwanted?*

This isn't just a conversation about the merit of choice in pregnancy. If it's okay to buy and sell sperm, eggs, and wombs, then why is it *not* okay to sell other human tissues or organs? If it's okay to sell one's reproductive parts, why is it not okay to sell one's *sexual* parts, as in prostitution? If it's okay to pre-sell and pre-order children via third-party reproduction, what is so wrong with buying and selling children who are already born or conceived?

It is naïve to assume decent people—like Bobby Lopez's CSU-Northridge students—won't be very confused by this tangled web. Commercial conception lives adjacent to abortion and eugenics as a disembodied face on the dice of human dignity. It is all tied together, for better or worse. The better is *much* better—and very much worth fighting for.

Notes

[1] International Children's Rights Institute, "Inaugural Conference-Save the Date", (Undated) www.internationalchildrensrights.com (Accessed December 29, 2014).

[2] Kelsey Harkness, "As His Wife Delivers Their Baby, LGBT Group Smears This Pro-Marriage Professor as International Criminal", *Daily Signal*, Society/News (October 20, 2014) www.dailysignal.com (Accessed December 29, 2014).

[3] See Alana Newman, ed., *AnonymousUs.org*. www.anonymousus.org.

[4] See Alana Newman, "Reproductive Technologies and the Quest for Immortality", *Public Discourse* (March 1, 2012) www.thepublicdiscourse.com (Accessed December 29, 2014).

[5] Rickard Newman, "Journey to Baby Gammy: How We Justify a Market in Children", *Public Discourse* (August 18, 2014) www.thepublicdiscourse.com (Accessed December 29, 2014).

[6] Kevin Rawlinson and agencies, "Interpol investigates 'baby factory' as man fathers 16 surrogate children", *Guardian*, Life and Style (August 23, 2014) www.theguardian.com (Accessed December 29, 2014).

[7] Cable News Network, "Nadya Suleman: Babies Disgust Me", *The Marquee Blog*, CNN Celebrities (June 30, 2011) www.marquee.blogs.cnn.com (Accessed December 29, 2014).

[8] Alana Newman, "The Rotten Root of an Infertile Culture: Why We Need A Revolution in Virtue", *Ethika Politica*, The Whole Story (September 11, 2014) www.ethikapolitica.org (Accessed December 29, 2014).

[9] Glynn Washington, Host, "Genius Sperm", National Public Radio, *Snap Judgment* (October 3, 2014) www.npr.org (Accessed December 29, 2014).

[10] Theo Colborn, "Endocrine Disruptors Dr Theo Colborn The Male Predicament", Lecture on YouTube (January 6, 2011), www.youtube.com (Accessed December 29, 2014).

[11] Trish Wilson, *Myths and Facts about Fatherlessness* (Free eBooks, 2002) http://thebooks.club.

[12] Rory Devine and R. Stickney, "Convicted Surrogacy Attorney: I'm Tip of Iceberg", NBC 7 San Diego, News Local (February 29, 2012) www.nbcsandiego.com (Accessed January 10, 2015).

[13] Elizabeth Marquardt, Norval D. Glenn, and Karen Clark, "My daddy's name is DONOR: A New Study of Young Adults Conceived through Sperm Donation", Report from the Institute for American Values (New York: Institute for American Values, 2010), 9.

[14] Ibid.

SECTION TWO

RECONSTRUCTING FAMILIES

Introduction

Jennifer Lahl

For over a decade, I have been an outspoken critic of assisted reproductive technologies, and more specifically, third-party uses of these technologies. Third-party uses include the buying and selling of eggs and sperm from those not intended to be the parent of the child, and/or the renting of a surrogate womb in order to have a woman carry a child for the sole purpose of surrendering that child at birth. Often these arrangements are driven by legal contracts, involving unequal power relationships between those who need money (the egg, sperm, and womb "sellers") and those who have money to buy. Such arrangements render the "sellers" powerless, which often leads to making decisions not in their own best interest but rather because of financial need.

As a paediatric nurse, I've raised many concerns about the safety of these technologies to the health of women and to the health and well-being of children created via these technologies. In addition, I have raised questions regarding the long-term psychological and social harms of these techniques to help infertile couples, single people, or same-sex couples have children. What I have seen, again and again, is that the needs of children are often woefully neglected in an insatiable desire to have a child. Children are in essence treated as products to be bought and sold, to be designed or discarded, or to be simply abandoned if they are deemed unfit. As these children grow up and make their struggles known, they are told that they should be happy they were so desperately wanted, and that their biological ties to mother or father and extended family are irrelevant and unimportant.

One of the things that has been quite refreshing in my work is the successes of building broad coalitional opposition to third-party conception arrangements. Men and women across religious and political divides have worked to raise awareness of the risks and harms. People from both the pro-choice and pro-life sides recognise the exploitation of women and the harms to women of lower socio-economic status. This is an area where people are not yet tribal or so firmly entrenched with their views that they have simply dug in their heels. I find that when people are confronted with the facts, the stories, and the known and unknown risks, it is easy to get people to agree that we need, at the very least, to stop and study these technologies so that further harm is not done.

What, exactly, is wrong with third-party assisted reproduction?

The health and psychological risks to women who serve as egg vendors or surrogates often go untold
The medical process required for egg retrieval is lengthy, and there are serious medical hazards associated with each step in the process. The most severe risk is Ovarian Hyperstimulation Syndrome (OHSS) from superovulation. Young, thin women are more at risk for OHSS, and young, thin women are the most sought-after for egg donation and surrogacy.

Risks to their own future fertility are possible along with other risks such as ovarian torsion, blood clots, and reproductive cancers. In addition, there are documented deaths of both egg donors and surrogates. Some of the drugs used on these women have never been FDA safety-approved for the uses to which they are being put. Given the high failure rates of assisted reproductive cycles, women are aggressively stimulated to produce dozens of eggs. Multiple embryos are implanted into surrogates in order to increase the chance of live births. Women are treated as commodities, paid vessels, a breeding class.

There are real health and psychological risks to the children of third-party reproductive arrangements
The medical literature is clear regarding risks children who are conceived through reproductive technologies face. They are more likely to suffer from premature birth, low birth weight, and fetal anomalies like

Beckwith-Wiedemann and Angleman Syndromes.

The risk of foetal death and stillbirth are higher too. In addition, surrogate pregnancy intentionally severs important mother-child bonding. Gamete donation creates children who will be intentionally separated from their biological identity, history, and extended family. Genealogical bewilderment is a phenomenon well documented in studies and in the testimonies of those born via donor conception. Studies even show that in the long run, many parents regret using anonymous gametes to create their children. Many experts conclude that anonymous conception arrangements simply should not be allowed.

Problems with commercialised conception

There are myriad problems, not the least of which are ethical bad actors preying on vulnerable people in order to make money. Consider the lack of central tracking of these pregnancies, the children born from them, the donors, and the parents, coupled with the global nature of what is now a multi-billion-dollar-a-year industry.

The standard medical model in third-party reproduction is not patients and doctors. Instead, the fertility industry has "clients" and "vendors" and "donors" and "carriers". Conflicts of interest in arranging contracts for the buying and selling of babies abound. According to the European Society of Human Reproduction and Embryology (ESHRE), the global failure rate of assisted reproductive cycles is 77%! Slick marketing offers large sums of money to "help someone have a baby" or "be an angel and make dreams come true", while harms and risks go unmentioned, making truly informed consent impossible. Money is coercive; the more financial need a person has, the more risks she will assume in order to meet that need.

For these reasons I find it impossible to support third-party contract pregnancies. While many suggest regulation is the way forward, regulation simply will not protect against these harms.

Chapter Twelve

SECULAR ISRAEL, GAYS AND SURROGACY

Brittany Klein

Israel's Minister of Health, Yael German, recently supported amending current surrogacy laws. As reported by Ynetnews:

> Same-sex couples will be able to become parents through surrogate birth in Israel instead of being forced to find proxy mothers outside of the country, Health Minister Yael German announced Wednesday.
> … German is promoting a bill that will amend the current surrogacy law to be submitted on January 15.[1]

Her endorsement of same-sex couples' right to use surrogates points out the ways that the left in Israel has naively embraced and championed a male-centered ideology. This ideology is steeped in a misogyny unknown in the west since white men owned black women. The move also highlights a deeply troubling disregard for the basic human rights of children and women, in favor of the so-called "civil rights" of a powerful moneyed male minority.

Simply put, this change in law facilitates the sale of human infants to men. It increases the number of the current breeding stock, and produces more babies. In reality the politics and legal changes are designed to provide better customer service in the sale of babies, and streamline what is taking shape as the new slave trade.

The new flesh trade comes at a specific cultural moment. It is in some measure rooted in a more general social anxiety that the left feels when they think about the growing population of haredi (sometimes known as "Orthodox"). Consider the nervousness about demographics when

Jewish leaders gather lately (this is just New York but...):

> Last week, new data released by the UJA-Federation of New York showed Orthodox and specifically haredi Jews were by far the single fastest growing demographic in the Jewish population of that city. According to the study, the 10 percent increase in the number of Jews living in the New York metropolitan area over the past decade – who now number 1.5 million – was largely due to high birth rates among the fervently religious. ... At the same time, the number of people affiliated with Reform and Conservative Judaism dropped and intermarriage rates among secular Jews remained high at about 50 percent.[2]

Assimilated Jews never imagined that the ranks of the haredi would grow. In an old and myopic hubris the left always assumed that the haredi would die out or recognise the inherent superiority of secular values. This did not happen. Now secular Israelis are crunching the numbers, or the numbers are crunching them.

If the low birth rates of the secular Jews and high birth rates of the haredi continue on their present trajectory, the secular will no longer be a clear majority. This may in part allow some people to accept reproductive slavery and the sale of children as a way to add to the secular population.

No doubt this is just one facet of the larger current culture war in Israel. Unlike the culture wars of America, in Israel it is the rich, white, educated and powerful who are attempting to maintain their hold, in light of their dwindling numbers. Part of the power play requires that they lay claim to being oppressed and at the same time maintain their pose—standing for "equality" and "tolerance". In this case, the left's idea of tolerance means they champion the use of women as breeders and erase basic human rights owed to children, in favor of the paying customer, who in the past had to travel to human breeding farms in the Third World in order to buy a baby.

This it seems a tad disingenuous for the left to continue to frame the haredi as "backward" or "primitive". The secularists have single-handedly reinstated the slave trade.

In some unfathomable fog of arrogance, Israel's left wing, the former champion of human rights, has the unmitigated chutzpah to frame this as a move toward "equality". The only analogy that makes sense in this case is when I remember opposite day in kindergarten: everything everyone said meant the opposite. Well, it is opposite decade for neo-liberalism worldwide.

The argument for surrogacy relies on a whole set of tropes trotted out by the LGBT lobby to derail any logic and concern for women or children. The tropes are fuelled by 'entitlement' gas. The discourse operates like some cheap Las Vegas grifter preying on many people's fear of being called a bigot or their phobia of being passé.

We are expected, from the beginning, to refrain from critically examining the things that gay men ask for, because they are "oppressed". Let's be reasonable. Do oppressed people own and live in exclusive enclaves located strategically in the most expensive areas of major cities worldwide? Do oppressed people have entire luxury resorts devoted to catering to their every need?

So oppression really is not an issue. It is just some smoke and mirrors. Rather entitlement is the issue. Entitlement allows people to imagine they are more socially progressive than the next guy. It plays to people's egos more than their sense of justice or even to reality. Most people know that white men are far from being oppressed. And no doubt it is easier to give in to their egregious demands, than it is to admit we might actually be making the lives of children miserable.

I can't help but wonder what has happened to people's critical analysis. To hear them tell it one isolated case of "homophobia" is a greater human rights violation than the hundreds of women and children murdered and tortured worldwide that same week. For instance, last month a guy was punched in the Ukraine by another guy because of sexual orientation.[3] Wow—men beating each other up is now earth-shaking news and counted as a crime against humanity! When well-positioned powerful white men have to live with the fear of violence, the presses must stop and something must be done. Everything else on the agenda must be tabled. So forget the twenty honor killings, the twelve bloody stonings, the women held in cages for years and tortured with cattle prods. Focus all attention only on the passing whims of men.

In this misogynistic worldview, women are of no value (except as breeding stock for men). The extension of misogyny is the argument that children don't need a mother. Hence, the very idea of needing a mother is met with "tisk, tisk" shaming and then tossed aside as bigoted

Nothing can eclipse the male interest in what the male wants. Dead women—please don't interject with trivia.

One can't help but note how manipulative it is too, but it works. Here is why it works: the neo-liberal's motivation and values are self-reflective, self-serving, uncritical, and often based on the image they want to present and how they imagine themselves. Call it the new politics of narcissism, based on ego-feeding and the never-ending need to look good. I suspect it will ultimately prove, in the final future analysis, to be more dangerous than the politics of hate.

In Israeli neo-liberal parlance, "equality" is a buzzword that means some people have no rights at all—not even the most basic human rights of a mother and father. This denial of basic human rights in current legislation engenders the codification of legal human rights violations reminiscent of Nuremberg. Today's trend is born out of a similar cultural arrogance.

Israelis should not kid themselves and imagine that selling human babies is good because it ups their numbers and thus helps keep world Jewry alive. Even India, not known as the epicentre for protecting the rights of women, has demonstrated more compassion toward both woman and children than current factions in Israel.

The worldwide LGBT lobby is a male-centered and moneyed network adept at using claims of their own oppression to annihilate the human rights of the two most oppressed groups in the world—women and children.

The question is: how did supposedly thinking people get to this point?

The basic argument is that in a secular country it is not unreasonable that two adults, same-sex or opposite-sex, have the right to love each other and enter into a committed relationship of whatever form. The familiar riposte to any objection is: they are not hurting anyone.

After all, everyone has the right to love whom they love. Most educated people living in the modern world accept this. It's a given that what two adults do is their business as long as they are not hurting anyone else. And here is where the truth of the arguments ends and the arrogant abuse of women and children begins.

One might note that using women as breeding stock (one as surrogate womb and the other as egg donor) and buying a baby might just push the envelope of "not hurting anyone". Check my maths but two adults' right to live their dream of parenthood just trampled the most basic human rights of two other people.

Which begs the question, how did "parenthood" become a "right"? This is not about what goes on between two adults. This is a whole country becoming complicit in making women breeder livestock to meet the whims of a group of men and then denying children created as saleable goods the basic right to a mother and father. "Not hurting anyone" falls apart unless people accept the premise that children have no rights and that women are breed animals for men. But this is finally about political power and these men do not care whom they hurt. That would require them to stop thinking about themselves, which is not happening in the near or distant future.

This is nothing new. Rich white men are especially privileged to exercise misogyny and have it codified into law and government-funded—that is as old as the hills. A child deserves a mother and a father. This is a basic human right. Parenthood is not a right.

No homophobia in the world even competes with this socially accepted dehumanisation of children. Just because men assert that women are worthless (except to exploit their wombs) and that mothers are not needed (because he says so, and because he wants a baby) does not make it true. It takes an inordinate amount of smug contempt towards women and children to pretend that the right to partner with whom you choose extends magically into the demand that reproductive slaves be provided and the price of the baby be lower.

Being called an "apartheid state" pales in comparison to this. Israelis at large should get off their high horse and just throw in the towel. What next, sell babies on eBay? Now there is a whole billion-dollar industry devoted to the sale of infants.

We see how as a community they come together in times of crisis. (For good and for bad.) One has only to recall the terrible 2009 Barnoar shootings, which were originally blamed on Orthodox Jews but ended up not being the fault of the haredi at all. There were vigils and speeches, and a few brief years of pleasure imagining the wild-eyed haredi monster

147

that slaughtered teenagers:

> Four years have passed since the murders at Barnoar, a club in Tel
> Aviv for gay, lesbian, bisexual and transgender youth. On August
> 1, 2009, a masked individual sprayed the club with gunfire, killing
> Nir Katz, 27, and Liz Trubeshi, 16. Others were wounded. Until
> not long ago, it seemed that the case would never be solved. We
> got used to living alongside it, as though it had never happened.[4]

Opportunity knocks so infrequently, so no need to mention that a good
hate crime oils the machinery of the cause, the photo ops, the strategy
sessions in cafés, just a drizzle of walnut oil, the role of victim. Work
the audience. Who cares that it was not a hate crime. It could have
been a hate crime. So what?

Does it matter if it was a revenge crime over a sexual entanglement
between an older man and a teen, and the intended target was a community
leader, LGBT activist, and director of the Youth Center? Some allege
that the man who was targeted (the shooters hit the wrong person) had
a taste for young boys and was having sex with the fourteen-year-old
brother of one of the criminals responsible. Is it homophobic to bring
that up—are points of information homophobic? The June 2013 *Haaretz*
reports:

> The fourth, most recent arrest in the case is apparently of an activist
> in the gay community. He has been detained for allegedly knowing
> the motive for the murders and obstructing the investigation by not
> sharing that information with police. It is believed this individual
> is directly connected to the motive, and that he was the target of the
> assassination, which involved revenge.[5]

In truth every demographic has its share of child molesters that prey
on children. But here's the snag: does anyone seriously believe for a
nanosecond that the intended target's dangerous dalliances were not
well known in LGBT circles in Tel Aviv? Only a number of gay guys
may be molesters and boy rapists but the ones who are will be protected.
In such a world, children have no rights. Search the records. You will
find precious few cases of abuse, sexual abuse or neglect reported by a
gay male to authorities.

No doubt the entire movement will go down in history alongside other breeding programs such as Lebensborn. The claim it will create more Jews is as repugnant as the idea of creating more Aryans.

Here's my prediction. The children bought and sold and bred to meet the whims of adults will have a voice in the future. They will reframe the narrative. Future footage of the Pride Parade will be shown in classrooms just as we now show footage of the rallies at Nuremburg. The teachers will be explaining, "Yes, men bought and sold women and babies." Children will be as wide-eyed as students are today looking at those terrible jack-booted parades.

I don't know the future but I know increasingly voices will be raised. I know because I was raised by LGBT parents and in the LGBT community. My mother was a lesbian and raised me with her female partners.[6]

There are many of us in out in the world. Our parents used us as little display objects. We existed only to make our parents look good, living breathing political statements. We existed to feed the insatiable egos that were our parents. Does that sound like a happy childhood? I am intimately acquainted with the manipulations, the intolerance, and the intimidation tactics, the punitive nature, their love of revenge. I can already hear the outcry—as the men mount the attacks against my lived experience, my character, and my little dog too.

Anyone who thinks this is a good idea, I invite you to talk to adults raised by gay parents. By that I do mean the adults with enough maturity and distance that their parents no longer manipulate them. Don't ask the six-year-old if she or he is happy. The toddlers have been trained to speak like a pet bird. They live in fear of what a parent will do if they dare to make the parent look bad. Don't go by the dog and pony show at the Pride Parade. Ask us, those of us who broke away from the culture that we grew up in. We will tell you.

History will be a harsh taskmaster. Children grow up. Trendy social causes are often revealed as bad ideas. I can say honestly that I don't know a single one of us—those raised in gay and lesbian households— who is going to tell you they had anything even remotely related to a happy childhood. How could we? We were just pawns. We existed only as a mirror, and there were not enough mirrors in the world to satisfy them.

It would behove people to reflect on the past. Israel has a checkered history when it comes to ideologies and children. There were Yemenite children stolen from their dark-skinned parents.[7] There were kibbutz children's houses and those children of the dream born to a system so socially superior that they could be raised as a group with only afternoon visits to their parents' room. They would spend all other times herded around by whatever *medapelet* they had that week.[8]

Does anyone imagine that either of those ideologies served children well? No, they served the ego and the arrogance of the adults. Do we see a cultural pattern emerging here? Mistakes can be forgiven, but premeditated wrongs carried out when cautionary counterpoints were available, but just disregarded, will not be forgotten. History will be a harsh taskmaster.

Notes

[1] Yaron Kelner, "Same-sex couples to be entitled to surrogacy services in Israel", *Ynetnews,* culture & leisure (November 12, 2013) www.ynetnews.com (Accessed December 30, 2014).

[2] Gil Shefler, "Haredi growth absent in talk on Jewish future", *Jerusalem Post,* Jewish World (June 20, 2012) www.jpost.com/Jewish-World (Accessed December 30, 2014).

[3] Versha Sharma, "Russian Neo-Nazis Are Now Beating Up Gays in the Ukraine", *Vocativ,* Culture/LGBT (November 7, 2013) www.vocativ.com (Accessed December 30, 2014).

[4] Doron Halutz, "Four years after Tel Aviv's gay center shooting, young Israelis look back at the night that changed their lives", *Haaretz,* Weekend>Magazine (July 27, 2013) www.haaretz.com (Accessed December 30, 2014).

[5] Yaniv Kubovich, "Israel Police: Hired Killer Opened Fire at Tel Aviv Gay Youth Center after Target Didn't Show", *Haaretz,* News-National (June 6, 2013) www.haaretz.com (Accessed December 30, 2014).

[6] See Brittany Klein, "This Lesbian's Daughter Has Had Enough", *American Thinker* (October 20, 2014) www.americanthinker.com (Accessed December 30, 2014).

[7] Sarah Helm, "Yemeni Jews Describe Their Holocaust: Sarah Helm in Yehud Reports on Claims That Israelis Stole 4,500 Children from Immigrants", *Independent,* News/World (April 17, 1994) www.independent.co.uk/news/world (Accessed December 30, 2014.)

[8] See Barbara Demick, "Daughter Learns Of Stolen Past, Reopening An Israeli Mystery. A Family Reunion And New Questions", *Philly.com,* News (August 28, 1997) http://articles.philly.com (Accessed December 30, 2014).

See also Abraham Balaban, *Mourning a Father Lost: A Kibbutz Childhood Remembered* (NOOK Book: Rowman & Littlefield, 2004). http://books.google.com

Chapter Thirteen

THE NY TIMES GLAMOURISES REPRODUCTIVE SLAVERY

Brittany Klein

Sometimes I feel like such a stickler. I am not nitpicking when I say there was a mistake in the pages of *The New York Times*' Fashion and Style section. There was a piece, "And Baby Makes Three" about the new drive to legalise paid surrogacy in New York, where it has been banned since the early 1990s. The major impetus for this new push comes from gay men who want children but do not want children's mothers as part of the deal.[1]

We must fall on the side of intellectual honesty. That title should have read "four", or "five" if one were to consider the actual human females involved in the production line of surrogacy these days.

The *New York Times*' telling omission reflects something ominous, the deep misogyny of a gay male community, which in turn has been accepted and championed by many people who consider themselves progressive.

More to the point, it demonstrates the total erasure of the female who supplied the egg and the second female in whose uterus the baby grew. It mirrors the blind eyes that society has toward marginalised women. Here both are factored out of the male equation. No less concerning is the reason—to obscure "motherhood" and deny the child a clear concept of mother.

No less chilling was the article's placement in the Fashion and Style section in the first place. No doubt this was done to deflect from what most people consider an important and serious topic—women and children's basic human rights. The omission and the placement taken together crystallise the narcissistic glibness of the "new civil rights" movement, in which rights include a supply of marginalised women to provide gay men with offspring.

Of equal importance was the article's timing.

In a rather cynical move the article appeared in time to support the overturning of the current law against selling babies in New York State, so that it might be replaced with new laws that allow women to be paid for the sale of babies.

The article strains in a clumsy attempt to argue that the old law is now archaic and was merely enacted through a fear-based over-reaction to Margaret Atwood's novel *The Handmaid's Tale*:

> Historically, the legal aversion to surrogacy stems from a sort of Margaret Atwood, "Handmaid's Tale" fear that it lends itself to unnatural social engineering and the subjugation of women. This led to an unusual alliance of feminists, civil libertarians and the Catholic church in the early 1990s, when the New York Catholic Conference joined with the New York Civil Liberties Union and the National Organization for Women to oppose surrogacy.[2]

And, according to the Article, Atwood was wrong. Really? The novel was a dystopic narrative about a future world in which men use women as incubators to produce white babies. Which is exactly where we've arrived through several detours, as a result of a gay movement that didn't do enough introspection.[3]

It is a good thing nobody took Orwell seriously. Once upon a time he wrote, "Politics and the English Language":

> Now, it is clear that the decline of a language must ultimately have political and economic causes: it is not due simply to the bad influence of this or that individual writer. But an effect can become a cause, reinforcing the original cause and producing the same effect in an intensified form, and so on indefinitely. A man may take to

drink because he feels himself to be a failure, and then fail all the more completely because he drinks. It is rather the same thing that is happening to the English language. It becomes ugly and inaccurate because our thoughts are foolish, but the slovenliness of our language makes it easier for us to have foolish thoughts.[4]

Foolish thoughts would likely include large numbers of people styling themselves as progressive because they buy and sell humans. Some of my LGBT friends have taken notice of the strangeness of this new definition of "progress". Consider what Doug Mainwaring says about the trend, speaking as a gay father who cannot accept the unethical implications involved in a commerce of human life:

Any infertile couple working with a reputable adoption agency knows that the window of opportunity for adopting newborns closes as you approach forty years of age. After that, you're cut off and must start considering adopting older children. In fact, agencies prefer that there be a comfortable distance between you and the big four-oh. ... But for white gay males, there are no rules, only endless options for accessorising their lives with human beings they have the means to acquire. They choose to purchase children because they are unwilling to create children in the natural way, and are unwilling to commit to a woman in order to form a family to nurture children.... So now we have a growing population of children who must pay the price for their Two dads' neglected functionality, or perhaps dysfunctionality, by foregoing a mom. Creating children is the most natural thing in the world, except for gays and lesbians, who disqualify themselves from nature's ample provision for procreation.[5]

Surrogacy is an equal-opportunity problem, with many heterosexuals such as Tagg Romney, Sarah Jessica Parker, Jimmy Fallon, and Melissa Harris-Perry engaging in the practice alongside famous gays like Neil Patrick Harris, Bryan Singer, Ricky Martin, and Perez Hilton. There is something delightfully democratic about this debate, despite the hideousness of what is going on. You do not have to be gay to be involved in such rank misogyny. You do not have to be straight to see that it is wrong, even if you are a man. We are all in this mess together.

But now what?

Now gay men and über-wealthy celebrities in their late forties have the civil right to use women's bodies to reproduce. Somehow, if we do not streamline this womb-to-market commerce, we are committing another violation of their civil rights.

You were told in Women's Studies 101 (an academic syllabus in the US) that traditional marriage was oppressive to women. If you think a system that forced husbands to commit their financial and social resources to supporting the mothers of their children was oppressive, just wait until you see the glamorous new world of baby farming for men who have no interest in permitting women in any part of their lives because they claim they were "born" gay. You have not seen anything yet.

All these taken together reiterate one clear message without nuance: there is no such thing as ethical surrogacy. But that is not the issue. The issue is equality. Equality has been posed, in an Orwellian fashion, as the uniformity of all marriages as the means to reproduce because, by some magic hereto unknown to me, random women of much lesser means now owe men access to their bodies.

The neo-liberals who raise their own little navel-gazers applaud while libertarians can't sell women into slavery fast enough because to hear them tell it, it is women's right to allow their bodies to be used.

Truthfully, there are only a few things I find more disturbing than white male entitlement: ebola, anthrax, a rats' nest in the chimney. Many feminists have started to note that the gay rights movement has been able to do what many men have been hoping for, for the last fifty years. Bring back socially sanctioned misogyny into the moneyed enclaves of culture where the power brokers just want to dump their binders of women.

It is a win-win situation—brilliant, right?

Human rights violations against women and children will be framed as LGBT civil rights. Anyone who suggests that maybe people do not have rights to other people's body or organs is a hater, a bigot, and a homophobe.

Well, that dog doesn't hunt. I grew up in a gay household and I know the arguments better than I know the pledge of allegiance. So save it— the missives, the threats. Don't prove my point to people about loving the gay community. They will turn and tear their own to shreds in a heartbeat. Because the fragile narrative has to be protected at all costs. Family is a photo op. And children are props.

Let's not kid ourselves about the cute photograph affixed to this *New York Times* article: that kid is not related to both of the "Daddies." That child has been denied one parent so that men could prove that two men can play at baby-making—and ironically the men needed two women to do it.

The message, if you have not heard, is that marriage is about reproducing and the fact two men can't is a form of discrimination (biological reality does not exist), which society must rectify.

So here comes the real test for the so-called allies. We all danced at their wedding. Who will turn over human females as breeders?

And it needs to be cheap. In their civil rights book they get to use one to two human females, including one to harvest eggs (she doesn't lay them!). The other is to gestate the baby designed to obscure and erase motherhood and provide legal protection to the buyer.

We are talking here about an invasive procedure that requires ovulation stimulation, which raises the risk of ovarian cancer. We must get the rest of the Big Apple on board to change New York State laws, so it is best to have a light touch, a breezy prose.

But back to civil rights.

The white man's civil rights trump two females' rights, the most fundamental right being not to be used as breeder animals. The article laments the fact that New York has laws about selling. Everything would be much easier if the buyer could purchase the product—a baby–locally, because as Mr. Hoylman said in the interview some people "have to take out a loan".[6]

Oh, the horror: a loan combined with the utter inconvenience of having to fly the red-eye out to California when his contracted surrogate gave birth. This is something that must be rectified post haste through new laws that erase women and children's rights.

I would have rather read a little breezy piece on Alexander MacQueen in the Style & Fashion section, but when you want to trivialise reproductive slavery, draw false equivalencies, and gloss over the basic human rights of women and children, what better way is there to present it than as a child, or two (aren't they to die for?) as the must-have fashion accessory for the well-heeled gay couple?

Make it stop. No, people. Children are not a right.

Notes

[1] Anemona Hartocollis, "And Surrogacy Makes 3: In New York, a Push for Compensated Surrogacy", *New York Times,* Fashion and Style (February 19, 2014) www.nytimes.com (Accessed December 30, 2014).

[2] Ibid.

[3] Margaret Atwood, *The handmaid's tale* (Boston: Houghton and Mifflin, 1986).

[4] George Orwell, "Politics and the English Language", posted by *National Public Radio*, Ombudsman blog (Undated) www.npr.org (Accessed December 30, 2014).

[5] Doug Mainwaring, "Engineering Children for Gay Granddads", *American Thinker* (February 28, 2014) www.americanthinker.com (Accessed December 30, 2014).

[6] Anemona Hartocollis, "And Baby Makes 3".

Chapter Fourteen

DIVORCE AND GAY MARRIAGE

Jennifer Johnson

Around March of 2013 I came across the words of a prominent LGBT activist named Masha Gessen:

> "I have three kids who have five parents, more or less, and I don't see why they shouldn't have five parents legally... I would like to live in a legal system that is capable of reflecting that reality, and I don't think that's compatible with the institution of marriage."[1]

Imagine having five parents. Imaging going back and forth between all those households on a regular basis, never having a single place to call home during your most tender and vulnerable years. Imagine having divided Christmases, other holidays, and birthdays—you spend one with one parent, and another with the other parent, never spending a single holiday or birthday with both parents. Imagine having each of your parents completely ignore the other half of you, the other half of your family, as if it did not even exist. Meanwhile, imagine each parent pouring their energy into their new families and creating a unified home for their new children. These experiences give you the definite impression of being something leftover, something not quite part of them. You live like that on a daily basis for 18+ years.

I don't have to imagine, because I had five parents. I had five parents because my mom and dad divorced when I was about three; my mom remarried once and my dad remarried twice. So I had a mom and two step-moms, and a dad and one step-dad. In this day and age children can already have five parents. That's how badly marriage has deteriorated already. The main difference between what Gessen advocates and my experience is that my stepparents were not legal parents; she advocates for all of the adults in her situation to be legal parents.

Based on my experience of going back and forth between the two households of my two legal parents my entire childhood, I can say that having more than two legal parents will be a nightmare for a child. I am making the reasonable assumption that the legal parents will not be living under the same roof, because there is no longer any societal accountability for adults to create a unified home for children. Thus, adding additional legal parents will create more disruption for children's daily lives, more chaos, more confusion, less unity. And why are we doing this? So that adults can have the sexual partners they want.

Masha Gessen had a mom and a dad,[2] so it appears that she benefitted from the socially conservative family structure. She was not raised under the family structure she advocates. That sounds about right. I've talked to many people who think deconstructing the family in favor of adult sexual choice is a good thing... and these very same people lived under the socially conservative family structure with their one mom who spent her life with their one dad, and they all lived together in their unified home. Since I lived under the family structure they advocate, I will sometimes ask them: would you trade childhoods with me? They either say no or they don't reply.

If what I had is so great, then why don't they want it? Here's my conclusion: they want it as adults but not as children. They want the benefits of the socially conservative family structure when they are children. As adults, they want sexual freedom, or at least they want to appear "open minded" and "tolerant" about others' sexual choices, even at the expense of children. They themselves would never want to live under what they advocate. It's a bizarre sort of a "win-win" for them, I guess.

It's very painful for me to have conversations with these people. They don't understand what they advocate, and they don't seem to want to understand.

Notes

[1] Qtd in Johanna Dasteel, "Homosexual activist says gay 'marriage' isn't about equality, it's about destroying marriage", *LifeSite*, News (May 1, 2013) www.lifesitenews.com (Accessed December 29, 2014).

[2] Russian profile of Masha Gassen, available at: www.peoples.ru.

Chapter Fifteen

PARIS

Robert Oscar Lopez

Consider two unforgettable images: one of James Baldwin, and one of Sharon Stone. They encapsulate my feelings right now, as I prepare for another presentation I'm going to make before the people of France.

In one of James Baldwin's essays, he speaks of his experience living in Paris. He found himself trying to explain to Europeans in French cafés and taxicabs why there was racial strife in the United States. Midway through the conversation he realised he was not going to accomplish anything by living in Paris and explaining America's problems to Europe. He had to grit his teeth and go back to America. Why? He had to solve the problems that he was waxing ecclesiastical about to foreigners. Here is how Baldwin describes it:

> One day it begins to be borne in on the writer, and with great force, that he is living in Europe as an American. If he were living there as a European, he would be living on a different and far less attractive continent.... This crucial day may be the day on which an Algerian taxi-driver tells him how it feels to be an Algerian in Paris. It may be the day on which he passes a café terrace and catches a glimpse of the tense, intelligent and troubled face of Albert Camus. Or it may be the day on which someone asks him to explain Little Rock and he begins to feel that it would be simpler – and, corny as the words may sound, more honorable – to go to Little Rock than sit in Europe, on an American passport, trying to explain it.... This is a personal day, a terrible day, the day to.... which his entire sojourn has been tending.

It is the day he realises that there are no untroubled countries in this fearfully troubled world; that if he has been preparing himself for anything in Europe, he has been preparing himself – for America. In short, the freedom that the American writer finds in Europe brings him, full circle, back to himself, with the responsibility for his development where it always was: in his own hands.[1]

I feel like Baldwin is speaking directly to me, though I have little notion of what he, a famous bisexual of color, would make of me, a non-famous bisexual of colour, caught in similar cross-currents.

If Baldwin's literary style is too heavy for you, picture Sharon Stone in *Total Recall*, kicking Arnold Schwarzenegger as she says, "That's for making me come back to Mars. You know how much I hate this planet."

My feelings about my native country are a mix of both things right now. America launched the ridiculous combination of shameless consumerism, totalitarian thought police, and sexual chaos that represent the "LGBT" movement, which I am squared against nowadays.

I will use the term ligbitism because it is easier than writing LGBT all the time. It's important to distinguish this "ism" from gay *people*, who are a complex community too rich in nuance to be reduced to ligbitist doctrine.

Put simply, ligbitism is to sexuality as Marxism is to class. Marxists wanted to fix class relations according to a utopian template. To some of them the only thing, and to all of them the most important thing, was class. Let me dust off my yellowing copy of *Antiquity and Radical Authority*, the dissertation that allowed me to call myself "Dr. Lopez". I find in the opening chapter a catch-all explanation of Marxism and its ideology, which is a preponderant preoccupation with economic class:

> For Marx, the key enlightening facility had to be a thinker's "ability to expound the real process of production, starting from the material production of life itself ... as the basis of all history; and to show it in its action as State, to explain all the different theoretical products and forms of consciousness, religion, philosophy, ethics, etc., and trace their origins and growth from that basis." Marx sees that the struggle over resources is played out in struggles over ideological beliefs. Hence, for him, "not criticism but revolution is the driving

force of history, also of religion, of philosophy and all other types of theory".[2]

Marxism became such a powerful intellectual and political force because it made "sense" to people. Who does not worry about money and making a living? The problem of class differences is immediately compelling to just about anybody.

Over a century and a half after Marx's *German Ideology* was published, people's role in the means of production is as contentious as ever. Not only the "Marxism" that took its name from Marx directly, but also a vast family of milder "isms", have sought to equalise class relations. They have little to show for their attempts to bring about an equitable division of the surplus derived from human labor.

The problem of class is easy to diagnose, but what to do about it becomes the far thornier question. Barack Obama's main attraction to voters was helping the "middle class" and narrowing the gap between rich and poor; yet the Pew Research Center found, in 2013, that well-intended egalitarianism usually produced the opposite effect from what it sought. Four years after the famous economic stimulus championed by the United States president, "In 2013, the median wealth of the nation's upper-income families ($639,400) was nearly seven times the median wealth of middle-income families ($96,500), the widest wealth gap seen in 30 years when the Federal Reserve began collecting these data."[3]

Barack Obama is not a Marxist in the formal definition of the term. If he is Marxist, then we all are—everyone who lived in the twentieth century was alive during a time when Marxian analysis dominated social discourse. Yet the focus on class did not fix the class system and may have made it even worse. Warriors for class equality found that in order to fix class, they had to control so many things that they eventually became an intolerable octopus that had to be put to sleep.

So it goes with ligbitists. The twentieth was the century of class. The twenty-first will be remembered as the century of sex. Obsessing about class did not mean one had class; nor does obsessing about sex mean one is having a lot of sex.

For ligbitists, the desire to reorder the material world is an aching and insatiable hunger. They dream of a future world with no prejudice against people with unusual sexual inclinations, a place where people can pursue pleasure without guilt. They dream of a world where no consequences befall any individual whose sex life, gender identity, or desires deviate in any way from their neighbours. But, to get to that point, they have to control so many things that they are also becoming an intolerable octopus.

The spectrum of ligbitists' control and manipulation is staggering. Largely to show solidarity with gay parenting advocates, the Obama administration will redefine the terms of the Immigration and Nationality Act. Under the new policy directive, "A gestational mother has a petitionable relationship without a genetic relationship to the child, as long as she is also the child's legal parent at the time of birth."[4] The pro-ligbitist arm of government redefines human relationships and rearranges the priority given to different people seeking to immigrate. Poor migrants desperate for seasonal labor to support starving families must take the line *behind* wealthy gay couples hoping to import babies bought from Thai surrogates. Those who take objection to such a transfer of power from the poor to the wealthy face a gauntlet if they question such a policy change. Draconian speech codes punish people labelled as "anti-gay".

The scope, depth, and purism of sexual movements may ultimately surpass the overreach and eventual implosion of the global movements for class equality. Ligbitists are creatures of overreach. Yet their modus operandi has ended up being even more invasive than Marxism, because what ligbitists regulate is intimate, pertaining to the pleasurable acts that were previously private.

When I am in France, I have to explain to countless Europeans why this ideology became so awful. America is to the ligbitist movement as the Soviet Union was to Communism. American universities articulated the theoretical framework for this movement in its most abstract form. Then the police state and financial power of the United States have kicked in to impose it nationwide, then globally. We can blame it partly on the Scandinavians but, honestly, how much could Sweden and Denmark have inflicted this on such a massive swath of the world?

It's Americans who unleashed this on the globe. John Kerry delivered a statement at an "LGBT Ministerial Event" at the United Nations on September 26, 2013:

The Global Equality Fund is one way in which like-minded countries can address this injustice and show their support for LGBT persons. Since the United States launched the Fund in 2011, it has allocated over 7 million in more than 50 countries worldwide. And the investments have helped to challenge the discriminatory laws that undermine human rights and bolster – and to bolster civil society organizations that defend those rights.... With support from a range of like-minded governments, including Netherlands, Norway, France, Germany, Iceland, Finland, Denmark, and private sector partners as well, we are expanding the scope of the programs that this Fund supports. Earlier this month, President Obama and the Prime Minister of Sweden Fredrik Reinfeldt announced an additional $12 million for this effort. And today, I'm happy to announce another 1 million contribution from The Netherlands, and we're grateful to you for that.[5]

Such arrogance befits the former Soviet Union. The United States Secretary of State brags that a slice of northern Europe intends to reinvent what people in the rest of the world do with their genitals, how they feel about it, and what they can and cannot say about it. Everything from breastfeeding to military billets to human trafficking will be drastically impacted by such engrossing changes to human society; the unknowns are enormous; the promise of positive change based on nothing empirically sound. Yet with all the confidence of a demagogue, the American diplomat cheers on the tiny fraction of world inhabitants who think it is a good idea to impose this vision on billions upon billions of people.

The gay thing is getting on people's nerves everywhere. You don't see 700,000 people assembling in Paris with pink and blue flags against "gender theory" for nothing. The irritation with American sexual ideology is real. Tomorrow capitals all over Europe will be part of another massive "Manif". Even while I sit here in a Parisian café, not too far from where James Baldwin wrestled with such questions some 55 years ago, I still hope that American exceptionalism will be as much the cure as the cause of ligbitist excess.

We Americans have broken the world's sexual machinery. We have it within ourselves to offer the tools to fix it again, or at least I hope we do. We *are* the nation that hypnotised devotees in Iceland and Denmark to go along with our ambitious "Global Equality Fund." But is that all we are? We are also the nation of staunch evangelical Christianity, pious Jews, and thriving Mormons. Our State Department forces Latin American countries to accommodate drag queens, yet we are also the home turf of mega-churches in Colorado Springs, Orthodox Jewish schools in Brooklyn, and some of the most vocal Catholic archbishoprics in existence.

It's hard to explain America when I am in Paris. My friends here wonder, "Why can't American gays be like our gays? So discreet, elegant, and unobtrusive? We have always loved our gays, because they take care of their mothers and have so much class. All of us have read Proust and many of us have read Genet. Foucault was never shunned in France. We didn't need to make things so unstable. So why now do your gays come over and get our gays acting like animals, dressing up in fishnet devil's outfits for gay pride, throwing things at churches, and demanding that we change our laws?"

My response is usually clumsy, for I know that such a perception of *their gays* is debatable. Many French homosexuals weren't happy with their quiet role in the nation's cultural life for so long. But their complaints, in a typically blunt Parisian style, do contain a fair amount of truth. In France, the number of homosexuals who have stood up to defy the LGBT agenda, even denouncing homosexual marriage and especially homosexual adoption, is amazing. Inter-LGBT, led by the handsome Nicolas Gauguin, feels and looks a lot like the Human Rights Campaign, only with much less native enthusiasm. The viciousness, pushiness, and relentless claims to victimhood, which have made American gay activists so unique in the world, have begun infecting France's gay life. But the infection is at the beginning stages and it has already generated strong antibodies.

The French ask me many questions: why the extremes? Why the excesses? Why do American gays go from being closeted and over-compensating with hyperbolic displays of masculinity, to being promiscuous caricatures of themselves, blogging catty swipes at each other and dancing in G-strings in front of children at their unseemly street festivals?

I wish I could answer with something more than American

defensiveness. My approach is to say, "there are so many good people in the gay community, but that is not the same thing as the gay lobby. The gay lobby doesn't speak for the masses of gay people in America, who are good people."

Such an answer used to work, but now it doesn't anymore. The French have more questions for me: "Who finances this lobby? Why do American gays not do as the French gays do, and stand up and shout into a megaphone that the lobby doesn't speak for them? How on earth did they get so much power?"

This is where I begin to understand so clearly what James Baldwin meant when he said, at last, he couldn't keep sitting in French cafés trying to explain America's strange personality disorders. He had to return to America and try to fix them, even if he knew he might fail, and even if he knew Americans would never appreciate him as much as the French did.

Each time I am invited to France to work on one of their manifs, I arrive on French soil and feel I can breathe again. They're complex! They believe in ideas. They don't get stuck in simple platitudes such as, "love is love", and those of "No H8" (a US LGBT campaigning group). Debate with them involves hours of discussion over wine and coffee, witticisms, and allusions to great thinkers. Even the leftist intellectuals in France have invited me to their homes—socialists, atheists, revolutionaries!— and engaged in rich discussion that goes on well into the small hours.

I am a whole person in France; not a two-dimensional poster boy, far less a shallow bumper sticker. When I give speeches, there are time limits of course, but we meet many times and go over each phrase with care and delicacy. Those who oppose you question you and try to challenge your premises. It does not become, as it does in the United States, a volley of insults back and forth. They don't begin their counterpoints by saying things like, "well you're obviously an unhappy person, so...." The personal is respected but not exploited to escape thought.

Nonetheless, James Baldwin was right. There is a limit to how French an American can become. Though the thought has crossed my mind to move my family to Europe, something always prevents me. When I dined with French scholars in Nancy in 2007, I remember one of the other Americans saying to the French faculty, "I always say I am Canadian when I travel now because I am so ashamed of George Bush." She thought the French would respect her, but they didn't, particularly after my response. I looked to everyone around me and said, "would you ever say you were Belgian because you were embarrassed by Sarko?" To a Frenchman, the thought is off-limits, almost an insult to imagine. So it would be impossible for me to become French, because the part of the French spirit I admire most is one's refusal to be anything but what one is.

On each trip, there is a sad farewell and a trip on the RER to Charles de Gaulle, hauling my gigantic backpack like an overgrown college student doing his junior year abroad. The plane takes off. The French words start fading. We land in whatever horrible hub in which I have to trudge through the immigration inspections—Detroit, Chicago, JFK. I go from James Baldwin to Sharon Stone. "Here's for making me come back to Mars. You know how much I hate this planet."

I have devoted my life as a scholar to studying America, not simply to understand her, but to celebrate her, because she is my homeland. I love her. For these reasons I make a point to read the *Aeneid* several times a year. When I read Virgil's verses, I hear the voice of a man who felt about Augustan Rome the way I feel about post-modern America. You're fascinated by your country, you love your country, but you cannot help narrating your country in such a way as it make her seem embarrassingly hypocritical.

Consider Aeneas. Called "the father of Rome", he is Roman in both his gallantry and his blunders. Virgilian heroism is as much a critique of the homeland as it is praise for it. Confronted by a sea tempest in Book I, Aeneas drops to his knees and cries out impotently in front of his followers that he wishes he'd been killed on the battlefield;[6] in Book II, Aeneas somehow manages to lose track of his own wife as he flees from burning Troy;[7] and in Book IV, he mishandles his breakup speech with Dido so badly that he brings on centuries of war with Carthage.[8]

The greatness of great nations is not without gigantic mistakes. The passion that leads ambitious countries toward exceptional leadership leads them, at times, to guide others into disaster. So it goes with ligbitism. When I was completing my Classics degree, other students viewed fans of Virgil as troglodytes, since *everyone knew* that the Greeks, especially Homer, were the truly cultured ones, not those violent hypocritical Romans. This made me sad. I adored the part of *Aeneid* when Aeneas' father guides him through the underworld, to see all the great ghosts who will be reborn and populate Rome; Anchises says:

> "Roman, remember by your strength to rule
> Earth's peoples—for your arts are to be these:
> To pacify, to impose the rule of law,
> To spare the conquered, battle down the proud."[9]

In other words, Aeneas' father was saying, "Let other people like the Greeks and Persians make classy art; we kick butt." You have to love that kind of brutal honesty. I feel this way about Hollywood, American religion, and the US military. In the San Fernando Valley studios that make children's cartoons in Burbank line one side of the highway; on the other side are dozens of porn studios and an amazing number of churches. The same country that prays prolifically also watches hours of dirty movies, just before cheering on the Marines to the next mind-blowingly destructive and completely senseless war.

The schizophrenic leaps from excess to excess, the cognitive dissonance and rank hypocrisy, with girls in go-go boots shaking it up for the troops before they go to bomb faraway lands with the blessing of their chaplains, are a horror show. Like horror films, the stuff draws you in. Look closely enough at America, and the American inevitably sees himself. I am everything I hate about America, but strive to become everything I love about it.

I'm a little James Baldwin and a little Sharon Stone.

Notes

[1] James Baldwin, "The Discovery of What It Means to Be an American", *Nobody Knows My Name* (New York: Vintage Books, 1961), 9-10.

[2] Robert O.P. Lopez, *Antiquity and Radical Authority 1773-1861*, Doctoral Dissertation (2003), 5. The Marx quotation leads back to: Karl Marx, *German Ideology*, ed. Robert C. Tucker, *The Marx-Engels Reader* (New York: W.W. Norton & Company, 1978), 164.

[3] Richard Fry and Rakesh Kochhar, "America's wealth gap between middle-income and upper-income families is widest on record", Pew Research Center, FactTank: News in the Numbers (December 17, 2014) http://pewresearch.org (Accessed January 6, 2015).

[4] Ben Johnson, "Obama administration grants U.S. citizenship to foreign surrogate mothers and egg donors", *LifeSiteNews,* Bioethics/Family (October 30, 2014) www. lifesitenews.com (Accessed January 6, 2015).

[5] John Kerry, "Kerry at LGBT Ministerial Event", US Department of State, USA Embassy Texts and Transcripts (September 26, 2013) http://iipdigital.usembassy.gov (Accessed January 6, 2015).

[6] Virgil, *Aeneid,* trans. Robert Fitzgerald (New York: Vintage Books, 1981).

[7] Virgil, *Aeneid,* 60.

[8] Virgil, *Aeneid,* 118.

[9] Virgil, *Aeneid,* 190.

SECTION THREE

SOCIETY AND GLOBE

Introduction

Stella Morabito

Social acceptance of genderless marriage is guiding society towards a major shift in power from individuals to the state. The "marriage equality" campaign and its inherent gender identity movement will have an existential impact on national and global societies. The impact is unanticipated by the heedless majority, but is broadly celebrated by those who seek centralised power by a bureaucratic state.

Few realise that the autonomous family serves as a buffer zone, a sanctuary, between the individual and the state. And the notion of same- sex marriage will prove to be the perfect vehicle for dissolving that autonomy and transferring power to the state.

Recognition of marriage (and benefits conferred) has been the state's way of encouraging biological parents to responsibly sire, bear, and raise their own children for the sake of their children, not themselves. That is the only legitimate state interest in marriage. The only valid way to recognise this is across the board, no matter any given couple's intent to have children. Romantic love has got nothing to do with a valid state interest in marriage, and we should all shudder at any notion that it does.

Ironically, the concept of same-sex marriage carries within itself the seeds of its own destruction. Since genderless marriage does not result in children produced autonomously, the state can – indeed, *must* – use a whole new legal standard for recognising virtually any grouping of individuals as families. Since same-sex couplings depend on third parties for reproduction, they invite government regulation on a massive scale, not just for same-sex couples but, eventually, and in the name of "equality", for *all* families.

In the same vein, the campaign to end legal recognition of marriage as a male-female union is poised to water down legal recognition of a child's biological mother and father as parents by default. As the state decides to recognise ever more varieties of relationships and families, the rationale for recognising "family" with any unique purpose evaporates. And in the absence of a rationale, it will sooner or later reach the point of not recognising any form of family at all. In this context, a child's biological mother and father are not presumed the legal parents, even if they are eager to take on their parental responsibilities together.

Brewing chaos

We're currently in a transitional stage of mounting chaos. We can already see some of the largely unexpected effects of genderless marriage, many of them tragic and all of them ultimately dangerous to family autonomy and human freedom.

Arguments for genderless marriage are now being used to promote polygamy and incest, and various other sexual "orientations" that clamor for equal rights. Mainstream media and Hollywood are celebrating and promoting sex changes not just for adults, but for children. And for parents. Transgender activists are also pushing for gender-neutral public facilities that invade privacy, especially for women and children.

We are also seeing more legislation that recognises three or more parents for a child. The buying and selling of babies and the biomaterials to produce them is on the rise. Women in developing countries are being trafficked as surrogates to gestate donor eggs in their wombs, adding another degree of separation between child and mother. An anonymous sperm donor can spawn dozens, even hundreds, of half-siblings in a geographic region who are unaware of their blood ties.

On top of all this, the LGBT lobby has gone global and intends to forcibly export the whole "rights" package to developing nations who want no part of it. Meanwhile, the current US administration threatens to cut off aid to poorer countries that don't get with the LGBT program.

As the institution of marriage unravels, the state can step into the vacuum with greater regulation of personal relationships. We're on the path to redefining marriage so that the state – not parents – has primary legal jurisdiction over children. It truly portends a central planning coup, and is the ultimate bait-and-switch.

It's a war on many social fronts: against language, identity, free expression, privacy, and free association

We can connect these dots by observing how the same-sex marriage movement is already affecting and controlling so many areas of our lives throughout society: the language, legal identity of persons, public discourse, privacy, and our relationships. The picture that emerges is not of a society of voluntary associations, but of atomised individuals, joined only at the pleasure of the state.

The fact that the genderless marriage movement seems to have become a juggernaut overnight reveals that it was never a natural progression, but inherently a very fragile campaign that cannot tolerate dissent. It subsists on control of language and relationships – particularly through hard core punishment of dissenters – as it moves to colonise every nation and every mind.

We are a society in the throes of conversion, not by freewill, but by the virtual sword.

Controlling the language

Words are symbols. As individuals, we use them to communicate our thoughts, and thereby establish relationships with other human beings. But this only works as long as people agree on the definition of terms and accept physical reality. If you corrupt the words, you sow confusion. Keep it up, and you sow delusion.

The transgender lobby, through various arms of the LGBT lobby, dictates language usage for media outlets. Its protocol is a labyrinth of pronoun usage and terminology that insists we deny the physical reality of a transgender person's sex and adapt our language to whatever the stated gender of that person is.

Non-compliance – and even slips – are punishable. From school sex education programs up to campus speech codes, everyone must practice this self-censorship regime until self-censorship is our default mode of life. People become ever more isolated from one another when their language is controlled and corrupted.

But this is just the beginning. As sex distinctions are erased in the law, we are inevitably required to reject the physical reality of our *own* sex as part of our *own* identity. The transgender lobby, after all, insists that being female and male does not exist in physical reality, but only in our minds. And we are in the process of codifying that into law.

At root, the transgender project is not about gender identity *per se*, or about equality. It acts more as an agenda to corrupt the language – our symbols of communication – so that every single person's perception of reality and everyone's self-concept is controlled by the usage. This makes it a perfect tool for central planning.

Controlling identity

"Marriage equality" insists upon the legal erasure of sex distinctions from the parties in marriage. And by extension through its transgender project, it insists on the legal erasure of everybody's physical identity as either male or female.

Until the US Supreme Court's *Windsor* decision that overturned the Defense of Marriage Act, the "T" for transgender in LGBT was barely on the public's radar. Today the transgender lobby has pulled out all the stops in a media and Hollywood juggernaut meant to promote more gender identity non-discrimination laws.

Each of those laws contains the presumption that nobody is born either male or female, and that each person's sex is arbitrarily "assigned" or "designated" at birth. This is an assumption of seismic proportions that seems to have gone largely unnoticed by legislators.

It redefines humanity *universally* so that in the end nobody is legally either male or female. And if no one is legally male or female, then nobody is legally a mother or father or a son or a daughter either. In fact, the terms "mother" and "father" are already being replaced on many government forms with "parent 1" and "parent 2".

Every human being – equally and without exception -- comes into the world as a child resulting from the organic union between one male and one female. Civil marriage has been society's way of recognising this fact across the board for each of its citizens. This recognition also presumes that the mother-father-child unit emerging from an organic union has the right to live and grow together as an autonomous family.

But this natural right – a right which we've always understood as *inalienable* and *self-evident* – is now under severe attack.

The implications for separating children from their biological parents should become clear when we recognise this attack on the physical reality of sex distinctions for what it is. And if you haven't yet heard the drumbeat calling for state licensing of parents, it will get louder. The idea of parenting by committee is gaining ground in the media too. The proposal – advanced by prominent gender legal theorists like Martha Fineman – is to replace legal recognition of families with legal recognition only of "care-giving units" that will be regulated by state bureaucrats.

Controlling expression of thought

The same-sex marriage movement is on a collision course with the free expression of religion. It demands that no corner of society has a different point of view or moral code in conflict with that agenda. The clash has not only come from outside of the religious institutions, but through penetration of those institutions. The Church of England is but one example of many denominations in which the LGBT lobby has succeeded in watering down, and ultimately destroying, recognition of the doctrine of matrimony by leaders on the inside.

But political correctness has penetrated just about every institution of society, enforcing conformity with the LGBT agenda and punishing dissent as severely as possible. We see this not only in the media and Hollywood, but in the speech codes that have blanketed all colleges and universities. It is visible in the enforcement of LGBT-sponsored sex education programs from kindergarten through high school. It has permeated the entire medical profession, particularly the American Psychiatric Association. We see it in the legal profession, in all major corporations, defense contractors. It's in the military, in the Boy Scouts. And a thousand other places. Wherever the LGBT agenda is put into place, a thought police works to squash independent thought.

Erasure of privacy

The whole notion of "gender identity non-discrimination" (midwifed by genderless marriage) is a formula for erasing privacy from our lives. As more and more people goaded by pop culture – especially youth – "overshare" about their sexual habits on the internet, we can see a watering down of the notion that sex is a private matter. Some have even come to accept the idea that we not only have lost privacy, but any claim to a right to privacy.

Genderless marriage and the transgender project promote a de-privatising of sex that's reminiscent of Aldous Huxley's *Brave New World*. We see this especially in the proliferation of legislation that serves to mix the sexes in public bathrooms and locker rooms and high school sports teams.

Sex distinctions become irrelevant under these laws also because gender identity is increasingly being permitted simply by proclamation and understood to be a fluid term. Under this scheme, males are by default given access to women's and girls' facilities.

But it is not just sexual privacy that is being erased, but privacy in all of our personal relationships. Political correctness is a regime that works to dictate all personal communication throughout all of society. It encourages a surveillance state that kills trust and intimacy.

Controlling personal relationships
Ironically, the campaign to open up marriage to any other type of relationship also serves as a vehicle to control relationships among all people. Once sex distinctions of "male" and "female" are written out of law, custody of a child by the biological mother and father becomes less a right inherently recognised and more and more up to state discretion or – as the drumbeat grows for it – state willingness to grant them a license to raise their child.

As we embark on an age that increasingly condones polygamy, incest, and baby-selling, the child stands ever more alone. We are casting the child out to sea, without any presumed bond to the mother who bore the child or the father who sired the child. Her existential question "Where did I come from?" is answered with silence.

There can be no automatically recognised mothers and fathers or sons and daughters in a society that does not recognise sex distinctions. And the dilution of family relationships will in turn create a chain reaction that dilutes every other personal relationship in society.

And when we are all legally neutered, we must stand alone before the State.

I have argued in the past that the notion of genderless marriage also provides the precedent by which singles' rights activists can argue that the very existence of civil marriage is discriminatory against single individuals. This would allow judges to apply a *coup de grace* to any state recognition of marriage, and therefore family.

Once that's done, the state will only recognise our spousal and parental relationships at its pleasure. It's a scheme that would render blood ties increasingly irrelevant and require that all "families" be domestic partnerships drawn up by contracts that are regulated by the State. (Cass Sunstein, President Obama's regulatory czar during 2009-2012 provided a blueprint for that scheme in his 2008 book *Nudge*, co-authored with Richard Thaler.) State licensing of parents and regulation of families as "care-giving units" will fly into that vacuum.

The separation of children from this basic organic unit – from their origins and the knowledge of and care by those who gave them life – is sure to create a panoply of pathologies in society. And the LGBT lobby intends to export it all worldwide.

It was always about central planning
Genderless marriage is wrought with internal contradictions because of the pesky fact that genderless marriages cannot autonomously create children. It requires that the state basically define marriage at the outset as a sterile relationship for all parties. It also requires that children – as biologically conceived, sired, and born to a couple – be written out of state interest in marriage. It's more a formula for separation of families, not for uniting them. Perfect for the centralised state.

These hidden realities don't fare well in the light of day. So the genderless marriage campaign has depended heavily upon the cultivation of public ignorance and a very stunted public debate. And though the campaign relies on an appeal to morality in its "equality" rhetoric, it requires the destruction of all religious codes of morality in order to survive.

As with all such totalitarian revolutions, the LGBT lobby could only win by ambush, by subterfuge, and by enforced compliance as well as a good dose of ignorant goodwill by the masses. It can brook no dissent, which is why it is being imposed globally in one of the most sweeping movements of cultural imperialism the world has ever witnessed.

The campaign had to permeate virtually all of the outlets of communication in order to make inroads. It's a vast network that includes the mass media, Hollywood, academia, school education, the institutions of medicine and law, corporate America, and religious seminaries, to name but a few. The agenda depends too much on the suppression and control of communication, too much on the putative dictates of political correctness and on such a massive scale, that it cannot possibly centre on truth.

And though the idea of genderless marriage was fragile in its nascent state, it's poised to usher in new regulations that will allow the State to consolidate enough centralised power to eliminate the family as a mediating institution. If this happens in the U.S., we will have moved into uncharted territory for a nation conceived in liberty. The casualties will be inestimable. And the costs of dissent are bound to be far greater than they are now.

Chapter Sixteen

BORDERS AND BLOOD

Robert Oscar Lopez

Over 50,000 children have been intercepted at the US-Mexico border. These all fit the classification of "unaccompanied minors" because they have arrived on American soil without permission to enter the United States. No adults are accompanying them. "Children" here include teenagers who very likely take adult roles in their home countries— overwhelmingly Honduras, El Salvador, and Guatemala.

Reactions to the plight of these migrant children have been largely sympathetic, though divided. Some American conservatives feel that this is an occasion to back away from partisan rhetoric on Obama's immigration policies and be charitable. Some American conservatives feel that it will only harm the children to be too charitable, thereby giving an incentive for more children to come.

Same-sex parenting: the background music

The same-sex marriage debate has altered the way we discuss family reunification, kinship, foster care, social intervention, and adoption. Immigration reformists routinely cite the "reunification of families" as a central urgency requiring the government to decriminalise people who immigrated illegally. Latino and LGBT advocacy groups are vague about whether immigration law should protect children by bringing their father and mother into the country under some kind of waiver, *or* by making it easier for couples in the United States to sever children from one or both of their biological parents and adopt them under a special visa.

"Whose child is this?" becomes the most important question. It is the one question that nobody is willing to pose, because it would mean pitting Latinos against gays.

An official statement from the National Association of Latino Elected Officials (NALEO) provides a list of reasons for the necessity of immigration reform. High on the list is keeping families together: "Currently, large immigration backlogs prevent many U.S. citizens from swiftly reuniting with their family members. It is important that our immigration policies recognise the efforts of individuals that have petitioned for loved ones through legal channels, and that we institute measures to ensure family reunification and a substantive reduction of the family backlogs." NALEO has an entire fact sheet outlining talking points about the Fourteenth Amendment protecting the equal rights of children.[1]

The Human Rights Campaign (HRC) has a document similar to NALEO's, outlining the reasons that immigration reform is an LGBT issue. The HRC also highlights the goal of keeping families together, but there is no mention by either NALEO or HRC of the inherent conflict between their mutual discussions of "reuniting" families. Same-sex parenting relies on the ability of gay couples to adopt or acquire (even buy) children from their biological mother and father; a key target demographic for such "adoptions" would be struggling immigrant children whose mother or father cannot make it into the country. NALEO's stance can rely on a stable reference of one "family" unit of mother/father per child; HRC's cannot.

The HRC must refer simultaneously to at least two family units: the biological pair of mother/father, and the adoptive pair of man/man or woman/woman. How can the federal government pass a law that meets the underlying definition of NALEO's call for reform and the underlying definition of HRC's call for reform? *They are in open conflict with each other*. Observe HRC's statement on families and reunification:

> Include the Reuniting Families Act in immigration reform. The Reuniting Families Act would reduce current immigration backlogs in order to ensure that families navigating our immigration system are reunited more quickly. Among other reforms, the Act would reduce wait times: (1) by amending Section 201(b)(2) of the INA so that *lawful permanent resident spouses, children and same-sex partners are classified as "immediate relatives" and exempted from*

numerical caps on family immigration, (2) by recapturing visas that have gone unused or unclaimed and (3) by increasing per-country visa limits from 7% to 10%.[2]

In a country that never answers the question, "whose child is this?", the solutions are bound to be ill-conceived. The news cycle was dominated by the border crisis story in June and July of 2014. The children were summarily dispersed to homes throughout the United States via the foster care system. They vanished, having not really been placed in a home with their mothers and fathers together. Then they receded from the national consciousness.

The Obama government contracted a host of religious charities, paying, among many others, the US Conference of Catholic Bishops $30 million and Baptist Child and Family Services $289 million, to transition these children into the "custody" of American homes.[3] At first unloaded on Christian charities, the children flowed into the foster care system. Advertisements in California circulated under the aegis of foster care agencies, offering homes a bonus of 23% higher incentives to take refugee children rather than American citizens in the queue.[4]

Faced with a sudden crisis for which people were largely unprepared, American policymakers had two competing definitions of "family reunification". There was not a lot of time to workshop or focus-group these two definitions to see which one matched the public's instincts. One notion of family would be the child's mother, father, and kin, regardless of how impoverished or struggling they are. The other would be the "loving" family that wants the child and can provide for the child. In the latter case, the loving family has some money to start with and knows the government is going to sweeten the prospect of adoption with tax breaks or subsidies.

The choice made by the Obama administration speaks volumes. Rather than rush to assemble some means of connecting these children to their birth homes and expediting a resolution of their parents' immigration status, the administration rushed to create new families that were not based on the child's origins and which were being blatantly influenced by financial motives. His administration treated them like wards of the state and channeled them into a charity system based on foster care and adoption.

How did we get here? The debate about same-sex marriage created a situation in which, in order for the LGBT movement to attain its goals, people had to be comfortable looking past biological kinship in favour of whichever custodial arrangement was most "loving", "wanted", "planned", and "in the child's interests".

Advocates for gay parenting have not been secretive about their ultimate goal—creating a system where children belong to adults who want them, not adults who conceived them. In Washington DC, on June 20, 2013, about one year before the border crisis broke in the news, Nancy Polikoff testified before the City Council Committee on Public Safety and the Judiciary. She was speaking on the occasion of the City Council's consideration of a plan to repeal the capital's law against surrogacy.

Polikoff is a longstanding and highly respected scholar for LGBT rights. She begins by explaining that gay people need family to be redefined so that they can found families in the first place. The legalisation of surrogacy, and with it the drastic redefinition of human kinship, is justified because it is necessary to match the demands of the LGBT community. The overriding prerogative is to satisfy gay dreams of parenthood; all other considerations are secondary. Here is part of Polikoff's speech:

> For more than 20 years advocates for lesbian and gay parents have emphasized that genetics is neither necessary nor sufficient to create parentage. In 2008 and 2009, I worked with this committee on parentage legislation, which the City Council enacted, ensuring that when a lesbian couple plans for a child conceived through donor insemination then both women are the legal parents of that child. The semen donor in such instances is not a parent, absent a written agreement to the contrary. The position that a semen donor is not a parent is consistent with the law in numerous other jurisdictions. This demonstrates the LGBT family law position that a genetic connection is not sufficient to create parentage.[5]

To say that genetics is neither necessary nor sufficient to create parentage is to change the way we think about human existence: where we come from, whom we are supposed to cherish, whom we are supposed to obey, whom we mourn, whom we model ourselves after. Polikoff's worldview demands that people who *want* us have a *claim* to our filial love and obedience, *because they want us* and *because they have money*. It is automatically in the best interests of every human being to be under the emotional sway of people with means and intent to acquire the person at a young age. It is automatically not in the best interests of *any* human being to be under the emotional sway of people who conceived the person by making love, *because the only thing that connects them to the child is that their sex act conceived the child.*

The LGBT population represents a tiny sliver of the world's population. While they might benefit from such a massive shift in social structures, the vast majority of people who will feel the after-effects of such cultural surgery will *not* be LGBT people. It will be everyone else. Untold billions of babies are born into vulnerable situations where people who conceived them want to raise them but do not have the means to raise them well right now. A common situation is that people who conceived them did not want them at all at the moment of conception, but will likely grow to feel love toward them, if not soon, perhaps in a number of years. Another common situation is that someone else who is not a biological parent might find a little child cute and adorable and *want* that child, with the result that it is easy to rationalise taking the child away from its parents by looking at the most obvious flaws in the biological progenitors. They are poor. They are not living together; maybe they were never married. They do not know how to raise children. They live in a bad neighborhood or an underdeveloped country. They did not *really* want this child and the child will figure that out.

But I want the child, and I have means. Give me that child!

The tireless efforts of the gay marriage movement to nationalise the mindset of Nancy Polikoff had already yielded significant fruit by the summer of 2013. The *Windsor* and *Hollingsworth* cases brought New York and California's marriage laws before the U.S. Supreme Court. *Hollingsworth* was sent back to the lower courts but the majority opinion on *Windsor* was written by Justice Anthony Kennedy. A major part of his written opinion hinged on the role of children in family life.

Justice Kennedy opined that children being raised by a same-sex couple deserved to have the benefits of growing up with married parents. It was even a *right* of the children being claimed by their parents as proxies. He made no statement at all as to whether children being raised by a same-sex couple had a right to their biological mother and father in the first place, let alone whether the federal government's constitutional duty to attend to the "general welfare" or "posterity" extended to requiring some protection of such basic birth connections as heritage, patrimony, and origins.

Justice Kennedy had no evidence that marrying two guardians who were not really the child's parents would help a child; the only substantiated point was that marriage was something that gay adults who had custody of children wanted for themselves. Regardless of the adults' marital status, the child will still figure out at some point that one biological parent is missing. He *did* have supposed evidence, thanks to the copious amicus curiae briefs submitted by doctors, sociologists, and the Obama Administration, that children raised in same-sex couples had no material or hygienic disadvantage. The studies on which the latter claims were based measured the very things that would reward couples with money and couples who premeditated an intent to have a child—"well-being", performance in school, access to health care—while penalising couples without money who were taken by surprise when the child was conceived.

Kennedy's decision dealt a stealth blow to the central aims of Latino immigration reform. Most Latinos grappling with immigration issues are poor. The *Windsor* decision was a way of saying on the sly, "Actually, we do not think poor people should raise their own kids, because kids of poor people are not really 'their' kids—they belong to other people who want and have means to raise them."

In writing the majority opinion for *US v. Windsor*, Justice Kennedy blithely tossed in a reference to children of same-sex couples. He was principally delivering an opinion involving a lesbian, Edith Windsor, who was suing the federal government over taxes, not parenthood:

> By this dynamic DOMA undermines both the public and private significance of state-sanctioned same-sex marriages; for it tells those couples, and all the world, that their otherwise valid marriages are unworthy of federal recognition. This places same-sex couples

in an unstable position of being in a second-tier marriage. The differentiation demeans the couple, whose moral and sexual choices the Constitution protects, see Lawrence, 539 U. S. 558, and whose relationship the State has sought to dignify. And it humiliates tens of thousands of children now being raised by same-sex couples. The law in question makes it even more difficult for the children to understand the integrity and closeness of their own family and its concord with other families in their community and in their daily lives.[6]

The *Windsor* case was based on married people deserving to keep their own money rather than pay higher taxes to the government. Why does Justice Kennedy assume that these couples will automatically be able to convey to their "children" the "integrity and closeness of their own family" by having more money? What is "their own family"? Why not implement laws that let these children be raised by their mother and father?

Wherever two gay men or two lesbians raise a child, there is a missing parent who exists or existed, but who isn't part of the child's family. If the courts and the US government does not see this as an appreciable loss or something painful to be avoided, then there is no real way to realise NALEO's dream of family reunification, which is so crucial to the call for immigration reform. At best, we will have HRC's dream for family reunification: likely a pattern of wealthy gay couples taking Latino children away from Latino parents who love them but are poor. Immigration reform will likely involve denying biological parents the right to immigrate from Latin America, since the state's real interest will be to place the stateless children into the homes of well-to-do citizens and grant the *child* citizenship through adoption.

Unexamined and unreflectively assumed was the axiom that children are happiest when they are wanted by rich people. Totally erased from the discussion was the inevitable distress felt by mothers and fathers who did not get to raise their children, and children who did not get to grow up with their mothers and fathers. That is where the national discourse stood one year later, when news broke of 50,000 children at the Mexican border whose parents were not with them.

What could have been done for the 50,000 border kids?
If a child has absolutely nobody to take care of him, then we must look into the best possible adoption. All signs point to the fact that the border children are neither orphans nor a good fit for the adoption system. They have families but we need to find those families and figure out how the kids can be with them.

We could have said, in the summer of 2014, "We have to find their parents. Most of them know where their parents are but won't tell border authorities right away. We need experts in human intelligence to interview the children, build up some trust, and then draw the information out of them. We will need translators, not only for Spanish but possibly also other languages. We need all seventeen branches of the Intelligence Community, ranging from the FBI to the CIA to the State Department to the Department of the Treasury, and yes the NSA (National Security Agency) too, to track down leads until we can confirm that we have found these children's parents."

We could have said: "We have to resolve the status of their parents and the children too. Once we have located their parents, we have to make contact with them. If they are not in the country legally, we may have to apprehend them. If they are in Central America, we may have to dispatch partners on the grounds there to interview them. We will need to undergo a host of legal procedures. Reports need to be filed to immigration judges. Lawyers need to get affidavits signed. Psychiatric and medical evaluations have to be turned over to the judges. Hearings have to be conducted, including hearings where the parents will have to be present; this may mean having to transport the parents to a location where temporary courts are set up. This means we need a lot of judges, attorneys, law guardians, translators, court advocates, consultants, and certified social workers to partner with medics, nurses, doctors, psychologists, and paralegals. They all have to be in some central location where they can meet with each other on short notice. The children have to be available for interviews and hearings at any moment. The ultimate goal is that there must be a disposition rendered quickly, but one that is sound and based on reliable information. Judges may decide that the entire family can remain in the United States and grant them legal residency and authorisation to work, or judges may decide to return them to Central America, in which cases there have to be liaisons with the consulates of Honduras, Guatemala, El Salvador, and Nicaragua to expedite such cases and develop a repatriation plan."

We could have said, "We have to keep the children safe. This is a refugee crisis but it has to be treated with a military rather than a humanitarian mindset. The children cannot be put in situations where they are a flight risk or likely to disappear. They should not be released into the custody of private homes that might not want to relinquish custody of them when the parents are identified. The children need some kind of group lodging under safe conditions where there are security guards supervising them during the day and night. They have to be reachable during the day at short notice by people who need to interview them. The perimeters of their billets have to be guarded. These children have been incredibly traumatised so they need to have access to psychiatric and medical care. Also, to keep this many children occupied while they are waiting to get through the system, we will need a small army of teachers and youth recreation experts to come and hold impromptu classes in trailers, set up little soccer leagues, do arts and crafts, and play games. We need kitchens and food preparation facilities that can handle feeding large numbers of kids, which means we need cooks, dishwashers, and cafeteria monitors. These children may be stuck in holding for more than a year, so we need to arrange for hygienic living conditions with clean bathrooms and showering facilities, laundry, and bedding. Tens of thousands of cots have to be retrieved from basements all over military installations; if they are torn or rusty, they have to be repaired and then sent along. We'll need large numbers of trailers or tents. People who are used to setting up such kinds of lodging will need to make sure that kids have some level of privacy or quiet for their sleeping areas—their own cot, a small table or nightstand next to them even if it's just a crate, their own trunk to keep things in, their own pillow. There are curtains that can be set up to section off one cot from another."

We could have said: "We have to find out who was behind this trafficking. Besides being a humanitarian crisis, this is a massive crime scene. Somebody orchestrated an enormous scheme to smuggle tens of thousands of vulnerable children into a foreign country in violation of international law. We know that a large number of them have been sexually abused so we have to investigate to see if the trafficking was tied to sex work in the first place. In order to do this, the FBI, CIA, and other intelligence gathering operations need to set up shop wherever the kids are so that they can investigate. We need to apprehend the perpetrators and bring them to justice."

The American people lacked the imagination and will to say any of those things. Congress stalled because of provisions in laws that would be impossible to alter without serious negotiation. The Obama administration rushed to a solution based on unexamined assumptions, largely influenced by the gay lobby yet falsely cast as bows to the Latino lobby.

The problem of border children may lead to a precedent of many more being lost to a diaspora. Charity groups like Baptist Child and Family Services do not have the authority to resolve these kids' and their families' legal status, which is the singular most important thing that has to be done. Throwing millions at an adoption-based charity for them to take care of kids for two years is a colossal misuse of funds.

Dispersing the children all across the country will slow down or totally derail the legal process. The most important thing is for the kids to be with their parents and have their legal status resolved. All the paperwork and investigation cannot happen if kids are scattered to the four winds and placed in foster homes with citizens who receive large monthly payments to care for them. Their guardians will have an incentive to slow the process so the kids never leave their care.

If the President asks for $4 billion and then says he is disbursing that to private charities who will place the kids in foster homes, that's a waste of money and potentially anti-humanitarian. The kids will vanish or get adopted and then run away. More kids will follow them and the human trafficking will keep proliferating.

If the President asks for $4 billion and he presents a serious plan to cut backlogs and reunite families through meaningful, *fully enforced* court orders, then the money is better spent now. A stitch in time saves nine.

Notes

1 Rosalind Gold and Gloria Montano Greene, "NALEO's Principles on Comprehensive Immigration Reform", National Association of Latino Elected Officials (Undated) www.naleo.org (Accessed January 7, 2015).

2 Human Rights Campaign, "Comprehensive & Inclusive Immigration Reform", hrc.org, Resources (April 2014) www.hrc.org (Accessed January 7, 2015). Emphasis added.

3 Lee Cary, "Crony Christianity", *American Thinker* (October 13, 2014) www.americanthinker.com (Accessed January 7, 2015).

4 Scott Mayer, "Throwing American Foster Kids under the Obama Bus", *American Thinker* (July 19, 2014) www.americanthinker.com (Accessed January 7, 2015).

5 Nancy Polikoff, Testimony on Bill 20-32, D.C. City Council Committee on Public Safety and the Judiciary (June 20, 2013) http://beyondstraightandgaymarriage.blogspot.com (Accessed January 7, 2015).

6 Justice Anthony Kennedy, Opinion of the Majority of the U.S. Supreme Court, *United States v. Windsor*, No. 12-307 (June 26, 2013), 22-23.

Chapter Seventeen

COWBOYS AND INDIANS

Robert Oscar Lopez

One day before Justice Kennedy issued his much anticipated decision on *U.S. v. Windsor* in the U.S. Supreme Court, Justice Alito issued a far less trumpeted decision in *Adoptive Couple v. A Baby Girl, A Minor Child under the Age of Fourteen Years*. The case involved a little girl named "Baby Veronica", a US soldier, an unwed mother, and an adoptive couple in South Carolina.

These decisions share a hostility toward intact biological families. Such a coincidence was lost on most readers. The alignment of judges in the two decisions belied any easy explanation of right and left political loyalties. Both cases ultimately decided that a child's "family" and "kin" were determined by who wants the child and has better resources to raise the child according to bourgeois sensibilities. Both cases added to the disdain for people who become parents as the unintended result of having sex.

The lineup of justices concurring and dissenting was topsy-turvy. In *US v. Windsor*, at stake was the definition of LGBT families as perfectly equal, regardless of the biological reality that they can never acquire children without taking them from someone else. In *Adoptive Couple v. Baby Girl*, at stake were the rights of a father and mother who made love and created a baby but were less stable than two biologically unrelated people in another state who had money and really wanted to raise the girl.

Adoptive Couple was decided on June 25, 2013, one day before the *Windsor* decision was published. Without the Court's strong indictment of biological parenthood and disregard for cultural genocide in the *Adoptive Couple* case, it is arguable that Justice Kennedy would not have had enough jurisprudential ammunition to decide *Windsor* in the sweeping way he did.

Justice Alito wrote the majority opinion for *Adoptive Couple*, and was joined by Justices Thomas, Kennedy, Breyer, and Roberts. The dissenters in the case included Justices Sotomayor, Kagan, Ginsburg, and Scalia.

The following day, the Supreme Court was at its most schizophrenic. Only one day after dissenting from Justice Alito and insisting emphatically that biological kinship *did matter*, the three women on the bench all signed on with Justice Kennedy's majority opinion conferring "equal" family status to LGBT homes—homes which can only include children if biological kinship *doesn't* matter.

Justice Scalia was consistent in affirming the role of biological kinship by dissenting from Alito's decision in *Adoptive Couple* and dissenting from Kennedy's decision in the *Windsor* case. Justices Thomas, Alito, and Roberts seemed to discount the role of the natural family by siding with the adoptive couple on June 25, but they voted with the dissent against gay marriage the following day. A casual observer could infer that they were more worried about moral and consequential arguments specific to homosexuality than they were about children's ties to their origins or the need to thwart cultural genocide.

Lastly there were two justices, Breyer and Kennedy, who were consistently comfortable with sweeping aside the natural family based on other social or political considerations. They voted with the majority in both cases, letting Baby Veronica's Indian blood be cast aside in favor of a wealthier white couple, and letting gay people enforce their guardianship over other people's children using the state's endorsement of homosexual marriage. These two, who are typically seen as the most "centrist" justices, seem to confirm a suspicion I had all along: it is the middle ground on the same-sex marriage question that seems to collect the worst of leftism and conservatism.

However one tries to make sense of this dizzying pair of decisions, the result is strong in one direction. The Indian Child Welfare Act of 1978 and the Defense of Marriage Act of 1996 were weakened so severely that one might say that they were disabled by the courts. Justice Alito's opinion in the *Adoptive Couple* case opens with extensive quotes designed to explain what the Indian Child Welfare Act was about.

"The Indian Child Welfare Act of 1978 (ICWA), 92 Stat. 3069, 25 U. S. C. §§ 1901-1963, was the product of rising concern in the mid-1970's over the consequences to Indian children, Indian families, and Indian tribes of abusive child welfare practices that resulted in the separation of large numbers of Indian children from their families and tribes through adoption or foster care placement, usually in non-Indian homes." (*Mississippi Band of Choctaw Indians* v. *Holyfield*, 490 U. S. 30, 32 (1989).) Congress found that "an alarmingly high percentage of Indian families [were being] broken up by the removal, often unwarranted, of their children from them by non-tribal public and private agencies." (§ **1901(4)**.C This "wholesale removal of Indian children from their homes" prompted Congress to enact the ICWA, which establishes federal standards that govern state-court child custody proceedings involving Indian children. (Id., at 32, 36; see also § **1902** declaring that the ICWA establishes "minimum Federal standards for the removal of Indian children from ... their families".) Three provisions of the ICWA are especially relevant to this case. *First*, "[a]ny party seeking" an involuntary termination of parental rights to an Indian child under state law must demonstrate that "active efforts have been made to provide remedial services and rehabilitative programs designed to prevent the breakup of the Indian family and that these efforts have proved unsuccessful." (§ **1912(d)**) *Second*, a state court may not involuntarily terminate parental rights to an Indian child "in the absence of a determination, supported by evidence beyond a reasonable doubt, including testimony of qualified expert witnesses, that the continued custody of the child by the parent or Indian custodian is likely to result in serious emotional or physical damage to the child." (§ **1912(f)**) *Third*, with respect to adoptive placements for an Indian child under state law, "a preference shall be given, in the absence of good cause to the contrary, to a placement with (1) a member of the child's extended family; (2) other members of the Indian child's tribe; or (3) other Indian families." (§ **1915(a)**)[1]

Justice Alito's decision overrode the three latter considerations. He did so largely by characterising Dusten Brown, the biological father of Baby Veronica, as irresponsible and contrasting his behavior unfavourably against the Capobiancos, the white couple who had sought to adopt the little girl through a private agency.

Justice Alito sweeps aside the law's concern about the importance of preventing the breakup of Indian families. This state interest is "inapplicable when, as here, the parent abandoned the Indian child before birth and never had custody of the child". Delving into further specifics, Justice Alito narrates the story of the child's birth and relinquishment with particular emphasis on the father's fecklessness:

> Birth Mother informed Biological Father, who lived about four hours away, that she was pregnant. After learning of the pregnancy, Biological Father asked Birth Mother to move up the date of the wedding. He also refused to provide any financial support until after the two had married. The couple's relationship deteriorated, and Birth Mother broke off the engagement in May 2009. In June, Birth Mother sent Biological Father a text message asking if he would rather pay child support or relinquish his parental rights. Biological Father responded via text message that he relinquished his rights.[2]

Why did Brown not have custody? Why did he relinquish his rights? Why did he not support the baby girl during the pregnancy and just afterwards?

The answer to these questions is not, "he was a bad person", and certainly not, "because he should have never been the father in the first place". Like the vast majority of children in the world, Veronica was born into an imperfect situation and had imperfect parents. Imperfections are common in communities that have high poverty rates, such as the Latino and Indian communities to which Veronica's parents belonged.

Dusten Brown was a soldier in the U.S. Army and wanted to marry the woman whom he had impregnated. He wanted his daughter to be born in wedlock and tried to pressure his girlfriend into making that possible. He used the threat of not supporting the girl financially as an incentive. It is not clear how else he could have compelled the baby's mother to do what he thought was right. He thought it best to provide Veronica with a married home containing her father and mother.

Living with the prospect of deployments and navigating an unstable relationship with a woman who had changed her mind about marrying him, Brown was not entirely prepared for his situation. The world is cruel to the lowly soldier living on soldier's pay. He was trying to make important decisions on his own in what must have been an emotional whirlwind. He was dealing with the baby's mother who did not want to help matters and who may have been pushing for an adoption to get back at him.

In the heat of the moment, many good men could make a mistake, neither knowing how deeply they really wanted to be with their daughter, nor anticipating that the situation might change and it might be possible to provide the child with a loving home later on. Brown learns that he has become a father. Then he learns that the child's mother does not want to marry him. He does not know whether he can remain in the country. The fact that he stated, in a moment of pique, that he did not want custody of the girl, could be understood in context by someone who approached this issue with a generous attitude about the strains fathers like Brown face, and about the value of a person staying connected to their origins.

Cultural genocide is what happens when people dismiss the importance of origins and biological kinship in favor of state-sponsored social engineering. Cultural genocide is what led to the passage of the 1978 law that this case challenged. The mentality underlying Justice Alito's decision leans frighteningly toward the logic of cultural genocide. The same logic would resurge the following day with Justice Kennedy's decision in the Defense of Marriage Act. Biological origins do not matter in this logic because children belong to couples who want them and who appear respectable in the eyes of bourgeois society—especially the genteel class to which so many gay and lesbian couples belong when they aspire to become parents.

Emphasis matters. Justice Alito emphasises peculiar details that paint a picture of an unfit father: Brown text-messages about his child's custody, does not want to support the child's mother unless she marries him, and "never had custody" (which Justice Alito does not fully contextualise: Brown was in a fluxing and unstable state when the baby was born and Veronica's mother was turbulent toward him, not to mention that he was still subject to possible deployment by the Army).

A similar tone was evident in much of the commentary about the case, such as this column that ran in the *Weekly Standard*:

Take the case of the Capobianco family of James Island, South Carolina. Matt Capobianco, who works at Boeing, and his wife Melanie, a psychologist, spent years trying to conceive a child, even going so far as to attempt *in vitro* fertilisation seven times. The couple ultimately decided to adopt, and found a pregnant mother in Oklahoma who was willing to give them her child. So taken with the Capobiancos was the birth mother that she even let Matt cut the umbilical cord when the little girl, whom the Capobiancos named Veronica, was born in September 2009. The child's birth father waived his parental rights, declaring that he "would not be responsible in any way for child support or anything else as far as the child's concerned", and Matt and Melanie took Veronica back to South Carolina, where they began to raise her as their own.... Four months later, Veronica's birth father, a soldier in the U.S. Army living in Oklahoma named Dusten Brown, changed his mind and initiated legal proceedings to gain custody of Veronica. Normally, this would have been an easy win for the Capobiancos; not only had Brown signed away his rights, he had also provided no support through the pregnancy. But there was a hitch.[3]

References to the Capobiancos' employment situation and expenditures on in vitro fertilisation are puzzling. Mr. Capobianco works at Boeing whereas Mr. Brown is a soldier in the Army; they both serve in the United States' defense industry except that Mr. Brown has to do the dirty work that takes him overseas and exposes him to lethal dangers. For this, he is punished by having to let Mr. Capobianco have his child.

Depending on one's assumptions, the fact that the Capobiancos tried so hard to have a child through in vitro fertilisation could go either way. It proves they want a child very badly and have a great deal of money. But it also proves that they didn't want Veronica in particular; they wanted a white child of their own and only turned to the adoption of Veronica when their original plan became unattainable.

Regardless of these tangential issues, the fact remains that the United States Congress passed a law in 1978 to protect American Indians from cultural genocide. The size of the fraction of Veronica's Indian bloodline does not negate the pretext for the law. Whole indigenous nations were wiped out in the United States. The only way to stop them from being erased entirely is to keep the few who have survived within the orbit of their origins. Perhaps the 1978 law was too narrow because it only cared about Indians being traumatised by having their children taken away, rather than the pain anybody would feel with the permanent wound of losing their own kin to a child services system corrupted by money. Even if that is a fair criticism, the problem remains that cultural genocide has happened in the past because of actions like the one that the United States Supreme Court took on June 25, 2013. The Court decided that children do not need to be raised by the mother and father that conceive them, if a more respectable (i.e., richer) couple wants and claims them. If you can prove a poor mother or father unfit, you can take away the fruit of their sexual intercourse, their children.

The next day, the Court applied this logic to marriage and decided that same-sex unions were equal in every way, not despite, but *because*, they acquire children on a financial and professional timetable rather than through the disorganised and unregimented rhythms of sex. Cultural genocide relies upon disdain for people who aren't like the dominant culture. The targets for cultural genocide have customs at odds with the more powerful group whose values represent the supposed standard for hygiene, love, and all that is dignified and worthy. Cultural genocide relies upon the state's power to seize the bodies of children and separate them from their parents, placing them in the power of non-parents who come from the dominant culture.

Same-sex parenting relies upon all the same things. The Supreme Court's majority decided that the only possible reason for the passage of the Defence of Marriage Act (1996) (which defined marriage as the union of a man and a woman) was merely "animus", because in this case the Court effectively rejected the notion that the state had any interest in preserving, or prioritising, a child's bond to his mother and father. The Court also accepted the metrics put forward by the social scientists who filed amicus briefs in favour of gay marriage. Those metrics emphasised the kind of economically skewed and superficially hygienic concerns that had been cited for over a century by people who were convinced that it was in the best interest of American Indian children to grow up in rich white homes rather than in poor Indian ones.

The Supreme Court's majority did not even consider, let alone respond to, the concept of a child's highest interest being served by growing up with a mom and dad, *let alone his own mom and dad*. The Court accepted the gay lobby's assertion that there was no real need, and indeed no legitimate right on the part of the government, to value the child's biological heritage and the child's need to access cultural norms by having a mom and dad even if the child is adopted. In fact, the Court asserted that people who value such things can *only* be motivated by hatred for homosexuals and must be irrational.

In order for gay marriage to be legally vindicated by the Supreme Court, the Supreme Court had to obliterate the reasoning behind the Indian Child Welfare Act. The Supreme Court could not say that animus is the only reason for valuing a child's maternal and paternal origins in one case, and then in another case say that there was a legitimate reason to value a child's cultural origins. If gay people had the "right" to acquire and maintain physical power over children to the exclusion of the child's biological roots, then this "right" had to exist above and beyond the consideration of racial vulnerabilities or questions of cultural integrity.

Notes
[1] United States Supreme Court Decision, *Adoptive Couple v. Baby Girl, A Minor Child under the Age of Fourteen Years, et al.*, No. 12-399 (Decided June 25, 2013) www2.bloomberg.com (Accessed January 8, 2015).
[2] Ibid.
[3] Ethan Epstein, "Mistreating Native American Children", *Weekly Standard* 17, no.45 (August 20, 2012) www.weeklystandard.com (Accessed January 8, 2015).

Chapter Eighteen

SLAVERY

Robert Oscar Lopez

Paragraph II of the Declaration of Independence includes these lines:

> We hold these truths to be self-evident, that all men are created equal, that they are endowed by their Creator with certain unalienable Rights, that among these are Life, Liberty and the pursuit of Happiness; That to secure these rights, Governments are instituted among Men, deriving their just powers from the consent of the governed.[1]

Free citizenship relies upon the descent of rights. Integral to freedom is the nature of a person's origins. The moment of birth is fundamental in setting the origin not only of our nation, but also of each of us as individuals. Paragraph II takes care to emphasise creation twice: "all men are created equal" and "endowed by their Creator". One must not necessarily read "their Creator" as strictly religious. One could interpret it as a reference to whatever forces bring people into the world.

Sex brings people into the world. Men and women have intercourse, the woman bears a child, and the child starts life. If this is left alone as the means by which citizens come into existence, then certain parts of the Declaration of Independence remain intact. Citizens are born free, according to a timetable that nobody has the tyrannical power to control. No matter how much money we have as individuals, children come into our lives based on factors beyond our will. Citizens are born with the entitlement given to them by the two people who made love; the mother and father are bound legally to support this citizen. They do not have a right but rather a duty to the child; the child does not belong to them as much as they belong to the child. Male-female sex, with all its surprises and unpredictability, is not a frivolous side issue for democracy. It is foundational for democracy.

For each citizen, how we were created is crucial in contextualising the rest of the declaration to follow. Each of us is created from the seed of a man and the egg of a woman. This makes us "equal". The rights that are inalienable to us are inalienable because they accrued to us when we were born. The inalienable rights listed are not exhaustive. "Among" the rights are life, liberty, and the pursuit of happiness. Other rights exist but are not named. We can infer those rights from the format of the paragraph. We identify such by seeing how we were "endowed" by the act of creation; in other words, what was "given" to us at birth. Whatever we own when we emerge from the womb and begin to *be* a "creature" or created being, is what can never be taken from us.

When we are born, we are naked. We own no clothes, no property, and no language, which makes it difficult for us to state our "consent", upon which governments derive their just powers. When we are born and know nothing, speak nothing, and own nothing, how can we consent to be governed?

The lines here present a conundrum. To be born a free citizen would seem impossible, because we must do something to achieve our free citizenship—consent to be governed—which is impossible to do as a newborn.

Let's go back to the question of what is inalienable from us. What do we own when we are born? At the moment of birth, to what are we entitled? We arrive, remember, from the body of a mother. She created us with the cooperation of a man, our father. These are the bare essentials that we own when we are born; we have a mom and a dad. Because they are our flesh and blood, they can consent on our behalf for us to be governed as free citizens. It is through this inalienable bond that we are able to do the impossible: be free and not even know it yet.

The other three listed rights—life, liberty, and the pursuit of happiness—derive from the first inalienable right, which is our birthright, our automatic entitlement to a mom and a dad, in essence the only thing we own when we begin to live. Just as government powers derive from the consent of the governed, so life and liberty and the pursuit of happiness derive from our natural-born right to a mom and dad, who must nurture us, teach us language, and endow us with the tools that make adult citizenship possible.

Our rights as free citizens hinge on sexual difference. Self-evidence is directly opposed to contrivance. It is self-evident that mothers are female and fathers are male. "Self-evident" means that if you change the words around, you still haven't changed observable reality. Call two men your two dads, and you've contrived a pseudo-truth but the self-evident truth is that those aren't your two dads. You have a mom and a dad somewhere.

Ethical adoption complicates this precept but does not nullify it. Not all adoption is good. Unethical adoption has been entangled with cultural genocides in the past, most notably, the American Indian cultural genocide. The 1978 law against adopting babies from American Indian reservations without exigent cause was written in recognition of the risks to free citizenship of too much adoption. Fathers and mothers are bound by the child's rights. The child's right compels them to care for the child they conceive wherever possible. When hard times require adoption, no drastic removes should ever be made. The baby came into the world with a mom and a dad, so those two entitlements must be restored by reconstitution in an adoptive home with a mom and a dad. Selling an abandoned baby to a chain gang or the circus is obviously not justified if there is, instead, a regular home with a mother and father willing to care for the child. The adoption can never be done in exchange for pay, because then the baby would not be born free. The baby would be alienably rather than inalienably bonded. That is to say, the bond between the baby and its caretakers would be contingent on money and not something granted by nature; hence it is an unstable bond that can be taken away or cancelled.

If you tinker with these inalienable rights, everything falls apart. If you displace a baby's mom so that the baby has two dads, you have begun the baby's life with denial of a self-evident truth. You have stripped the baby of one basic right, its ownership of a mom. From there, all the baby's rights fall apart. The discipline under which the baby will grow is not something to which the baby consented; its flesh and blood have been alienated from it, and with the alienation, the baby, lacking cognition or agency, becomes a mere animal, a chattel. The two men raising the baby have begun a basic tyranny, for they are not defined by the baby's right to own them, but rather, by their power to own the baby. Make such changes on a massive, sweeping scale—for instance, by pushing a national legal framework through which same-sex parenting is forcibly equated to natural parenting—and you will destroy the very basis of our republic. Not only this baby, but all babies become the property of people by whom they have not consented, by nature, to be governed. Their life is not an inalienable right, but a product designed for their owners, who are not their creators but rather their purchasers.

This is why I made the statement in Minnesota, when I testified on gay marriage before that state's legislature: "the transformation of all of us from free citizens born into the care of the man and woman who conceived us, into the property of whatever two adults have acquired us". People thought I was speaking gobbledygook.

Democracy is fragile. The question of where our rights come from can seem a murky matter. The contradictions of "free birth" are delicate and can splinter easily. Gay couples can love children by volunteering at youth clubs, mentoring, teaching, coaching, serving as foster homes, or doting on nephews and nieces. If they want someone to live with them who is theirs and nobody else's, they can always get a dog. They shouldn't try to own a child as if they were a mom and a dad bound by natural rights to a baby.

At issue here is "free" birth. Unfortunately, same-sex couples who want to own children undo the whole basis of our identity as free citizens. That's why I testified the way I did in Minnesota.

The tale of two amendments
If you peruse the briefs filed in the Supreme Court case *Hollingsworth v. Perry*, you will see that the Fourteenth Amendment is the main constitutional basis for the claim of an inherent right to marry. In the fall of 2012 there was much anticipation for the prospects of a Supreme Court ruling on same-sex marriage. Observers were heavily focused on the California case involving Proposition 8 (*Hollingsworth v. Perry*) rather than on the New York case involving the tax code (*U.S. v. Windsor*). As history played out, in fact, California's case was never decided by

the Supreme Court; rather, *Hollingsworth v. Perry* was sent back to the lower courts based on a technicality. It was the *Windsor* case that rather led to Justice Kennedy's historic decision on June 26, 2013, paving the way for a national wave of same-sex marriage.

In *Hollingsworth v. Perry*, the case was a different legal maze from *Windsor*. California had a constitution barring gay marriage, whereas New York had the opposite. No constitutional amendment had ever passed in New York to prevent same-sex marriage. Au contraire, New York's state legislature had legalised gay marriage in June 2011, with a vote of 33 to 29 "in a packed but hushed Senate chamber", according to the *New York Times*.[2] Had the Supreme Court decided on gay marriage using *Hollingsworth*, the justices would have been subordinating state law to the federal government, overturning a state constitution based on the federal constitution. In deciding on *Windsor*, the Court did the opposite: they invalidated a federal law (the Defense of Marriage Act of 1996) using New York's rights as a basis.

The Fourteenth Amendment was not as central in the *Windsor* decision, though it was involved. *Windsor* focused primarily on whether the government could withhold tax refunds to people in different states depending on whether their marriage was legal or not. *Hollingsworth* spoke to a different landscape. In the writ of *certiorari* submitted to the Supreme Court in 2012, petitioners hung all their hopes for gay marriage on one question: "Whether the Equal Protection Clause of the Fourteenth Amendment prohibits the State of California from defining marriage as the union of a man and a woman."[3]

The Fourteenth Amendment passed in 1868 and guaranteed to blacks "equal protection" under existing due process. While race is not mentioned in the text of the amendment, its historical *raison d'être* comes from the context of trying to protect freed black slaves. Scholar Mark Graber explains the genesis of the Fourteenth:

> Time quickly revealed that the constitutional ban on slavery did not adequately protect the fundamental rights of newly freed slaves. The Black Codes in the South demonstrated that, "notwithstanding the formal recognition by those States of the abolition of slavery, the condition of the slave race would, without further protection of the Federal government, be almost as bad as it would before." The

Fourteenth Amendment was designed to remedy those identified weaknesses in the rights protected by the Thirteenth Amendment [abolishing slavery].[4]

The 2004 documentary *Corporation* was produced by Mark Achbar and Jennifer Abbott. It expressed a sentiment—popular then and even now—to the effect that over time the Fourteenth Amendment was hijacked by corporations. Many progressives believe that the amendment has been abused because of nineteenth-century decisions that allowed corporations to assume the role of "individuals" and receive protections that were supposed to help black people.[5]

Progressives have persuasive reasons for lamenting the way corporations claimed to be "people" in order to siphon legal protections away from oppressed communities toward elite shareholders. The same lament should also apply to the ways in which the Fourteenth Amendment was hijacked to offer legal protection to gay couples interested in paying laboratories, adoption agencies, lawyers, and vulnerable parents for ownership of children. Banning slavery is meaningless if somehow the country finds a way to buy and sell human beings under a different title. That is unfortunately what is happening now with gay marriage.

Cases like *Plessy v.Ferguson* and *Brown v. Board of Ed.* produced a court history holding "separate" anathema to "equal". Gay activists have managed to argue—successfully, in the Ninth Circuit Court of Appeals—that civil unions or domestic partnerships are akin to racial discrimination, insofar as they target the gay race, assuming there is a gay race, for second-class citizenship by making "separate but equal" terms for marriage. To argue as much, activists have had to promulgate an entire ideology based on biological determinism. Within this logic, the only remedy is to offer people of the same sex "marriage" and all its rights without creating any distinctions, even to differentiate between relationships that are generally able to produce new human life, and those that are absolutely unable to. If certain marriages conferred the right to be parents as well as spouses, while other marriages did not come with such a presumption, then according to activists the equal protection clause of the Fourteenth Amendment would be violated. Therefore gays had to have equal access to children. Simultaneously and concomitantly children could not have equal access to their biological origins.

Many free-market libertarians now support gay marriage. This is perhaps because equating same-sex couples to male-female couples goes handinhand with equating corporations to people. Together these two dubious equivalencies open the way for a remarkable convergence of interests between the gay community and big business. Gay family-building depends on a highly organised market for acquiring sperm, eggs, wombs, and babies away from their biological progenitors and into the custody of "intended" gay parents. The sale of sperm, sale of eggs, farming of babies, and renting of wombs could all proceed smoothly under the free-market philosophy that drove the push to grant corporations Fourteenth Amendment rights. Whether intentionally or not, gay marriage's ascendancy under the Fourteenth Amendment will represent the ultimate triumph of neo-liberalism and corporate power. The last frontier will be conquered when businesses can patent not only DNA but also the humans who are born with such DNA, then sell them to couples whose ownership of people is protected under the Fourteenth Amendment. Both *Citizen Kane* and *Truman Show* were films about boys adopted by corporations. Gay marriage would be a major step toward making these fancies a reality.

The possible abuses of gay marriage law get even worse upon further reflection. At least when corporations emerged as the predominant force in the American economy after the Civil War, they were doing so as a replacement for the far worse slave plantation. Post-Civil War corporations arose and presented a solid counter-system against slavery, which had been abolished. Now we have a drift backward. Once corporate structures are used to buy and sell people, the corporation and the plantation are no longer polar opposites. They become metaphors for one another. Corporate capitalism is no longer the antidote to slavery, but the pinnacle of it.

The amendment preceding the Fourteenth bans "slavery" in all forms. This Thirteenth Amendment, glorified in Spielberg's film *Lincoln*, cannot survive if gay marriage becomes protected under the Fourteenth. In legal terms, gay marriage equality means that motherhood and fatherhood are effectively removed as principles from the entire nation's judicial system, replaced with "parenthood" based on intent, contract, and payment. With gay marriage equality decreed by the Supreme Court, there is no way for any State to express investment in the rational desirability for a child to be under the "custody" of those who conceived the child.

Instead, in order to comply with the Fourteenth Amendment, children would be placed under the control of two adults who acquired their rights to the child, either by taking it from someone else, uncompensated, using the force of the state; or by purchasing the child. In the former, the government becomes the means to pirate human bodies from their natural guardians, while in the latter, human beings are being bought and sold. In either case "slavery" is occurring, with very predictable social ills. A quick gloss on the history of human bondage that led to the Thirteenth Amendment is worth keeping in mind.

Much to the worry of philosophers from Aristotle to Rousseau, human beings are born helpless. They need the dominion of adults in order to survive and develop during childhood. Under whose dominion should babies and children fall? So long as marriage is defined as a husband and wife, the answer is relatively simple. Impressionable dependents are to be the charges of those who conceived them through lovemaking, first and foremost, before any other arrangement is decided upon by the state. Only under extraordinary measures would a biological father or mother be legally replaced by, and would his or her dominion be transferred to, a second mother or second father not biologically interested in the child. If the parents died, abandoned, or proved unfit for the child, then of course an adoption could occur. Otherwise, the force of the state would always, in a basic ethical sense, wish to avoid chattel slavery by prioritising the parental powers of actual parents, always by definition a man and a woman.

Slavery had existed for thousands of years before Samuel Sewall wrote "The Selling of Joseph" in 1700. This was arguably the first anti-slavery document in English. In some ways it is shocking that Sewall even thought to question the moral legitimacy of something that had always been taken for granted. He did question it, though. In this critical early text, Sewall lays out the basis for his new doctrine:

> Originally, and Naturally, there is no such thing as Slavery. *Joseph* was rightfully no more a Slave to his Brethren, then they were to him: and they had no more Authority to *Sell* him, than they had to *Slay* him.[6]

To understand what precisely was abolished in the Thirteenth Amendment, one must first see what the word "slavery" meant to people in the eighteenth and nineteenth centuries. It is tempting to picture physical degradation, racism, or violence. Labor is naturally part of slavery, so one might picture very difficult work, long hours under the hot sun, and massive cruelty from overseers.

If "slavery" always and only meant harsh physical conditions, then we would not have to worry about the burgeoning present-day practice of gay couples buying other people's offspring. We could point out that gay couples are actually adopting people into tidy upper-middle-class homes and emancipating them when they become adults, so there is no common ground whatsoever with the horrors that led to the Civil War and the Thirteenth Amendment.

Not so fast. All of the physical abuses we associate with slavery coincided with slavery, certainly, but they could also exist where slavery did not exist. One must consider what life was like for the vast majority who were free in the pre-industrialised world. Labour was hard. Discipline rather than gentle understanding was the rule of parenting. Corporal punishment was common in virtually all walks of life. People ate little. People died young. Husbands beat their wives. Mothers beat their children. Children beat each other. The world was a violent place, whether one was white or black, free or enslaved. The key line in Sewall's initial declaration against slavery involved the word "*Sell*". It was the exchange of money in return for control of another human being that defines—and *is*—slavery.

Citing Joseph as the example of slavery, Samuel Sewall is consciously choosing a well-known allegory. This choice comes from the book of Genesis. It offers us some guidance as to what "slavery" really means. Joseph was not born of a different race from that of those who sold him—he was sold, in fact, by his own brothers to his own cousins (the Ishmaelites, who later sold him to Egypt).[7] When he went to Egypt, Joseph did not remain a slave for his entire life. He was not only emancipated but also rose up to a high position under the Pharaoh. He is placed in charge of all Egypt.[8]

To the biblically trained minds of eighteenth and nineteenth-century abolition, slavery was not evil because it was physically difficult or racist. Slavery was evil because buying and selling people was evil. It did not matter if the purchase of a human being was done out of love, or to help oneself, or as an alternative to something worse for the slave. Today there are pundits who defend surrogacy and other same-sex parenting arrangements based on the idea that the "loving" nature of the gay home outweighs public apprehensions about buying children. They ought to retread the history of slavery to see how much they echo the great villains of America's haunted past.

By the mid-nineteenth century there had been plentiful examples of slavery apologists claiming that they loved black people more than abolitionists who often wanted to deport them back to Africa. The very first poetry collection published by an African American was *Poems on Various Subjects*, by Phillis Wheatley, who was a teenager when the volume came out in England in the 1770s. Included in her collection was "On Being Brought from Africa to America", a poem that began with the line, "'Twas mercy brought me from my pagan land."[9]

Imagine how many generations of readers took Phillis Wheatley's expression of thanks to her masters at face value and walked away believing that the lines reflected her feelings about her own situation and slavery in general. The fact that her master Wheatley was looking over her shoulder as she wrote did not compute with people until decades later when they saw other signs of slaves' discontentment. Are we to take at face value the testimony of a nineteen-year-old who declares, "I love my two moms", in front of state legislators who are debating over gay marriage? Are the moms watching?

There are innumerable passages in early black literature testifying that sometimes masters loved their slaves and at times slaves loved them back. Such passages appear more often than not in texts written by narrators who hope to show readers how deeply twisted slavery is, by showing how normal emotions like love are used for evil. Any inquiry into the tragedy of American slavery must incorporate a scathingly honest appraisal of the abuses justified by the phrase, "but I love them like my own family". The inherent antagonism between sentimentalism and abolitionism was a major preoccupation of the sixth chapter of my 2011 book, *Colorful Conservative: American Conversations with the Ancients from Wheatley to Whitman*. See this excerpt:

SLAVERY

The role of sentiment is somewhat contested in African American writing prior to *Uncle Tom's Cabin*. ... Most antebellum black writing was actually at odds with sentimentalism. ...

In 1836 black autobiographer Jarena Lee says that the Spirit becomes a garment and she is clothed in God's glory,[10] but she never goes so far as to echo William Blake and to say that the Deity resides in the human breast. Likewise in 1846 Zilpha Elaw says "like Enoch, I walked and talked with God" without a cloud to intervene,[11] but the Spirit does not come inside and stay inside; at each point Satan walks besides her and clouds her judgment, making it necessary for her to call upon God again and again. Thus in her mind it would never be safe to write "whim" on the lintel of her doorpost, as Emerson does in "Self-Reliance".[12]

For these writers, sympathy and sentiment are not always the means to find communion with the Holy Spirit. Religious black autobiographers often prefer deliberation to affection, echoing obliquely the taste for temperate reason that one finds in Sewall's work. Zilpha Elaw writes that "many in some parts of the United States ... readily sacrifice their intelligence to their prejudices, and possess more knowledge than wisdom".[13] The stirrings of the heart which Stowe deems transformative are problematic in Elaw's view—they might be passions and whim, closer to what Elaw calls "baubles of the skin" than to wisdom. When Stowe rejoices that "the heart of the dominant race" at last is "turned toward her [the Black race] in mercy",[14] she is locating spiritual deliberation among the heartstrings, seeing victory not as the subordination of prejudices in general but the replacement of an exploitative prejudice with a merciful one. This keeps the discourse of the Spirit on a level of sentimental appetites where Zilpha Elaw and many other African Americans are wary of engaging whites in discussion. What the heart feels may not always be love, and the heart's fickleness keeps it only one remove from the flesh. In William Wells Brown's slave narrative, he misses an important chance to run away, because the slavers are able to capitalise on his own affections toward his mother:

I looked into her face, as the tears coursed swiftly down her cheeks, and bursting into tears myself, said –

"No, I will never desert you and mother."

She clasped my hand in hers, and said–

"Brother, you have often declared that you would not end your days in slavery .... If we cannot get our liberty, we do not wish to be the means of keeping you from a land of freedom."

I could restrain my feelings no longer, and an outburst of my own feelings, caused her to cease speaking on that subject. In opposition to their wishes, I pledged myself not to leave them in the lands of the oppressor.[15]

The black writer often has to decide where to situate the "heart," when the heart is deployed as a means to dissuade him from escaping the system that keeps him in bondage. The Pauline attitude that imbues Thoreau and Equiano sometimes evolves into a differentiation between love, as the fulfillment of the law, and the fickle turns of the heart, belonging to the flesh. The body and the passions are most accessible to white violence, and least under black control.

Both theologically and pragmatically, earthly feelings are a hopeless route for social change. Henry Bibb issues his variation of Pauline philosophy when he says, "I felt as if I had too much at stake to favor either horse flesh or man flesh. I could indeed afford to crucify my own flesh for the sake of redeeming myself from perpetual slavery."[16]

The publication of William Wells Brown's *Clotel* in London, in 1853, demonstrated many of these tensions and differences surrounding white and black views about sentimentality. Not surprisingly, *Clotel* leans more toward the conservative distrust of sentiment. In Stowe's text, Miss Ophelia solves her impasse with Topsy by feeling affection and relaxing her rigid way of thinking. She must open her heart like little Eva and let herself be impassioned by Topsy's humanity, rather than deal with her according to the sober code of Northern decorum. For Brown, the matter is entirely different. In Brown's *Clotel*, sentiment is still secondary to a more cerebral enlightenment. In one key passage of Brown's novel, the white characters Carlton and Georgiana overhear slaves rejoicing upon her father's death, singing:

He's gone to where the slaveholders go.

Hang up the shovel and the hoe

Take down the fiddle and the bow,
We'll dance and sing
and make the forest ring,
With the fiddle and the old banjo.[17]

There is little need of decoding here: Georgiana hears the slaves jubilantly sending her father's soul to Hell. Georgiana must subdue her daughterly affection and listen, instead, to her intellect.

She tells Carlton, "it is from these unguarded expressions of the feelings of the Negroes that we should learn a lesson". Brown's text does not diminish the importance of feelings; one can learn lessons from them. But Georgiana cannot learn from the song if she gives in to her own heart, wherein dwells the love for her father. There is a time for emotion (the Negroes read their surroundings and know when to be unguarded), but ultimately the thinking mind has to be the organising and structuring force in Brown's model. This speech follows:

> you may place the slave where you please; you may dry up to your utmost the fountains of his feelings, the springs of his thought; you may yoke him to your labour and put him under any process which, without destroying his value as a slave, will debase and crush him as a rational being; you may do this and *the idea that he was born to be free will survive it all*. It is the ethereal part of his nature, which oppression cannot reach, it is a torch lit up in his soul by the hand of the Deity and never meant to be extinguished by the hand of man.[18]

Brown italicises the phrase beginning with *idea*. The part of the black person that cannot be reached by oppression is the thing that consumed Plato's and Hegel's philosophical pursuits: the idea, the conception. This, as in Thoreau, is the part closest to God and farthest from the animal flesh of man. Sober clarity is closely linked to honesty; the affections, to flattery and fancy.

When Brown refers to the perfidy of white men he sees intimate discourse with whites as an impasse. In virtually all the slave narratives from Equiano to Douglass, accounts include details of white tricksters defrauding the black subject of money or work. No promise, no compliment, no expression of goodwill is ever entirely past suspicion of irony or inversion. It is partly the artifice of polite speech that Zilpha

Elaw warns against when she tells readers to "give preference therefore to the Holy Scriptures", keeping guard against "the scavenger of scandal, the harlequin of character, the masquerade of morals and the burlesque of religion". She iterates that her vision of racial equality comes from an unbiased reading of the ancient Book of Acts, not an ideal of sympathy.[19] Given the black writer's fear of sophistry and emphasis on keeping the departure from ancient scripture to a minimum, Stowe's sentimentalism and her emotional glossary of Biblical text might have bordered, for Elaw, on the "harlequin of character ... and the burlesque of religion.[20]

Americans had already had sufficient examples of slaves expressing gratitude or other loving emotions toward their masters (and vice versa) and claiming to be happy in their condition. By the early nineteenth century objective visitors had figured out two caveats. First, even if they loved their masters, their masters were inflicting a grievous wrong on them, and the fact that they loved them made the entire atrocity more tragic. Second, nothing the slaves said about how they felt toward their masters could be trusted because they faced unspeakable horrors as retaliation for saying anything negative.

Not all Americans had the critical insight necessary to see through the multifarious ruses that characterised life in a pro-slavery society. If observers were to judge slavery according to the outward signs, they would probably conclude, as so many did, that slavery was a justifiable and even glorious act of caring for needy dependents who would not be able to survive on their own. In his famous *Narrative of the Life*, Frederick Douglass cautions about the inferences one might draw: "I have often been utterly astonished, since I came to the north, to find persons who could speak of the singing, among slaves, as evidence of their contentment and happiness. It is impossible to conceive of a greater mistake. Slaves sing most when they are most unhappy".[21]

Many casual visitors to a plantation could be tempted to conclude that the conditions there were not much worse than the deprivations forced on free labourers who had no security or regular access to health care. To arrive at an abolitionist ideology an American had to disbelieve cursory comparisons of physical conditions and turn cold to sentimental appeals. Buying people was wrong because it was unholy to reduce a human being—a child of God—to the same status as livestock, or worse, a piece of unthinking property. In Exodus, the freed Hebrews cry out repeatedly to return to the "fleshpots of Egypt" because they remember having more security when they were slaves. Moses has to push them to accept the vicissitudes of a harsh life as the price of freedom. This concept of slavery as an evil apart from questions of hygiene or physical comfort is crucial in understanding what the Thirteenth Amendment was targeting for abolition when it passed. It was not trying to ban hardship; it was trying to eliminate forever any arrangement where people were bought and sold.

Back in 1700, Samuel Sewall mentions the unclean conditions of the slave ships, but this reference comes after, and seems subordinate to, his reference to the shattering of natural relationships in a pro-slavery society:

> It is likewise most lamentable to think, how in taking Negros out of *Africa*, and Selling of them here, That which GOD has joyned together men do boldly rend asunder; Men from their Country, Husbands from their Wives, Parents from their Children. How horrible is the Uncleanness, Mortality, if not Murder, that the Ships are guilty of that bring great Crouds of these miserable Men, and Women.[22]

Slavery is unholy in Sewall's reckoning because of what the exchange of money does to human bonds. To honour contracts for the purchase of people, men have to be removed from their country, men and women who should build lives together are prevented from dwelling together, and children are taken away from their parents. Had gay marriage never become entangled with the need for institutions to transfer control of children from their parents to gay couples, then there would be less concern here. I would have never become such a staunch critic of same-sex marriage. Unfortunately, though, pro-gay advocates consciously conflated their fight for marriage and their seeking of parental rights over children who are not biologically theirs.

A classic example came in the Fifth Circuit Court of Appeals. In January 2015, attorney Roberta Kaplan emphasised that gay marriage had to be legal so that children of same-sex couples would not suffer the stigma of being raised out of wedlock. Thus reported the *Washington*

Times on hearings that took place in New Orleans:

> The Mississippi argument featured gay rights lawyer Roberta Kaplan, who famously won the landmark Windsor case that struck down the federal Defense of Marriage Act. Ms. Kaplan told the court that no "logic, common sense and even simple human decency" should cause them to deny kids of LGBT couples right to have married parents, according to Lauren McGaughy, a reporter for Houston Chronicle.[23]

Underlying Roberta Kaplan's argument is a profound sense of ownership on the part of the gay couple. They have acquired a child. They will control the child. Society must give the gay couple what *they* want. No distinction is even permitted between what the gay couple might want and what the child has a right to. This is the way owners speak about things they own. Rather than captivity or a hostage crisis, this is couched as love.

Courts tend to ignore altogether the problematic issue of how the children end up under the power of two adults, one or both of whom are not biological parents. Debates proceed as if the babies were dropped on gay people's doorsteps or children sprouted in cabbage patches in their backyard. The ugly reality of taking children away from other people through financial contracts or the invasive power of the state gets obscured by terms like "logic", "common sense", and "simple human decency". Advocates argue for gay marriage by saying it is necessary to formalise the parenthood of a gay adult who *got a child* by buying or seizing the child from an excluded biological parent. Gay marriage advocates are asking to roll back the Thirteenth Amendment by beating it down with the Fourteenth Amendment. It is not so much a constitutional crisis as it is a constitutional implosion. The Constitution's immune system is attacking its own organs.

Slavery plodded along in the United States' early history because colonists and antebellum Americans showed a similar reticence to speak directly to the ethics of buying and selling people. The Declaration of Independence and the U.S. Constitution both bear the marks of the young nation's agony over the persistence of this evil on their soil. Thomas Jefferson drafted a passage of the Declaration of Independence, which was famously taken out of the final document in order not to aggravate the signatories who depended on slave labour:

He has waged cruel war against human nature itself, violating its most sacred rights of life and liberty in the persons of a distant people who never offended him, captivating and carrying them into slavery in another hemisphere, or to incur miserable death in their transportation thither. This piratical warfare, the opprobrium of infidel powers, is the warfare of the Christian king of Great Britain. Determined to keep open a market where men should be bought and sold, he has prostituted his negative for suppressing every legislative attempt to prohibit or to restrain this execrable commerce.[24]

In a way similar to Samuel Sewall's, Thomas Jefferson's document mentions physical hardships ("incur miserable death") but hinges his condemnation of slavery on the essence of buying and selling people ("execrable commerce"). In the end, this passage did not matter because the other drafters had the lines erased from the document so slave-owners would not be confronted with such a hurtful attack on their livelihood and families.

Jefferson would be away in Paris when the Constitution was drafted. At that time, the framers struck a similarly cautious note on the slavery question, appeasing those who were sensitive about their dependence on slavery by avoiding the word itself. Article I of the Constitution states:

Representatives and direct Taxes shall be apportioned among the several States which may be included within this Union, according to their respective Numbers, which shall be determined by adding to the whole Number of free Persons, including those bound to Service for a Term of Years, and excluding Indians not taxed, three fifths of all other Persons.[25]

Slave owners felt they needed the government to reflect the added responsibility they bore for the care of the human beings they owned, but they compromised on having each slave count as a whole person for representation in Congress. Opponents to slavery were naturally resistant to allowing slave owners to count slaves as full people for the purpose of having more voice in Congress. The latter would offer an incentive to do more of what was already becoming a problem—enslavement—in order to hold more sway with the government. Rather than attack slavery as wrong, opponents got a small concession and deferred the issue. Lest free states start trouble with slave states by encouraging blacks to run away, Article IV of the Constitution stated that nobody "held to Service or Labour in one State, under the Laws thereof" could "be discharged from such Service or Labour, but shall be delivered up on Claim".[26]

The deferral broke down quickly, though. Twenty years later, William Wilberforce was forceful in pushing the issue of slavery toward the forefront of debate in Britain. As Matthew Mason points out, "In the spring of 1807, as Great Britain's Parliament and the U.S. Congress debated withdrawing from the trade, proponents of abolition in each body used national rivalry to their advantage. They urged their colleagues not to let the other nation seize the honor of acting first in this great cause."[27] Thomas Jefferson ended up having the honour of signing into law the abolition of the Atlantic slave trade.

The ending of the Atlantic slave trade was supposed to lead to a gradual dwindling of slavery and its inevitable disappearance. That didn't happen. To replace fresh shipments of new slaves, masters resorted to forced breeding. This way they replenished plantations once older generations died off. The appetite to own people was insatiable; the tricks used to perpetuate slavery seemingly infinite. The institution carried on, stronger than ever, for another six decades, thanks to the incipient and crude forms of today's artificial insemination, surrogacy, and baby farming.

The term "breeder" today is often used by gay men to describe heterosexuals. In antebellum America it meant a bondswoman used for forced conception of slaves to add to the master's bevy of human inventory. Frederick Douglass says of the awful Mr. Covey: "Mr. Covey was a poor man; he was just commencing in life; he was only able to buy one slave; and shocking as is the fact, he bought her, as he said, for *a breeder* ... After buying her, he hired a married man of Mr. Samuel Harrison, to live with him one year; and him he used to fasten up with her every night."[28]

Imagine the extent of suffering and wretchedness caused by the failure to have a direct and frank debate about the ethics of buying and selling people. Dancing around the issue with semantics and euphemisms contributed immeasurably to the scars wrought on the United States by slavery. Finally in the closing moments of the Civil War, the Thirteenth Amendment passed:

> Section 1. Neither slavery nor involuntary servitude, except as a punishment for crime whereof the party shall have been duly convicted, shall exist within the United States, or any place subject to their jurisdiction. Section 2. Congress shall have power to enforce this article by appropriate legislation.[29]

Note first of all that slavery is not limited to simply being forced to work against one's will. The phrasing is specific: "neither slavery nor involuntary servitude". The text reflects the American understanding that there was more to slavery than simply being made to do hard labour. Slavery was a larger system of buying, selling, and owning human life.

The text doesn't make an exception saying that children can be bought and sold as long as the purpose is the good-faith desire of loving adults to have a child that they can't conceive. The text does not state that as long as conditions are documented as decent, livable, even beneficial, it is appropriate to buy, sell, or own human beings. The Thirteenth Amendment had to be passed *because* the American republic, as well as other nations of the nineteenth century, determined that regardless of the qualify of life, the very idea of buying, selling, or owning human beings as property was harmful to society and a crime against humanity. It was an evil in and of itself.

Gay marriage is the single most prominent means of reversing the Thirteenth Amendment and bringing slavery back to the United States, even under many of the same guises. "Gays" have been deemed a race with biologically ordained rights not to share property with the opposite sex, as a result of the Fourteenth Amendment's being applied to their case. Simultaneously, the courts have warmed to the idea that gays cannot be guaranteed marriage equality in the fullest sense without also having the right to children. In fact, much of the argument for gay marriage has shifted to the demand that the state give "protections" to the children raised by same-sex couples. These "protections" amount to contracts that bind children to obey people who are not their parents. Hence gays are a race biologically ensured the right to buy and sell babies of the straight or mixed races. Like Southerners in antebellum America, gays have been given a pass on scrutiny since their peculiar situation requires that they set up families by purchasing people. In the South, the plantation was a way of life, "the way we are". For gays, homes assembled with other people's children are a way of life, "the way we are".

If gay marriage is given the full force of law, children are no longer the natural charges of mothers and fathers who conceived them through lovemaking. Rather, they are the property of two adults who have stolen or bought the power over such children—not only in the de facto sense of extraordinary circumstances arising (such as a divorce) *but in the de jure sense*. Gay marriage equality guarantees that the two adults who have bought a child can demand that the police, family court, schools, and other public powers use force, if necessary, to keep their charges under their control, should a child run away, misbehave, or be taken up by its excluded biological parent. Article IV of the original Constitution, with its warning not to "discharge" people bonded to others, is back, wrapped up with the need for "protections" for gay people's children. This is how the world got the case of *Dred Scott v. Sandford (which in 1857 upheld slavery)*, because slave-owners argued that for their full property rights as citizens to be respected by law, the state had to constrain charges who wanted not to be under their power.

The emerging gay community's sense of ownership over children is frightening. When Brittany Klein and I came forward with honest accounts of our difficult experiences growing up in the gay and lesbian community, the backlash against us was not merely condemnation. It consisted of hot pursuit and violent threats reminiscent of the ways masters caught runaways and brought them back to their plantation. The Human Rights Campaign literally issued a *Wanted* poster putting me "On Notice" and encouraging its 1.5 million members to hound me at my job or wherever they could find me. As the child of a lesbian, I was not a member of their community to be respected and heeded, but rather a sub-human pet to be whipped into submission for betraying my owners. It should not have surprised me as much as it did. A community that argues for their constitutional right to own human beings who are not really their children will fall prey to its own tyrannical hubris. Whether such "children" are fourteen or forty, the community feels entitled to control and punish them. Certainly they believe it is their right to silence them as if a blood contract bound gay couples' children to a lifelong gag order. After all, for many gay parents, there *is* a contract binding children to them in just such a manner.

All sense of interpersonal boundaries is lost in slavery; the division between the charge's thoughts and the owner's thoughts is blurred. The owner relates to the subordinate by way of a price, a legal boilerplate, and a list of what the owner wants. All of this strays dangerously far from the relationship between parent and child that exists when someone makes love and suddenly finds that a child is on the way. In the latter scenario, the child comes into the world by a schedule of nobody's choosing. The parents become parents at the same time that they realise that their urges have consequences and their ambitions have limits. Heterosexual parents learn, when they become parents, that life is not always about them. Gay parents learn, when they do, that life is *always* about them and children are part of the larger world that exists to satisfy them. That is what makes slavery evil. Not the racism. Not the hard labour. Not the whips and chains. It is the destructive arrogance of believing that people *belong to you*, especially if you have paid for them.

Notes

1 Declaration of Independence, ed. William E. Cain, *American Literature Part I* (New York: Penguin, 2004), 346-350.
2 Nicholas Confessore and Michael Barbaro, "New York Allows Same-Sex Marriage, Becoming Largest State to Pass Law", *New York Times,* NY Region (June 24, 2011) www.nytimes.com (Accessed January 9, 2015).
3 Supreme Court of the United States, Petition for a Writ of Certiorari, *Hollingsworth v. Perry,* (July 30, 2012), i.
4 Mark A. Graber, "Subtraction by Addition?: The Thirteenth and Fourteenth Amendments", *Columbia Law Review* 112, no. 7 (November 2012), 1501-49.
5 Mikela Jay and Rob Beckwermert, *Corporation,* Directed by Mark Achbar and Jennifer Abbott, Big Picture Media Corporation, 2004.
6 Samuel Sewall, "The Selling of Joseph: A Memorial", Massachusetts Historical Society, Collections Online (June 24, 1700) www.masshist.org (Accessed January 9, 2015).
7 Genesis 37:28.
8 Genesis 41:41.
9 Phillis Wheatley, "On Being Brought from Africa to America", posted at www. poemhunter.com. (Accessed January 12, 2015).
10 Jarena Lee, *Life and Religious Experience of Jarena Lee,* in *Sisters of the Spirit,* ed. William L. Andrews (Bloomington: Indiana University Press, 1986), 29.

[11] Zilpha Elaw, *Memoirs*, in *Sisters of the Spirit*, ed. William L. Andrews (Bloomington: Indiana University Press, 1986), 67.

[12] Ralph Waldo Emerson, "Self-Reliance", in *Selected Writings of Emerson*, ed. Donald McQuade (New York: Modern Library, 1981), 133.

[13] Zilpha Elaw, *Memoirs*, 85.

[14] Harriett Beecher Stowe, *Uncle*, 3.

[15] William Wells Brown, *Narrative*, 386.

[16] Henry Bibb, *Narrative of the Life*, in *Slave Narratives*, eds. William L. Andrews and Henry Louis Gates Jr. (New York: Library of America, 2000), 534.

[17] William Wells Brown, *Clotel*, 134-5.

[18] William Wells Brown, *Clotel*, 135.

[19] Zilpha Elaw, *Memoirs*, 52.

[20] R.O.P. Lopez, *Colorful Conservative: American Conversations with the Ancients from Wheatley to Whitman* (Lanham, MD: University Press of America, 2011), 217-220.

[21] Frederick Douglass, *Narrative of the Life of Frederick Douglass, An American Slave, Written by Himself* (Boston: Anti-Slavery Office, 1845), republished in: Eds. William L. Andrews and Henry Louis Gates, Jr., *Slave Narratives* (New York: Library of America, 2000), 267-368; .

[22] Samuel Sewall, "Selling of Joseph".

[23] Cheryl Wetzstein, "Gay marriage arguments heard in 5th Circuit", *Washington Times*, News (January 9, 2015) www.washingtontimes.com (Accessed January 9, 2015).

[24] Thomas Jefferson, draft of Declaration of Independence, from *Autobiography of Thomas Jefferson*, excerpted in William Cain, ed., *American Literature Vol. I* (New York: Penguin Books, 2004), 346-50.

[25] Constitution of the United States, in ed. Jack N. Rakove, *Founding America: Documents from the Revolution to the Bill of Rights* (New York: Barnes & Noble Classics, 2006), 397-409.

[26] Ibid.

[27] Matthew Mason, "Keeping up Appearances: The International Politics of Slave Trade Abolition in the Nineteenth-Century Atlantic World", *William and Mary Quarterly 3rd Series* 66, no. 4 (October 2009), 809-32. Pg. 809.

[28] Frederick Douglass, *Narrative*, 324.

[29] Constitution of the United States.

Chapter Nineteen

INHUMANITIES

Robert Oscar Lopez

Address for the European Bioethics Institute
Brussels, November 26, 2014
[Translated from French to English]

I would like to thank the organisers of this conference. It is a great honor for me to be here because only six days ago we celebrated the International Day of the Child. On November 20, 2014, I spoke in Washington, DC, on the subject of the importance of children's rights. One of the great problems that poses challenges for us is academic, even disciplinary. Here I do not speak of disciplines in the terms of punishment or chastisement. I speak rather of intellectual discipline.

How can we confirm that there exists something called a child's right? How can we know whether the right has been violated? This is a type of epistemological mystery: how do we know what we know and how do we diffuse our knowledge to others?

In speaking of the child's rights in the Anglophone context things get complicated. There is a lot of confusion about the term "children's rights". This term is sometimes reduced to its strictly epidemiological meanings. Those who fight for children's rights who use the title in English are very worried about issues such as child poverty, physical abuse, health, vaccinations, and the like. Very often these experts take aim at "justice" while basing their objectives on statistics and figures: the percentage of children who finish their studies, their grades, the proportion of children who suffer from illnesses be they physical or mental. This positivist emphasis lacked, for the most part, a vocabulary with which to doubt or question the philosophy behind the figures.

Among childhood advocates, in the name of reducing child poverty, scholars give great preference to wealthy parents and communities. That is to say, in light of the fact that rich people may buy more things for their children, if an expert measures the differences among children he will decide that rich people's children are happier, more acceptable, more representative of all that society seeks in its idealism. Wealthy people's children have better grades, fewer sicknesses, tidier bedrooms. These statistics are "proof" of the happiness designated by statistical experts.

There are those children's rights advocates who support abortion, transsexual surgery, and same-sex parenting because the studies find figures that confirm, analytically, that these events are "better" for children or at least "just as good". Hence children who are affected by such life decisions "do better" or "do just as well" in general.

We must say that this generation of children's rights experts arrived at their conclusions by way of social sciences, avoiding philosophy, history, and letters. Thus I will pose the question: how does it enlighten us to measure happiness in a child with a tally? What is the worth of reducing a child's life to a ponderous mathematical equation? My subject here introduces into the heart of our debate the forgotten voices of philosophy, history, and letters.

Two years ago, in France, something very different began under the name of *droits des enfants,* something rather at odds with "children's rights" in the Anglophone context. Protesters began to say "no" to ideas, to which scholars were saying, "yes". At the core of this battle between the academic and the popular, we have a chance to ask: Why such a huge difference between points of view? Can one impose an academic science on and against popular common sense? For common sense in France was deeply opposed to surrogacy.

I will argue that the populace can resist academic pressure and the pressure of political correctness. I find it absolutely necessary. There are three very powerful lobbies exported by Americans: the artificial reproduction lobby, the adoption industry, and LGBT groups. All three perceive a benefit either economic or social in weakening the ties between the child and his biological parents. All three have many liberal allies in American universities, who provide a large number of experts who feed rhetoric to the liberal governments of countries now deemed "progressive". Note that in 2013, there were massive advances of this deracinated vision of children in England, the United States, and France. It was purposeful that these three nations, seen so widely as lodestars for human rights and the academic humanities, would all be overwhelmed simultaneously by scholarly claims devoted to uncoupling children from their natural origins.

Najat Vallaud-Belkacem (French minister of women's rights), Pierre Bergé (leading socialist financier), and Christiane Taubira (French attorney general), were telling the people that social science was *on their side*. They said with much confidence that there existed a consensus in the United States and the consensus is: children with or without their biological mother and father score high on happiness indexes, especially if they are raised in comfort. And if one accepts that a child is a measurable index and that it is possible to place the child's worth into a mathematical equation, well, they were right.

In the United States, there are several associations relevant to this topic: The American Sociological Association, American Association of Pediatrics, American Medical Association, many adoption and foster care groups, the American Psychiatric Association. All these influential groups agreed upon certain "studies". They added up arbitrary indicators, which they classified as "health" and "happiness" factors—and in Australia, for example they reported that after studying 500 children of same-sex couples, many conceived through surrogacy, the scientists had to conclude that gay homes produced happier children.

Now, there was something troubling in these tendencies: We were speaking effectively about selling and buying human life, biomaterials, and even children. In the United States with a heavy history of slavery one would expect more forbearance and circumspection. But it wasn't so. The social sciences were comfortable justifying the purchase and sale of children.

In America, these notions went without much resistance. In France it was different. Since I do a lot of work in both countries, I wonder why. Let me explain how I got into this debate: I speak French because as an adolescent I spent time in a youth school on the border of Québec. In

2012 there were some Catholics who read the Vatican's references to a text written by Gilles Bernheim, the French grand rabbi. They asked me to translate the text. I found a very interesting argument against same-sex parenting expressed by a tradition that was Talmudic and Judaic more than scientific. Due to my work as a translator, there were people in France who discovered my personal story, including my childhood with a lesbian mother and my writings based on my experiences. But more important than my biography would be my work as a humanities scholar, trained in Greek and Latin, and tutored in the theories of Michel Foucault, Gilles Deleuze, and many other French philosophers with much influence in the US.

Having had a lesbian mother is important to mention when I fight for children's rights but it is equally important that there are intellectuals who use the full range of art and literature to give to the discussion a breadth and rigor *outside of figures, outside of social sciences*.

Surrogacy is the buying and selling of children. That is what it is. But we must keep on searching for the best possible means of explaining the deep consequences of this practice.

We must first remind ourselves that money too is a system of numbers. Many people who wish to legalise the merchandising of procreation are rich, because the rich have the money necessary to buy children. Hence the social sciences do favour the richest lobbies. And maybe it is ironic, but supposedly the Left is the side that is supposed to keep eye on abuses by the rich; the Left is supposed to care about the poor. In this case the Left is remiss.

If we step out of the mindset of the social sciences, we can drift into literature, philosophy, art, and history; there we find copious evidence that the human being has an eternal desire to come into a family without being bought or manufactured. Every boy and every girl has a natural yearning for a father and mother. The human being is irresistibly drawn to his own origins — this is the very reason for history as an art and as a discipline. The question is posed constantly: "Where did I come from? Why do I exist?" History shows three graphic examples of suffering because of the human error of disrespecting these eternal desires: slavery, cultural genocide against the Indians, and eugenics.

Until now the American conservative mainstream has taken control of the project of defending the family. They made the error of trying to resist the merchandising of the child by citing more studies and more social science. The overreliance on the study by Mark Regnerus suggests itself as an obvious example. Social-science studies are not the main way to make conclusions about human dignity, and how it is encroached upon in the way children are placed.

Here the problem is something I discussed at the Université d'Eté in Paris in September 2013. The right was actually in agreement with our left wing, concerning a positivist vision of the world: the liberal vision comes together with the progressive vision and locks up the discourse for the free market.

In truth, regardless of what social science can do for good, it is not on our side in resisting surrogacy. At least, social science does not help us if it is our only plane of discussion. We must look to art, trans-historic literature, history, and philosophy, because we must express in concrete terms what we know by instinct. Even if a child is sold by his poor mother to a stable and rich couple, even if that child has better grades, earns more money, and scores higher on happiness tests, this is not a measure of true happiness. There are always unjust impacts that become irreparable—denial of origins, separation from a parent, abandonment, sale, purchase, or conception of a human being in a test tube without love … These cause a spiritual wound that comes from having been an object, having been sold.

This work of explanation falls upon translators, writers, professors— the bards of the world. And thus I have come upon the work that I do. I have gathered a team of experts in literature, law, philosophy, history, and the like, from seven nations: England, France, Belgium, Switzerland, Italy, China, and the United States. On October 3 we launched an institute and brought to light the research of 120 scholars in Los Angeles, who made eighty exhibits on the culture of antiquity and nineteenth-century culture, in order to visualise the natural reality against which four modern tendencies strike: surrogacy, sperm donor conception, divorce, and adoption. This evening we speak of surrogacy but there are other links between surrogacy and these related trends. I would like to bring to your attention three of the sources that researchers presented among their eighty exhibits. What do the humanities tell us about surrogacy?

First let us consider Oedipus. Was Sigmund Freud right when he said the play symbolises incest? Perhaps, but also there are other levels on which to read the text. The problem for Oedipus was that his biological father abandoned him and he was raised elsewhere without knowing his origins. His real identity was taken away by his family, supposedly for his own good. But he lives in confusion with fragmented filial relations. When he kills his father he does not recognise that *it is his father*, and when he sleeps with his mother he does not know who she is. The broken tie of *filiation* is the cause of his fall.

Then let us consider Bacchus in Ovid's *Metamorphoses*. He is born of Jupiter's thigh. According to Ovid, the birth of Bacchus is the result of a cruel tragedy. His mother Semele was a mortal who had an affair with Jupiter. Because of Juno's jealousy she died in a horrible lightning accident. Jupiter seizes the egg from the cinders of the dead woman, and plants the embryo in his leg to gestate. This myth describes surrogacy: Semele gave her ovum so that Jupiter could have a child; she also gave her life. Jealous Juno erases forever the woman who gave the child half his origins to protect her marriage. The message of the myth is that this means of having a child while doing away with the mother is always a horror carried out by cruelty. In effect Juno contrives Semele's violent death by burning. From Bacchus's point of view, his mother was burnt alive by this father's wife.

Lastly, consider the case of *Uncle Tom's Cabin*, the most popular book in the United States in the nineteenth century. Many historians give this book the honor of having incited the Civil War, which ended with the emancipation of American slaves. But which is the passage that's most emblematic and unforgettable for us Americans? It is when Liza knows that if she does not escape with her baby, the slavers will take the child away to sell to another. She jumps from ice block to ice block across the river between Ohio and Kentucky during winter, with the babe in her arms. This is the image of the mother who refuses to lose her flesh and blood—the image that always embodied in starkest terms the evil of slavery. In 1700 Samuel Sewall, the first American abolitionist, cited three crimes as the gravest of slavery, and among these violence and racism are not counted. He cited three separations: that of children from parents, men from women, and people from their origins. Thank you.

Chapter Twenty

THE SIREN'S SONG

Robert Oscar Lopez

I respect Dr. Michael Brown and like a lot of what he writes. But I want to look critically at his column in *Charisma*, where he laments Governor Jerry Brown's signing of a law that will replace the words husband and wife with "spouse":

> Note to California: A woman cannot be a father and a man cannot be a mother. Further note to California: The terms "husband and wife" are neither discriminatory nor outdated. Further, further note to California: Your social experiment will fail. I do not deny that there are same-sex couples who love each other deeply and who are committed to each other long-term, and I do not deny that there are same-sex couples who are absolutely devoted to their children. I am simply pointing out that their union cannot rightly be called "marriage" (regardless of what the courts might say) without rendering foundational words and concepts meaningless, a sure recipe for cultural chaos. To repeat: The implications of redefining marriage are staggering, and those of us who love and cherish marriage and family need to redouble our efforts and renew our courage to stand up for what is right and what is best, making a fresh determination to swim against the current flood tide of semantic and social confusion. True marriage and family will prevail in the end.[1]

I like the confidence when Brown states unequivocally "a woman cannot be a father and a man cannot be a mother."

But then why say, "I do not deny that there are same-sex couples who are absolutely devoted to their children"?

First of all, this is not true. Who are "their" children? To whom does a child in a same-sex couple's home belong?

The statement about loving same-sex couples with children can't be true if we follow the premise that a woman cannot be a father and a man cannot be a mother. Same-sex couples know they won't have their own kids when they begin a lifelong commitment to each other. They chose to acquire someone else's kid anyway, effectively inflicting a double whammy on a helpless child.

Whammy No. 1: The child has been forcibly cut off from at least one of the parents who gave the child life.

Whammy No. 2: The child is being held captive under the faux parental authority of at least one adult who is not the child's parent.

Let's say one of the same-sex adults is the biological parent of the child. What right does the other gay adult have to expect the child to provide filial affection, obey orders, and honor that person? The unrelated gay adult has no right to expect the child to love him/her as a parent. That gay adult has no right to tell that child what to do. *That gay adult is not the child's parent.* The child is essentially being held prisoner and in servitude to an adult who acquired but did not conceive the child.

This is increasingly not a case comparable to traditional adoptions, since in almost all cases of same-sex parenting, the infliction of a non-related parent onto the child's life was a bureaucratic and legal act executed to suit the needs of the two adults, not to meet any pressing need on the part of the child, and in no way to serve the child's best interests.

How is it anyone's best interests to have someone extra thrust into the person's life and given authoritative power over everything the person does, including bedtime, leisure time, chores, whose birthday to celebrate, who can come over for "play dates", and the ilk? If you don't have a boyfriend but a man inserts himself into your life and starts saying he is your boyfriend and forcing you to call him your boyfriend based on his desire for you, and contrary to your impulses, this is called stalking, rape, or abduction. If someone—let's call him Mr. Miles—is not your employer and you never worked for the person, but Mr. Miles shows up, tells you to work for him, tells the whole world he's your boss, and implicitly threatens to deny you food and shelter unless you say, "yes, he's my boss", does it matter that Mr. Miles really wants to be your boss and therefore you are "wanted"? Would anyone call that situation a loving workplace? Probably not, since they would be too busy trying to figure out what seems like trafficking, enslavement, imprisonment, or captivity.

For some reason the parent-child relationship escapes the ethical and legal safeguards that protect us from rape, stalking, captivity, and slavery. The basis for same-sex parenting and the claim that these couples "love" "their" children rests upon the notion that subordinate children can be coerced into emotional relationships in a way that others in society cannot be coerced. The side statement made by Michael Brown—"I don't deny that same-sex parents are absolutely devoted to their children"—negates the real issue in its rush to clear the way for the moral question of homosexuality and gender conformity. That "a woman cannot be a father" only matters because, from a child's point of view, the imposition of a non-related lesbian parent onto the child amounts to a parental version of "stalking". The fact that she's a lesbian matters too much to Dr. Brown while the fact that she has no business forcing herself upon the child's life matters too little to him.

Homosexuality is like the siren on a seaside rock, luring rhetorical sailors to their doom again and again. Something about the topic of homosexuality makes even sensible and well-intended people lose their focus, forget children, forget human rights, and obsess about the titillating but emotionally charged (and draining) question of a man sleeping with a man or a woman sleeping with a woman. On cue, opponents of same-sex marriage lose sight of the child's stake in the question and drift toward what really excites them: the glamour of sin and sex, the erotic matter of whether adults of the same sex really ought to be doing the things in the bedroom that we all know they are doing. The moral question of homosexuality can be a bottomless pit of discussion: once you fall into it, you can plummet into a darkness and can never come out. Meanwhile, the children who are the ones who have a true stake in the debate are forgotten with the thoughtless caveat, "gee, I can't deny that the two same-sex adults who are forcing you to live in their home based only on their tyrannical desire to own you love you and are perfectly entitled to keep you there. Let me get back to the main issue, which is that I think what they do in bed is disgusting and we shouldn't let them get married."

Of course, with arguments like these the LGBT lobby slaughtered the traditionalists in court. I might have decided the way some of the judges decided in the gay marriage cases, had I had to listen to hours of this argumentation and read through thousands of pages of our side's briefs. At the core, the disproportion in their focus betrays a lack of coherent reasoning: *If you think gay couples are good parents and ought to have children, then why the heck can't they marry?* The tiny concession seems thrown out as a throat-clearing preamble so that we can move on to the more popular question of whether homosexuality is a sin. Except that the preamble is not that tiny. It destroys the legitimacy of people who argued against gay marriage.

Sometimes, too, I cannot help the nagging feeling that our side deserved to lose. Why did they spend so many waking hours campaigning against gay marriage and do so little about gay adoption or artificial reproduction? Why did they go missing on divorce, often not even wanting to have a national debate on the topic? Why have they been so silent on the reform of adoption and foster care?

I have asked these questions but I have always feared the answer. The answer, I suspect, is exactly what our critics have alleged: they care disproportionately about stopping men from having sex with men and women from having sex with women. They are debilitated by their crushing obsession with homosexuality as a moral question.

The old adoption dodge
Oh wait, the gay parenting enthusiasts are going to bring up adoption in the old dodge: *What if there is a baby that nobody wants, and the only way for the baby to have a loving home is to be adopted by a gay couple?*

Let's just take care of the dodge before we continue: No such baby exists anywhere on earth. There are long waiting lists of heterosexual couples that want to adopt. There are 101,000 children in foster care waiting to be adopted, of various ages. But 12-15% of heterosexual couples who want children find it impossible to conceive because of infertility; in fact over one million women in such couples seek infertility treatments each year.[2] Add to this the huge number of fertile heterosexual couples who are also willing to adopt, and you reach the conclusion that the baby who needs to be adopted out to a gay couple is a figment of gay parenting advocates' imagination.

You will never run out of heterosexual adopters. You will never run out of heterosexual foster parents. You will never need to give a ward of the state to a gay couple. Ever. Unless you are doing the gay couple a favour. Which you should not.

These are the main ways that gay couples acquire children (remember, they must always acquire someone else's child, even if one member of the couple is a biological parent):

(1) One of the gay lovers had a heterosexual relationship and then after the heterosexual opposite-sex parent of a child died or wasn't in the relationship anymore, the parent came out as gay, jumped into a relationship with a new gay lover, and then got legal custody of the child.

(2) The gay couple bought biomaterials through a fertility clinic or surrogacy broker and paid to manufacture their child through a contract binding the child to be in servitude to both gay adults even though one is not actually the child's parent, and also forbidding the opposite-sex provider of half the child's identity from being loved, respected, or obeyed by the child as the actual parent.

(3) The gay couple went to an adoption agency knowing that there were other homes that had a mother and father in it willing to adopt, and the gay couple just pushed to get someone else's child anyway.

Doesn't all that sound ugly? It is ugly.

These are not people who are absolutely devoted to their children. Not in the least. They are mistreating children. They are forcing children into a Cinderella syndrome, having to do chores for a step-parent, or they treated their child like property to be bought and sold, or they basically gamed the system to force the child into their custody when they were not the best home.

Why didn't opponents of gay marriage ever deal with this issue up front?

So let's get back to my main point about Michael Brown's article. Why do so many opponents of same-sex marriage make the mistake that Michael Brown makes here? Why do they shrink from calling out same-sex parenting for the abusive practice that it is? Do they think that gay couples are going to be softened up and won't be as hostile? Why on earth would a gay couple be more open to your telling them that they make good parents and ought to have children, but just shouldn't be allowed to get married because that's "against your beliefs"? Of course they want to tell you off. Of course they go and try to sue your bakery, photography studio, or floristry. You're telling them, in fact, that what they're doing to kids *is okay*, but according to you the problem is that *they are a gay couple*.

That's doubly offensive, because it shows disregard for the children forced into these people's homes, and then places us in the position of intruding into the consensual loving relationship between two adults.

A tale of two California certificates

So it is less important that the Governor of California eliminates the words "husband" and "wife" from marriage certificates. Even if he calls them "spouses", we all know what husbands and wives are, apart from what the government says. Folks may be morally outraged, but the fallout of such a change in human relationships is still relatively limited to the two adults who are choosing to engage in the act.

I *do care* about the fact that when Dr. Brown wrote this, in California there was another bill pending—AB 1951—which was to allow male mothers and female fathers on birth certificates. That's the bill that people should have been upset about, yet people aren't talking about it enough.

I wrote a letter urging the governor to veto AB 1951. My letter had no effect. But my reason for opposing the birth certificate bill was deliberate. Changing the birth certificate language means violating a child's human rights. To have two male parents or two female parents on a birth certificate is a blatant lie. It makes the birth certificate a bill of sale. It forces the child to grow up not knowing his or her own origins. And it makes the child a prisoner/captive/slave of at least one adult who isn't actually the child's parent and therefore has no business demanding obedience and love from the child.

Yet all along, people who argue against gay marriage get infinitely more riled up about the immorality or "confusion" involved in what the two gay adults do in their bedroom, instead of the self-evident fact that gay "parents" aren't really parents, but rather people who are forcing other people's children into an emotional relationship with them and holding them captive.

This is a major problem. I don't know what more I can do. I don't think this inconsistency in the traditional marriage side comes from malice. It just comes from a lack of attention to children in the entire debate.

People who oppose gay marriage still tend to oppose it because they do not want men sleeping with men or women sleeping with women. They mention children, but usually as a last-ditch effort to knock down gay marriage. They make a few arguments about the importance of mothers and fathers, cite a few studies that measure whether kids "do better" (whatever that means) in straight or gay homes, and then print a few signs with messages like "every child deserves a mom and dad" or "children do best with a mom and dad" or "children need a mom and dad".

But then while they are waving these signs, they are also saying, for some reason, that they believe gay people can be loving parents. Often this is because they are just as susceptible to the charm offensive of cute gay family photographs as anybody else is. Or they feel guilty because they are divorced or abandoned a child. Or they have a sister or neighbor who went to a sperm bank and they feel bad saying that she and her lesbian lover don't love their kid. Or they worry about offending their friends who are single parents or adopted children.

Whatever the cause, I can't blame the American public for being bewildered and inferring that opposition to gay marriage is really all about opposing homosexuality itself.

Guess what, folks: not every child does best with a mom and dad (there are lousy parents and sometimes kids are better off being rescued from them). Not every child feels the need for a mom and dad (some kids, like me for instance, are just resilient in the face of everything life throws at them, and they do fine without the traditional configuration). *But every child has a mom and dad.* The child has a relationship, at birth, to a man and a woman who gave the child life. Those two people give the child gametes, an identity, origins, and a cultural framework. The child is entitled to know those people and must receive their love and support. If one of the people dies, the child is entitled to know where the remains are kept, to visit the site and reflect upon the child's origins. No ifs, ands, or buts about it. Other people do not have the right to replace those people unless there is an adoption carried out because the biological parents cannot look after the child, and it had better be an urgent situation as opposed to some glorified captivity narrative. No child should be forced to treat a non-parent like a parent, because that is the filial equivalent of stalking.

Modern captivity narrative: alternative families

The only legitimate adoptions are ones that take place when a tragedy has severed the child's bond to mother and father. The adoptive family must then restore to the child precisely what the child lost, namely a mother and father. Any other kind of adoption that takes place to suit two people who want a child, whether it's due to infertility or homosexuality or cupidity, is unethical, because it unfairly renders a child subject to the power of someone who isn't a parent.

You can't force someone to marry you because you love them. You can't force someone to have sex with you because you love them. You can't force someone to call you a parent because you love them, when in fact you are not their parent. Only in a handful of cases involving ethical adoption would such a transfer of love be appropriate. Gay people can be doting aunts and uncles, helpful babysitters, inspirational coaches, foster guardians to help kids until parents get back on their feet, loving neighbours. Gay people may marry the opposite sex and conceive children to live in a home with a mom and dad.

But a gay couple cannot raise a child and be considered "absolutely devoted" to the child. Having the child under their power is an abuse of adult strength and a misuse of state authority. It's not devotion of any kind, rather cruelty and selfishness. So stop going easy on same-sex parenting. There is little that can be done about the kids who are already living with gay couples. Their gay guardians probably won't let them read what I am writing right now. And even if they did read this and felt hurt, that hurt would not compare to the wrong done to them already by two adults who took advantage of their child-like helplessness and cut them off from half of where they came from.

Once you surrender your logic and place disproportionate emphasis on adults' sexual hang-ups rather than the rights of children, you begin the process of losing the gay marriage debate.

The supporters of gay marriage will seize upon your statement that "gay couples can be absolutely devoted to their children" and they will press that issue, beating you over the head with it, until you end up having to concede that if they are doing a great thing for children, letting them get married is probably best for the child since what's good for devoted parents is probably best for the children to whom they are absolutely devoted.

During the whole gay marriage debate, kids lost out because nobody put them first. Gay marriage advocates used them for photo ops. Gay marriage opponents spent more time worrying about what adults do sexually and didn't ask themselves if their slogans made any sense from the child's point of view.

That's why in this war over gay marriage, everybody lost.

Notes

[1] Michael Brown, "I Now Pronounce You Spouse and Spouse", *Charisma News,* Opinion (July 14, 2014) www.charismanews.com (Accessed January 12, 2015).

[2] For links to some of the sources for these figures, I suggest two places to start. First my piece on *American Thinker* about gay adoption: Robert Oscar Lopez, "On Gay Adoption, S.E. Cupp is out to Lunch", *American Thinker (*April 24, 2014) www.americanthinker. com (Accessed January 12, 2015). Also, see: Jennifer Wolff Perrine, "Many couples struggle with infertility in silence", NBC News, Women's Health (August 5, 2010) www.nbcnews.com (Accessed May 10, 2014).

Conclusion

Brittany Klein

We have used the story of Jephthah's daughter as a kind of pulse point throughout this book. It is often overlooked, as are many of the issues we have tried to address.

It seems to follow then that I start my discussion of Judges 11 from an unusual place—not to deflect from any discussion of Judges 11 but because I started from an unusual place. I was raised in the gay community in the 1970s: those pre-AIDS days, that one long party that spilled over to the suburbs. On the painted side of the white picket fences other people were also having good times: doctors, lawyers, their wives. The cool people were swinging and drinking Sangria. I wish I lived with them. As I remember it there was no culture of hate or homophobia. The dominant attitude that had taken root among the educated was "live and let live".

By the middle of the decade there was The New York Dolls (the American hard rock band) before they became well known. The hippies had receded and everything had a sharper "gay" and urbane edge. For the sake of survival I had to learn to empty a lot of ashtrays and clean up messes because the adults around me sprawled in bed until three in the afternoon. Sometimes I hated them but I kept my mouth shut. I knew even then if I opened up, I would not stop. Readers will be relieved to know that I have acquired restraint on the page.

The guiding themes in Judges 11 are obviously judgement, or lack thereof, and sacrifice. We all have judgement. Some of us have poor judgement or rash judgement. Popular culture tells us judgement is wrong despite the fact it is needed to survive. The other main issue in the text is even less popular. Sacrifice does not play well in a culture dominated by entitlement. The idea of sacrifice as enacted in the Biblical narrative is too often seen either through the limits of theology by true believers or through the opposing ideological positions and impulses that push against dominant theology by the doubters or the rebels. I think in order to begin to see the nuance here of "killing your own kid", which indeed is not nuanced, we need to look at both the idea of judgement and the idea of sacrifice.

Love and other platitudes

The story that best illustrates judgment and sacrifice is the story of the two women who come before King Solomon. Each woman claims to be the mother. One of these women has rolled over in her sleep and killed her own infant. His dilemma is obvious. There is only one mother. The "other" woman who is not the mother sees the baby as a possession, something she wants very badly. She is grief stricken at the loss of her own baby; and she *wants* a baby and we feel for her in this. She feels entitled because she "loves" the baby and her "love" makes it hers. Well no.

Unfortunately there is a cruelty born out of selfish desire here in this mother's love. She is willing to have the child cut in half and killed because she "loves". While both women may in fact love the baby one will sacrifice and suffer the loss because she realises the baby is a living human and not a possession—that one is the mother. So love is not the end-all and be-all. Stalkers also love their victim. And their feeling of "love" does not make them wanted additions in the victim's life. The solution Solomon offers is to cut the baby equally in half and give each woman her half. Enforced equality, so to speak. It does not take much to see that such a judgment based on an equal portion would result in a dead baby.

Equality in general is not an ethical position, but here we are at the dawn of new millennium and one of the only guiding principles that we hear is making everything *all same-y* or *even Steven*. The woman who was not the mother in fact had no "right". She did have the ability to obscure the truth. Only in desperate situations does real motherhood not matter. Are the judges willing to take a sword and start halving children?

Do not call "differences" equality

Here's a problem and not a small one. The notion of equality is not an ethical system, not a moral system, in this case not even a system that reflects reality. It is a word being used deceptively. The courts can make taxes fair but they can't pretend differences need to be corrected. Same-sex marriage would like us all to enter into a world of doublespeak and distortions. Men can't become pregnant. That is the reality for all males for millions of years. It makes me wonder how dumbed-down we have become by the media blitz.

Turn off your TVs, people—do it now. I am here to tell you gay men are not "infertile" women. Infertile women are women with a medical problem.

A same-sex marriage between two men has no right to demand or even expect to be provided with other people's children. That requires a denial of children's basic human rights. Nobody has a "right" to children. We could rattle off the relevant documents: conventions on adoption, trials after famous genocides, the United Nations Declaration of the Rights of the Child, the Thirteenth Amendment to the US Constitution—other amendments are worth noting as well—the Declaration of Independence, papal bulls, declarations from grand rabbis, etc. The point is clear; history's lessons speak loudly. Children have the right to be born free, not bought or sold. They have a right to a mother and father. They have a right to their own cultural and ethnic heritage.

Gay parenting is toxic to these rights. It results in the denial of rights to a larger number of people. Three people—a mother, a father and a child—all give up rights so two same-sex adults do not cry "bigot, hater and anti-gay".

According to the conventional wisdom of today, the rights of a predominately wealthy male group trump the rights of the child and two heterosexuals who made the child—three people denied rights. This will disproportionately affect minorities and the poor. The timing could not be worse for the poor, as the gap between the haves and the have-nots widens and the billion-dollar baby selling industry grows.

Gay marriage and future families depend on racial inequality and poverty to provide minority mothers and young, disenfranchised fathers with no support and not enough money to buy access to the courts and assert their parental rights. How progressive. It does not help poverty or the poor when their children are taken. That is an offensive lie that smacks of "the white man's burden". In the future it will be considered a form of cultural genocide. It strangles the black family in its cradle.

We are not supposed to question and many don't. Two decades of lies and rhetorical diversion have left us pie-eyed and stupid. To understand how the rhetoric of the movement operates one needs to understand the basic con. It taps into our vanity with chatter about the "right side of history". The narrative is fragile and built on logical fallacies as well as emotional appeals. It cannot withstand scrutiny, questions, or critical analysis. It has created a history linking itself to the civil rights movement. We are meant to accept that a bar in the urbane West Village called Stonewall and its patrons were exactly like entire black families with three generations forced into share-cropping, impoverished and barred from access to schools, hospitals, and voting. This is just offensive given the fact that quite possibly descendants of share-croppers are those whom rich gays can adopt quick and easy. They have a stake in maintaining inequality. They benefit from it as long as it is women who breed.

They say the victor writes history. In this case the victors make it up out of whole cloth. And this extends past the run of-the-mill false equivalence. It arrives at a newly minted history of victimisation that justifies entitlement to other people's children. We have lost all sense of judgement because justice has been reduced to fashion and emptied of deep ethical principles and definitions. Relativism depends on ignorance and the bandwagon appeal.

Back to Judges 11. The story of Jephthah's daughter has a kind of chilling effect. Rash behavior and missed opportunities all coalesce to create a human tragedy of broken families and loss. Judges of Israel were picked based on military prowess, not wisdom. Jephthah is a judge of undeserved prominence. While he overcame his own less than ideal birth and had a successful military career, he was poorly suited for the position. He on many levels represents so many of us. His accomplishments do not protect or spare him from grief and loss. His prowess and courage as a solider do not matter and are not talents that will serve him as a judge.

We have arrived at a cultural moment in which we are not able to apply a critical analysis because we have been raised in a culture that abhors judgement and ethics. In today's parlance judgement is seen as bigotry and oppression. Judgement requires analysis and a good deal of critical acumen. It also requires a set of ethics that are more nuanced and versatile than "live and let live".

Fathers and mothers die. Some women get pregnant only to find that the man is not interested in marriage and family; she can choose to raise that child alone as a single mother. Her choice and her right are not transferable to a commercial endeavour. She has the right to her reproductive freedom as an individual right. This does not mean that, because women can have babies and men can't, babies are a new civil right.

The answers to ethical dilemmas are not found in prime-time media, not honed by platitudes repeated over and over, not reached by general consensus of the élan for the few on the green leafy quads. Ethics and the rights of children separate from adults' demands may not serve to appear politically correct; they are not answered by talking points and the networks' lineup, not crafted by long-view strategies or financed by fortunes amassed in hedge funds. They exist once people are willing and able to cut through the thicket of diversions, exaggerations, shaming, and abusive name-calling, and be honest.

The next big thing
There will be a dark and Orwellian inheritance. Kids grow up and they will reach financial independence. They will be rightfully enraged at the society that consigned them to a life mirroring adults' distortions, so that society could feel the conceit of what social justice has become. In the past few years we have swelled in rank. More and more of us are coming forward. We are not good at public relations for the movement. In fact I take their threats of violence very seriously and live very differently. I think of Zach Wahls (raised by two lesbians and conceived by artificial insemination and now an LBGT activist) who they say is "too good to be true", and I think of his moms, all their connections, their commitments,

and the whole lengthy grooming process. I don't feel sorry for him; he was able to play the game, good for him. He will be amply rewarded for that until he can no longer play—then I will feel for him. He knows what he has lost, as we all do, because one thing we all had to develop early on was a honed instinct for self-preservation. That's the price of being denied your own emotional life, your own identity. That's the price extracted.

I never experienced any bullying because of my mother. To be honest, not a single kid I know who grew up in an LGBT home experienced it. I wonder if the children of single mothers or unmarried co-habituating parents are tortured because their parents do not have a marriage license. It seems like an odd thing to be on a child's mind.

Gay marriage gives dignity to children? This is what Justice Kennedy said in 2013. I do not buy it. I see children trained from an early age as props for the public to tell people on cue "let my mommies marry". "Love makes a family" rings rather hollow.

ABOUT THE AUTHORS*

Robert Oscar Lopez (ICRI, EM) is Professor of Humanities at Southwestern Baptist Theological Seminary, having previously been Professor of English Literature and Classics at California State University. He is the author of *The Colorful Conservative*, *Johnson Park*, *Melville Affair* and *Gay Wars*. He serves as President of the International Children's Rights Institute.

Brittany Klein (ICRI, EM) was raised in New York and has lived in Israel. She holds a Master of Fine Arts degree in Writing from the University of Virginia. She now teaches college English. She serves on the Executive Board of the International Children's Rights Institute.

Jennifer Johnson (ICRI, EM) is the Director of Outreach for the Ruth Institute and has written for *Clash Daily*, *English Manif*, *Christian Post*, and *Ricochet*. Her work defends traditional marriage, particularly to the libertarian community. She remains a fighter against divorce culture.

Sam Johnson (EM) is a recovering atheist and, as his pseudonym suggests, an Englishman. Both parents married three times, so he understands the importance of stronger marriage and family protections in law and culture.

Jennifer Lahl (ICRI) is founder and president of the Center for Bioethics and Culture. Her writings have appeared in publications including *San Francisco Chronicle* and *American Journal of Bioethics*. She is on the Academic Council of the International Children's Rights Institute.

Stella Morabito has written about marriage and family for *Federalist*, where she is a senior contributor, and for several other publications. In her previous work in intelligence she focused on communist propaganda. She has an MA in Russian and Soviet history.

---

*Authors with (ICRI) after their name serve on one of the boards of the International Children's Rights Institute. Authors with (EM) after their name were contributors to *English Manif* when it was live (January 2013-December 2014).

Alana Newman (ICRI) is the founder of The Anonymous Us Project and The Coalition Against Reproductive Trafficking. She is from San Francisco, CA and now resides in Louisiana. She is on the Testimonial Council of the International Children's Rights Institute.

Dawn Stefanowicz (ICRI, EM) is the author of *Out From Under: The Impact of Homosexual Parenting*. Many of the testimonies she compiled from other adult children of gays can be found on her website, which is http://dawnstefanowicz.org. She is on the Testimonial Council of ICRI.

Benoît Talleu (ICRI, EM) belongs to the French movement "*la Manif pour Tous*" and debates on homosexual marriage and adoption. He is member of the Testimonial Council of the International Children's Rights Institute (ICRI) since 2013. He focuses on orphans and adoption.